POWER 3™

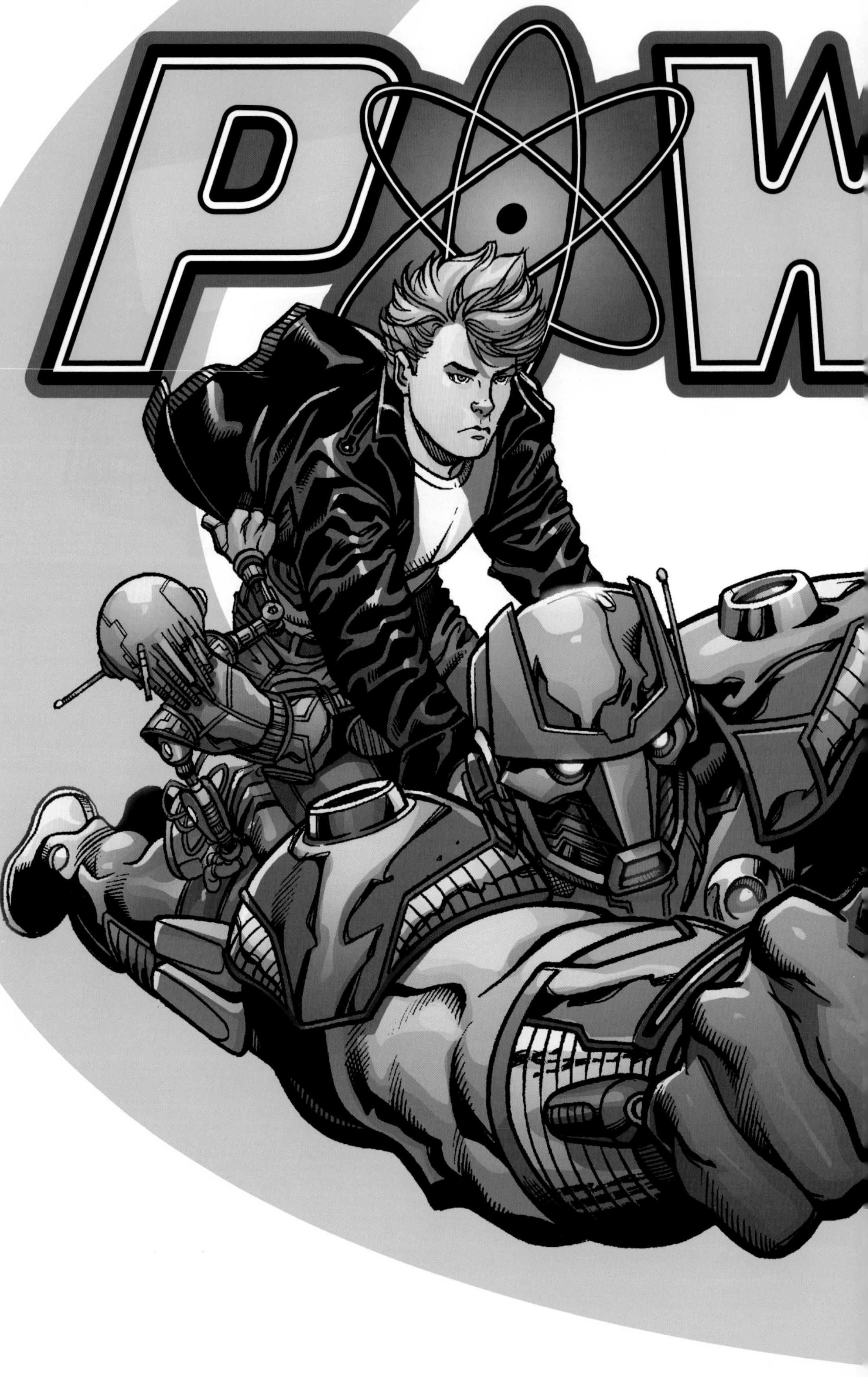

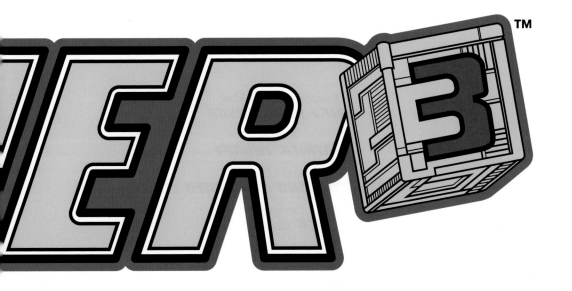

Written and illustrated by
AARON LOPRESTI

Inks by
MARK MORALES—chapter 2
MARC DEERING—chapters 3, 4

Colors by
HI-FI DESIGN

Letters by
MICHAEL HEISLER

Cover and chapter breaks by
AARON LOPRESTI

DARK HORSE BOOKS

President & Publisher
MIKE RICHARDSON

Editor
PATRICK THORPE

Assistant Editors
EVERETT PATTERSON & CARDNER CLARK

Designer
RICK DeLUCCO

Digital Art Technician
CHRISTINA McKENZIE

Thanks to Mike Richardson for the opportunity and to Shelley, Sammi, Faith, and Josh for the love and support. — *Aaron Lopresti*

Special thanks to Annie Gullion.

This volume collects issues #1–#4 of the Dark Horse Comics series *Power Cubed*.

Published by
Dark Horse Books
A division of Dark Horse Comics, Inc.
10956 SE Main Street
Milwaukie, OR 97222

DarkHorse.com

To find a comics shop in your area, call the Comic Shop Locator Service toll-free at 1-888-266-4226.
International Licensing: (503) 905-2377

First edition: May 2016
ISBN 978-1-61655-876-5

1 3 5 7 9 10 8 6 4 2
Printed in China

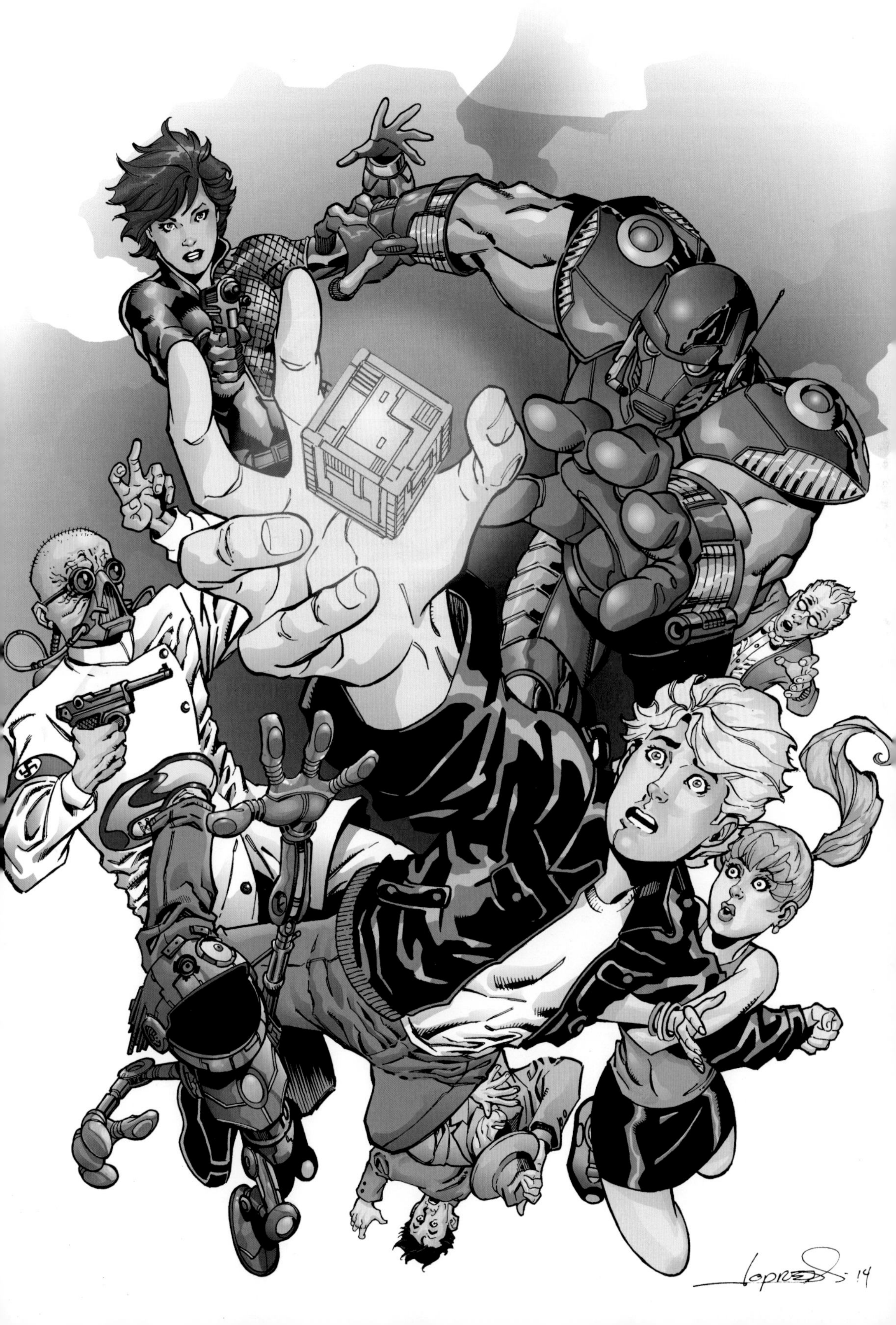
Lopresti '14

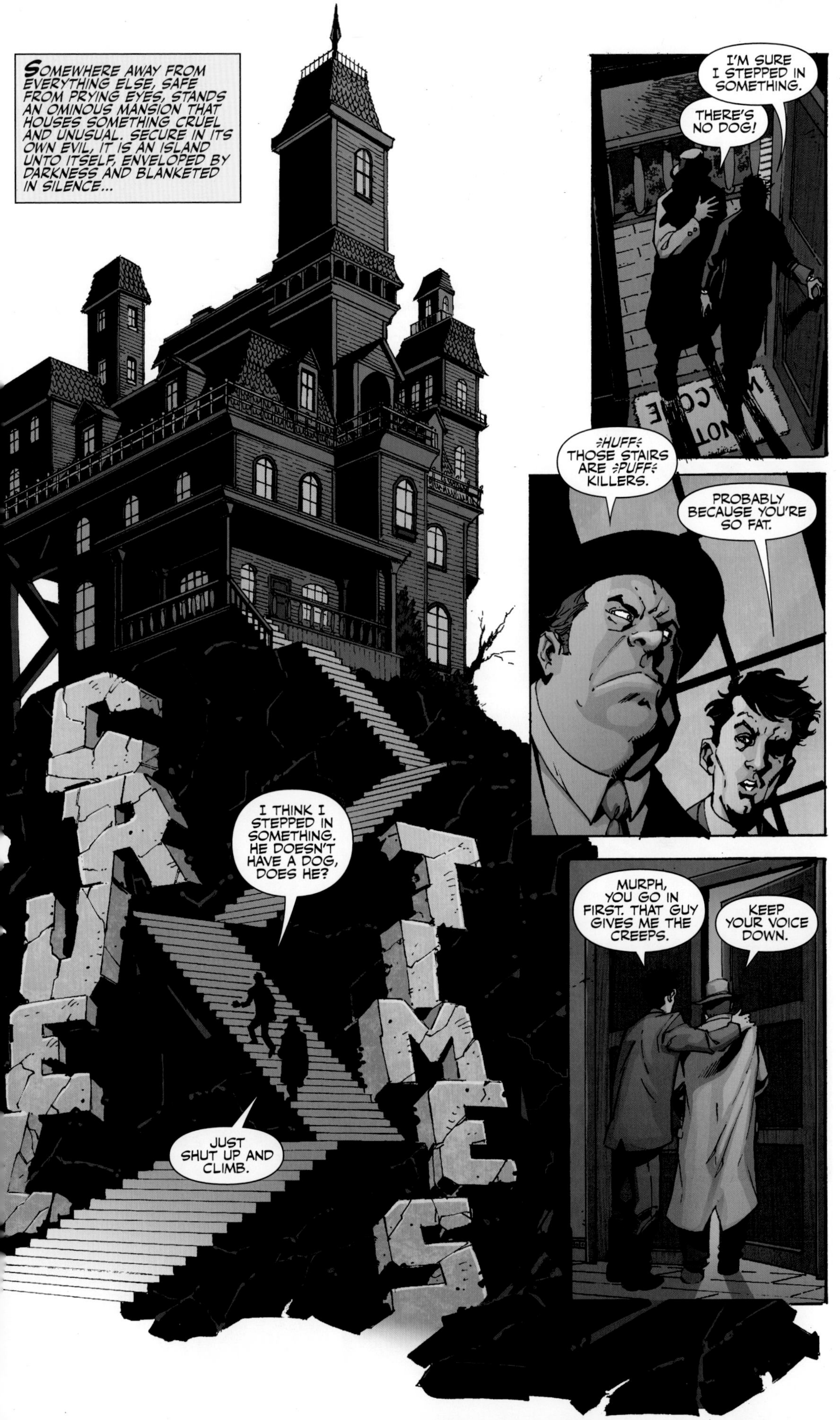
SOMEWHERE AWAY FROM EVERYTHING ELSE, SAFE FROM PRYING EYES, STANDS AN OMINOUS MANSION THAT HOUSES SOMETHING CRUEL AND UNUSUAL. SECURE IN ITS OWN EVIL, IT IS AN ISLAND UNTO ITSELF, ENVELOPED BY DARKNESS AND BLANKETED IN SILENCE...
I THINK I STEPPED IN SOMETHING. HE DOESN'T HAVE A DOG, DOES HE?
JUST SHUT UP AND CLIMB.
I'M SURE I STEPPED IN SOMETHING.
THERE'S NO DOG!
HUFF THOSE STAIRS ARE *PUFF* KILLERS.
PROBABLY BECAUSE YOU'RE SO FAT.
MURPH, YOU GO IN FIRST. THAT GUY GIVES ME THE CREEPS.
KEEP YOUR VOICE DOWN.

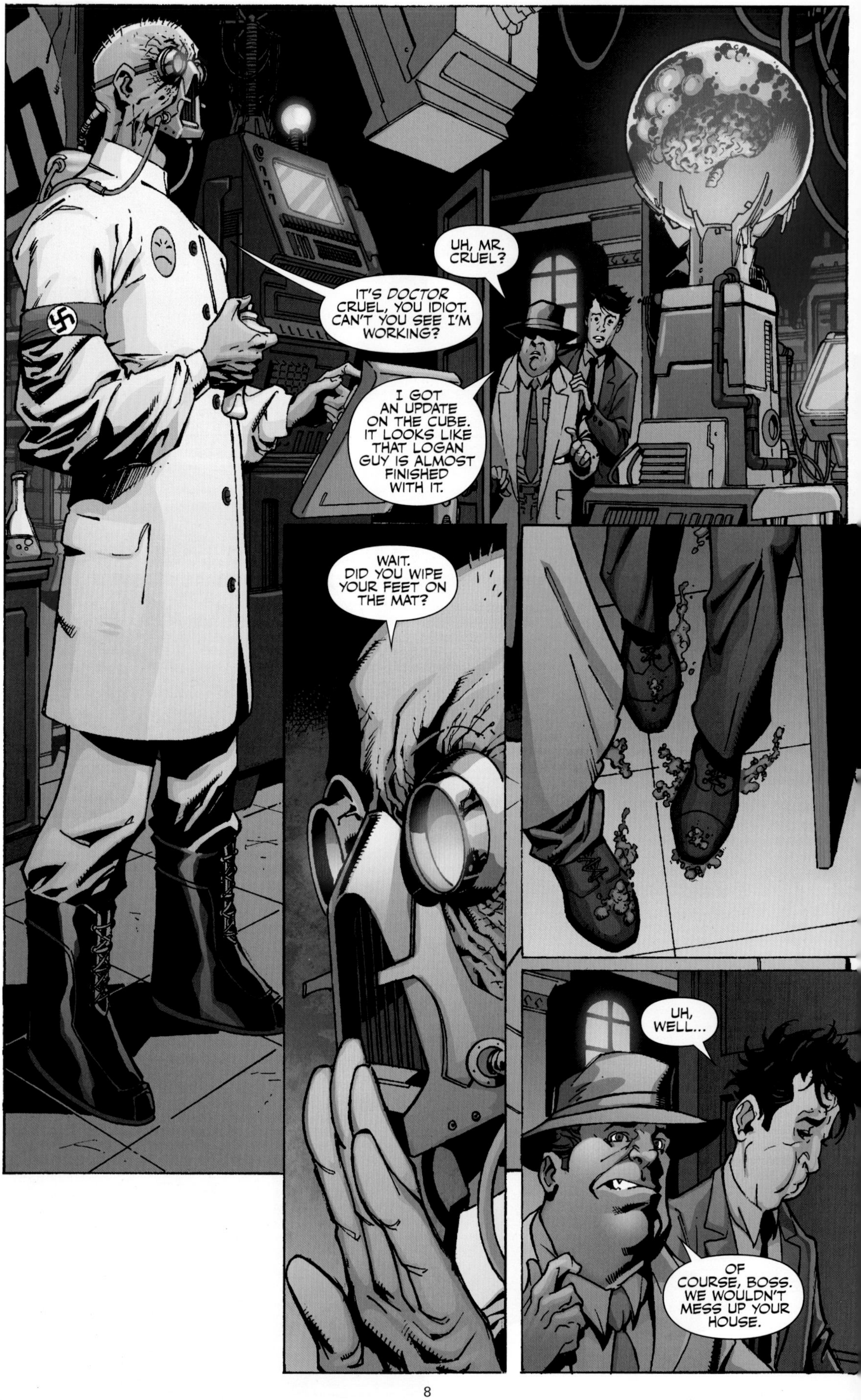

UH, MR. CRUEL?
IT'S DOCTOR CRUEL, YOU IDIOT. CAN'T YOU SEE I'M WORKING?
I GOT AN UPDATE ON THE CUBE. IT LOOKS LIKE THAT LOGAN GUY IS ALMOST FINISHED WITH IT.
WAIT. DID YOU WIPE YOUR FEET ON THE MAT?
UH, WELL...
OF COURSE, BOSS. WE WOULDN'T MESS UP YOUR HOUSE.

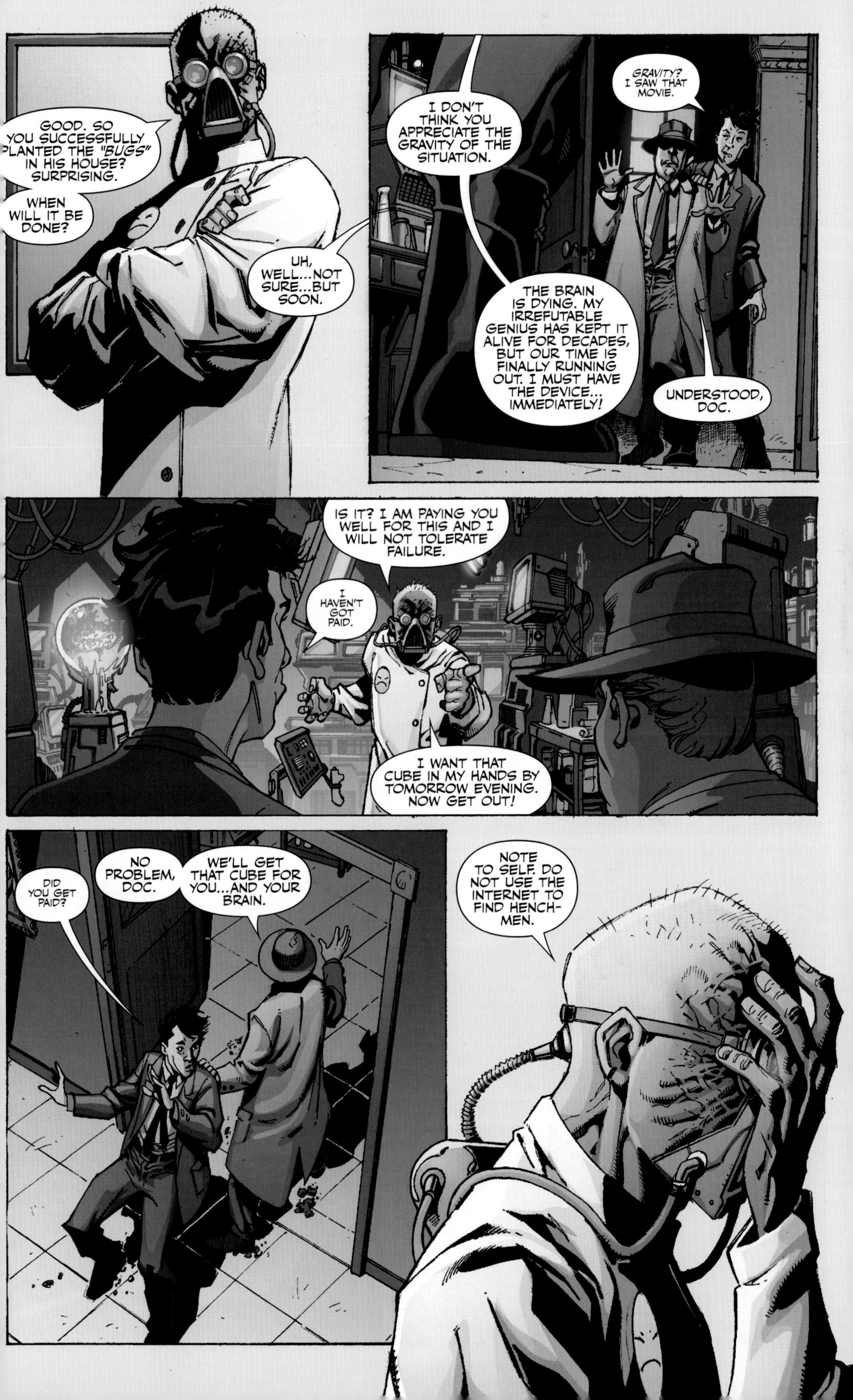
GOOD. SO YOU SUCCESSFULLY PLANTED THE "BUGS" IN HIS HOUSE? SURPRISING.
WHEN WILL IT BE DONE?
UH, WELL...NOT SURE...BUT SOON.
I DON'T THINK YOU APPRECIATE THE GRAVITY OF THE SITUATION.
GRAVITY? I SAW THAT MOVIE.
THE BRAIN IS DYING. MY IRREFUTABLE GENIUS HAS KEPT IT ALIVE FOR DECADES, BUT OUR TIME IS FINALLY RUNNING OUT. I MUST HAVE THE DEVICE... IMMEDIATELY!
UNDERSTOOD, DOC.
IS IT? I AM PAYING YOU WELL FOR THIS AND I WILL NOT TOLERATE FAILURE.
I HAVEN'T GOT PAID.
I WANT THAT CUBE IN MY HANDS BY TOMORROW EVENING. NOW GET OUT!
NO PROBLEM, DOC.
WE'LL GET THAT CUBE FOR YOU...AND YOUR BRAIN.
DID YOU GET PAID?
NOTE TO SELF. DO NOT USE THE INTERNET TO FIND HENCH-MEN.

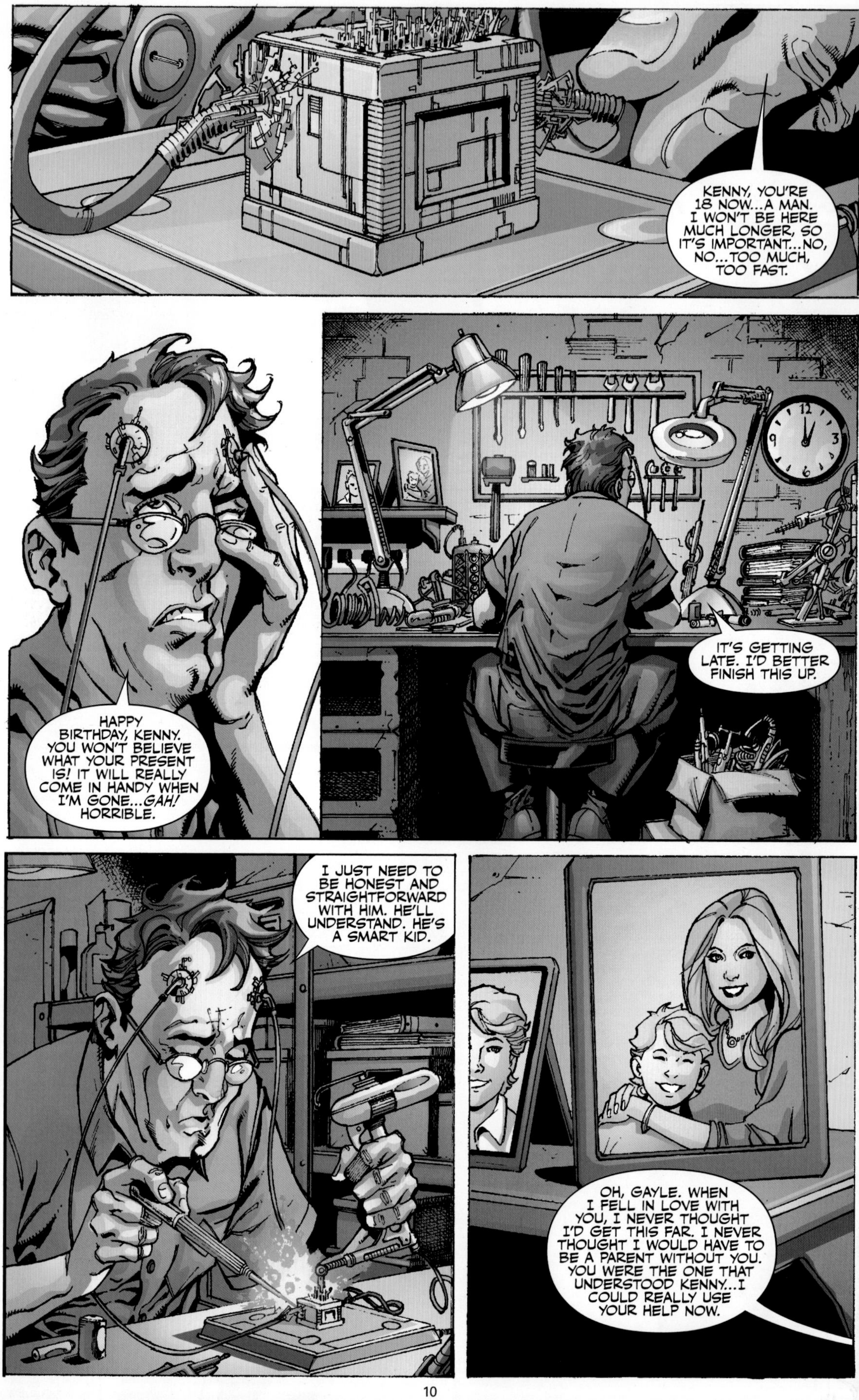
KENNY, YOU'RE 18 NOW...A MAN. I WON'T BE HERE MUCH LONGER, SO IT'S IMPORTANT...NO, NO...TOO MUCH, TOO FAST.
HAPPY BIRTHDAY, KENNY. YOU WON'T BELIEVE WHAT YOUR PRESENT IS! IT WILL REALLY COME IN HANDY WHEN I'M GONE...GAH! HORRIBLE.
IT'S GETTING LATE. I'D BETTER FINISH THIS UP.
I JUST NEED TO BE HONEST AND STRAIGHTFORWARD WITH HIM. HE'LL UNDERSTAND. HE'S A SMART KID.
OH, GAYLE. WHEN I FELL IN LOVE WITH YOU, I NEVER THOUGHT I'D GET THIS FAR. I NEVER THOUGHT I WOULD HAVE TO BE A PARENT WITHOUT YOU. YOU WERE THE ONE THAT UNDERSTOOD KENNY...I COULD REALLY USE YOUR HELP NOW.

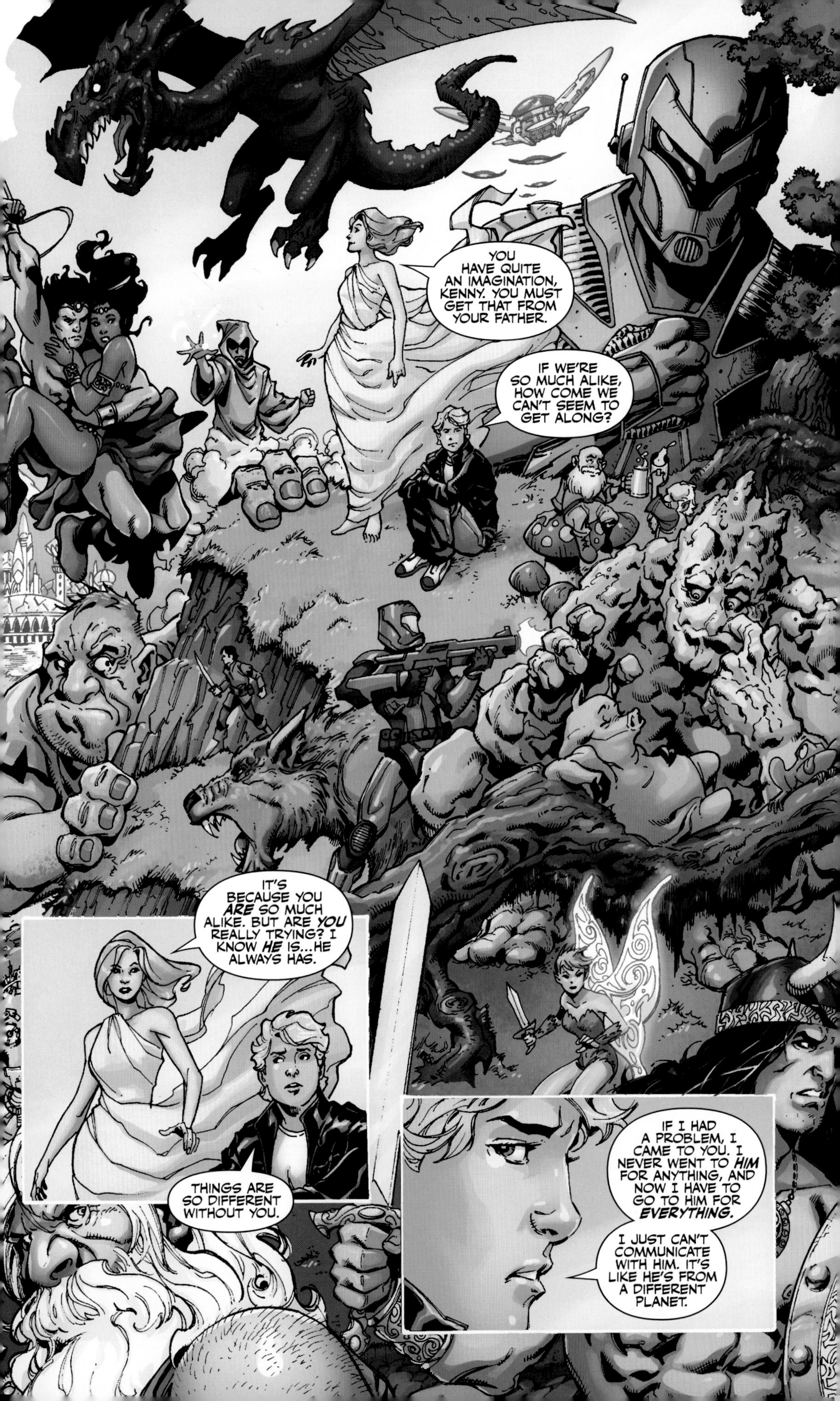

YOU HAVE QUITE AN IMAGINATION, KENNY. YOU MUST GET THAT FROM YOUR FATHER.
IF WE'RE SO MUCH ALIKE, HOW COME WE CAN'T SEEM TO GET ALONG?
IT'S BECAUSE YOU ARE SO MUCH ALIKE. BUT ARE YOU REALLY TRYING? I KNOW HE IS...HE ALWAYS HAS.
THINGS ARE SO DIFFERENT WITHOUT YOU.
IF I HAD A PROBLEM, I CAME TO YOU. I NEVER WENT TO HIM FOR ANYTHING, AND NOW I HAVE TO GO TO HIM FOR EVERYTHING.
I JUST CAN'T COMMUNICATE WITH HIM. IT'S LIKE HE'S FROM A DIFFERENT PLANET.

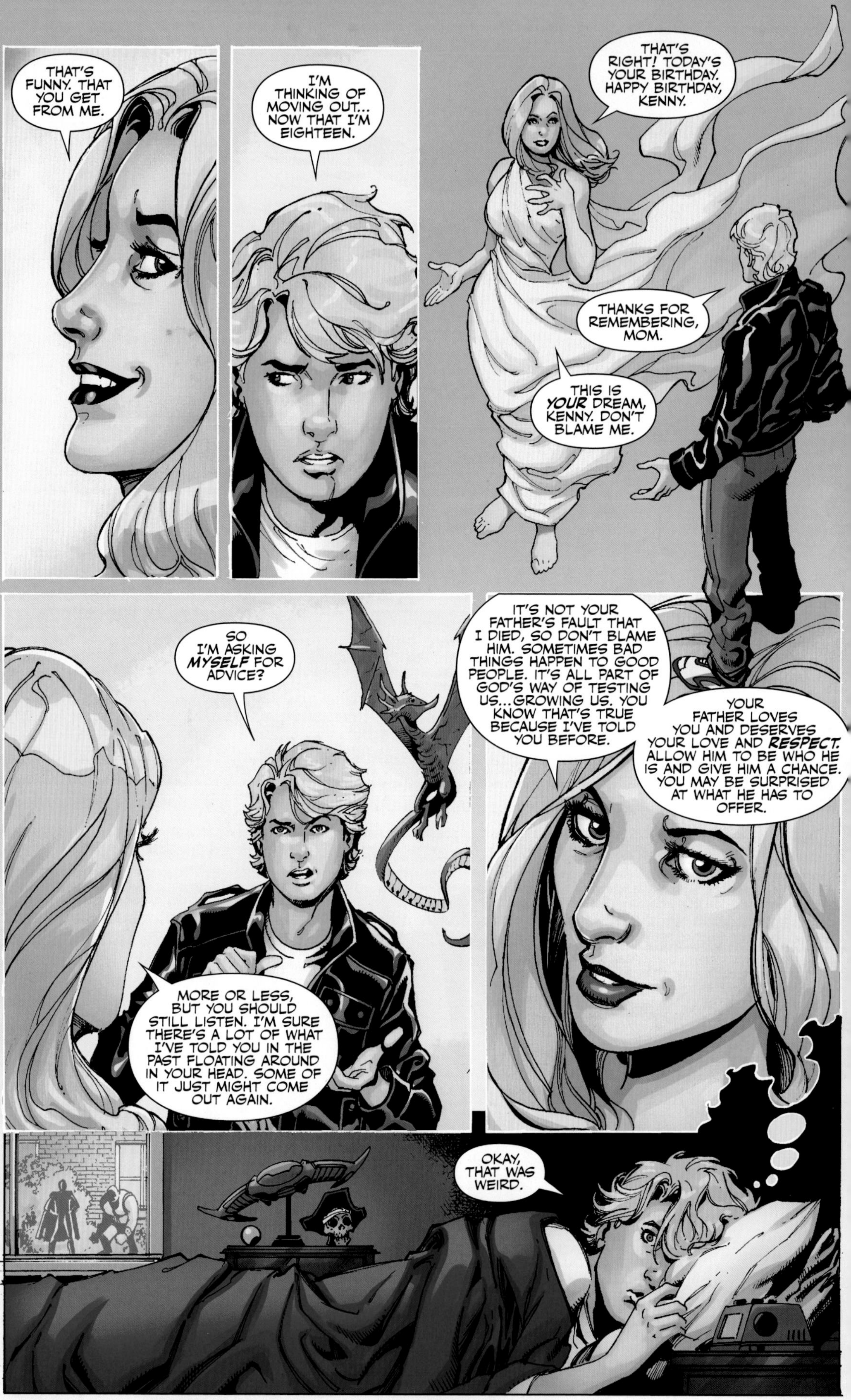
THAT'S FUNNY. THAT YOU GET FROM ME.
I'M THINKING OF MOVING OUT... NOW THAT I'M EIGHTEEN.
THAT'S RIGHT! TODAY'S YOUR BIRTHDAY. HAPPY BIRTHDAY, KENNY.
THANKS FOR REMEMBERING, MOM.
THIS IS ***YOUR*** DREAM, KENNY. DON'T BLAME ME.
SO I'M ASKING ***MYSELF*** FOR ADVICE?
MORE OR LESS, BUT YOU SHOULD STILL LISTEN. I'M SURE THERE'S A LOT OF WHAT I'VE TOLD YOU IN THE PAST FLOATING AROUND IN YOUR HEAD. SOME OF IT JUST MIGHT COME OUT AGAIN.
IT'S NOT YOUR FATHER'S FAULT THAT I DIED, SO DON'T BLAME HIM. SOMETIMES BAD THINGS HAPPEN TO GOOD PEOPLE. IT'S ALL PART OF GOD'S WAY OF TESTING US...GROWING US. YOU KNOW THAT'S TRUE BECAUSE I'VE TOLD YOU BEFORE.
YOUR FATHER LOVES YOU AND DESERVES YOUR LOVE AND ***RESPECT.*** ALLOW HIM TO BE WHO HE IS AND GIVE HIM A CHANCE. YOU MAY BE SURPRISED AT WHAT HE HAS TO OFFER.
OKAY, THAT WAS WEIRD.

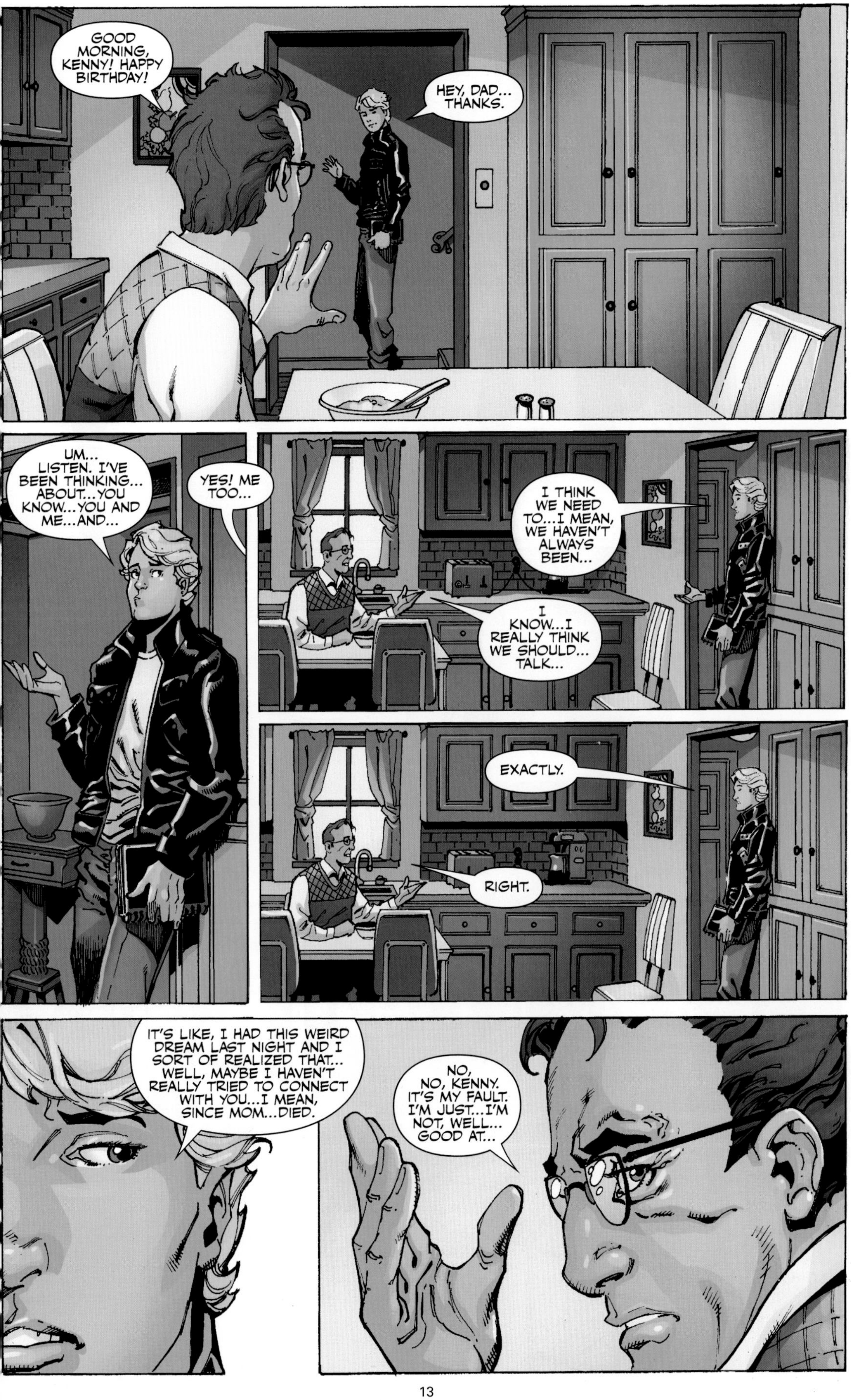

GOOD MORNING, KENNY! HAPPY BIRTHDAY!
HEY, DAD... THANKS.
UM... LISTEN. I'VE BEEN THINKING... ABOUT...YOU KNOW...YOU AND ME...AND...
YES! ME TOO...
I THINK WE NEED TO...I MEAN, WE HAVEN'T ALWAYS BEEN...
I KNOW...I REALLY THINK WE SHOULD... TALK...
EXACTLY.
RIGHT.
IT'S LIKE, I HAD THIS WEIRD DREAM LAST NIGHT AND I SORT OF REALIZED THAT... WELL, MAYBE I HAVEN'T REALLY TRIED TO CONNECT WITH YOU...I MEAN, SINCE MOM...DIED.
NO, NO, KENNY. IT'S MY FAULT. I'M JUST...I'M NOT, WELL... GOOD AT...

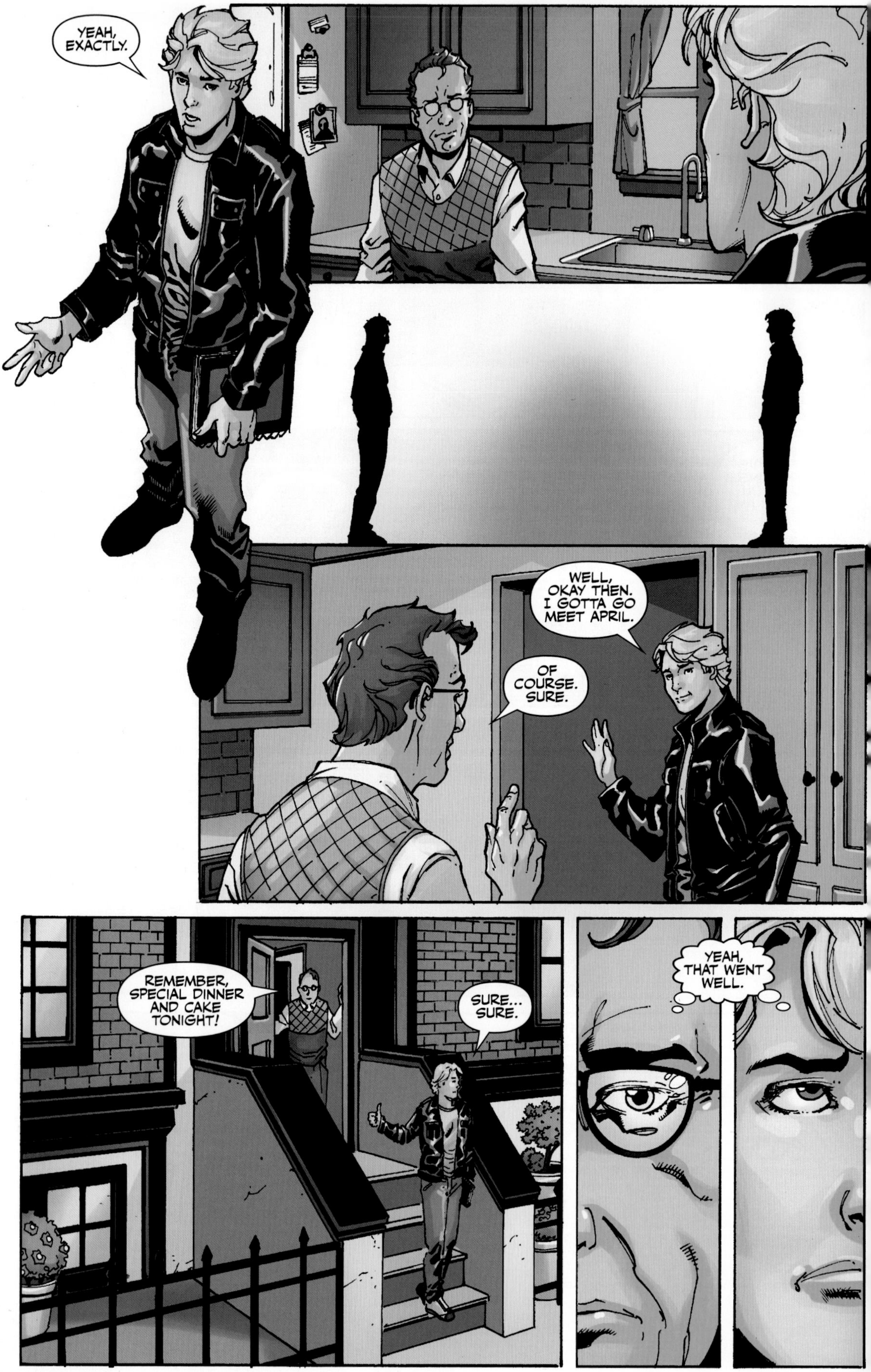
YEAH, EXACTLY.
WELL, OKAY THEN. I GOTTA GO MEET APRIL.
OF COURSE. SURE.
REMEMBER, SPECIAL DINNER AND CAKE TONIGHT!
SURE... SURE.
YEAH, THAT WENT WELL.

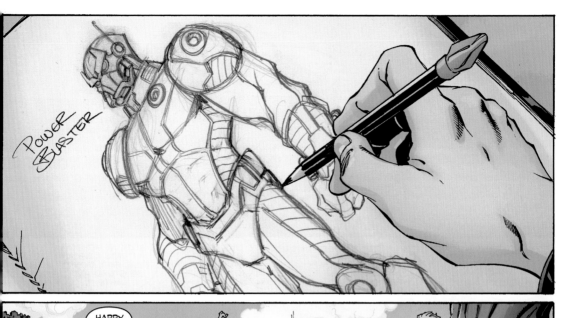

POWER BLASTER

HAPPY B-DAY!

THANKS.

WHAT'RE YOU DRAWING?

SOMETHING I CAME UP WITH... IT'S A ROBOT THING...

POWER BLASTER... COOL!

YOU SHOULD GO INTO ANIMATION OR SOMETHING AFTER SCHOOL.

I DON'T KNOW. IT SEEMS LIKE GETTING PAID FOR IT WOULD TAKE ALL OF THE FUN OUT OF IT.

SERIOUS? GETTING PAID FOR IT *IS* THE FUN, RIGHT?

YOU KNOW WHAT YOU SHOULD DO? YOUR DAD IS ALWAYS MAKING COOL WEIRD STUFF. YOU SHOULD DESIGN ALL OF HIS COOL WEIRD STUFF. THEN YOU GUYS COULD, LIKE, MAKE COOL WEIRD STUFF TOGETHER AND GET RICH!

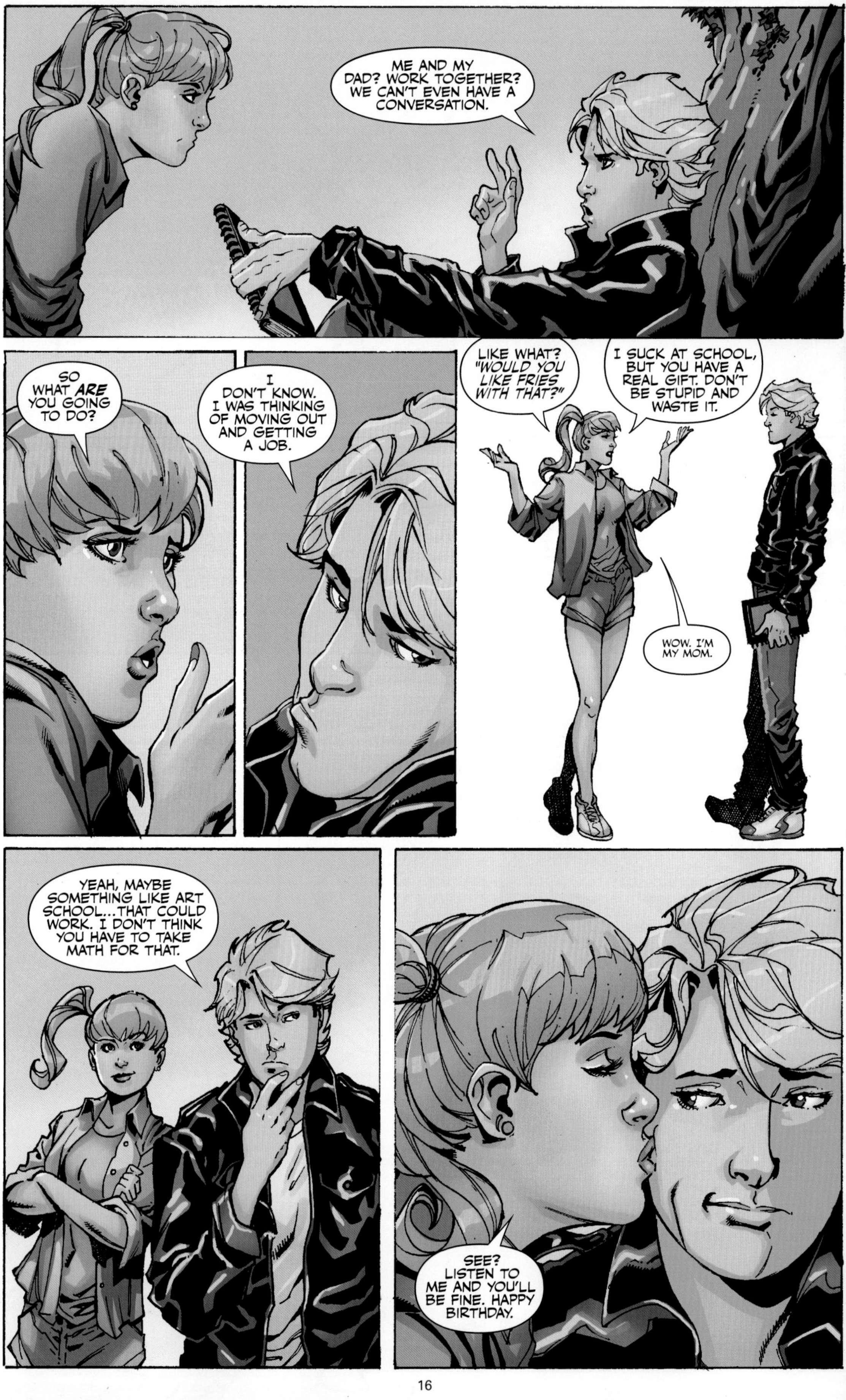
ME AND MY DAD? WORK TOGETHER? WE CAN'T EVEN HAVE A CONVERSATION.
SO WHAT *ARE* YOU GOING TO DO?
I DON'T KNOW. I WAS THINKING OF MOVING OUT AND GETTING A JOB.
LIKE WHAT? *"WOULD YOU LIKE FRIES WITH THAT?"*
I SUCK AT SCHOOL, BUT YOU HAVE A REAL GIFT. DON'T BE STUPID AND WASTE IT.
WOW. I'M MY MOM.
YEAH, MAYBE SOMETHING LIKE ART SCHOOL...THAT COULD WORK. I DON'T THINK YOU HAVE TO TAKE MATH FOR THAT.
SEE? LISTEN TO ME AND YOU'LL BE FINE. HAPPY BIRTHDAY.

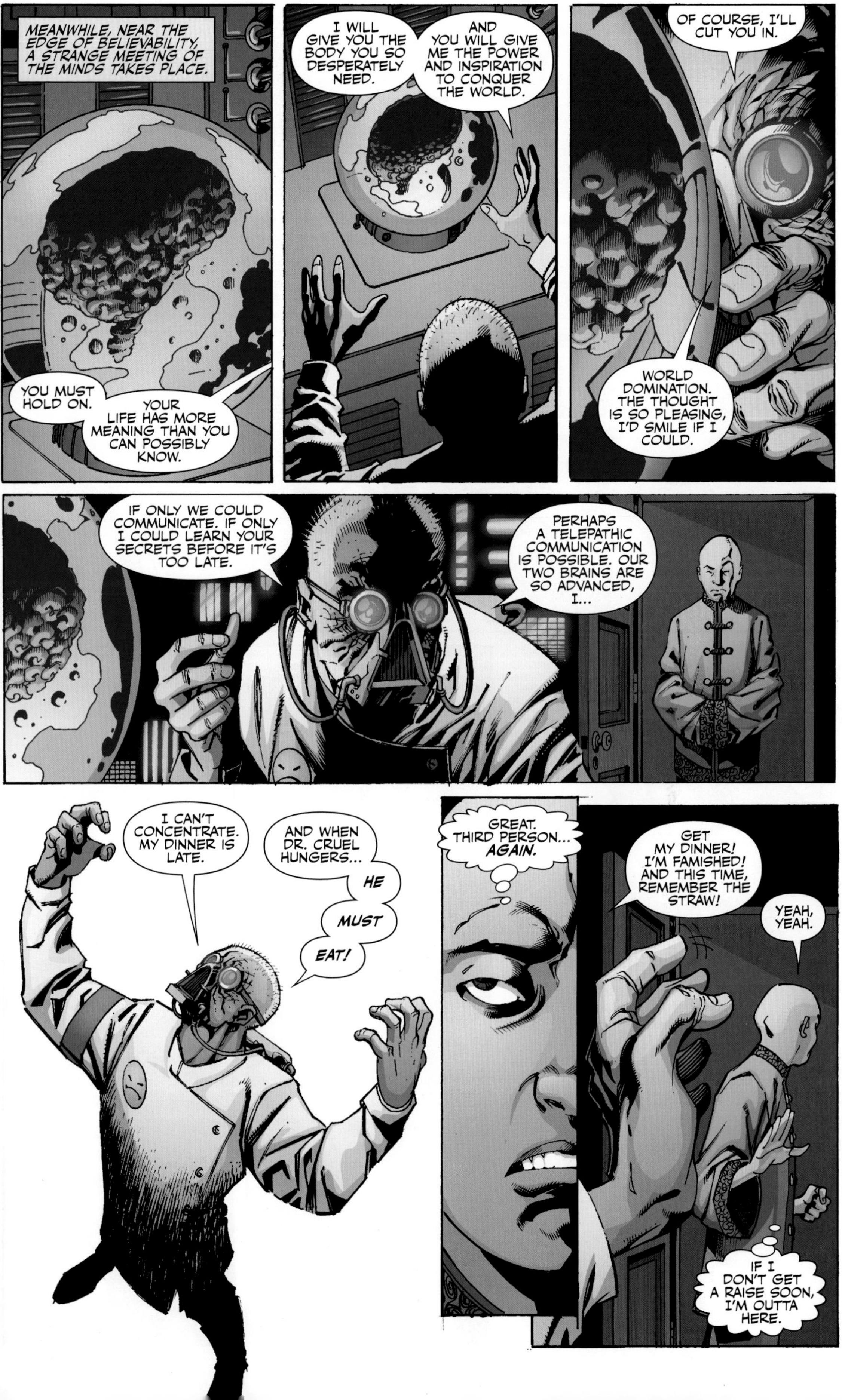
MEANWHILE, NEAR THE EDGE OF BELIEVABILITY, A STRANGE MEETING OF THE MINDS TAKES PLACE.
YOU MUST HOLD ON.
YOUR LIFE HAS MORE MEANING THAN YOU CAN POSSIBLY KNOW.
I WILL GIVE YOU THE BODY YOU SO DESPERATELY NEED.
AND YOU WILL GIVE ME THE POWER AND INSPIRATION TO CONQUER THE WORLD.
OF COURSE, I'LL CUT YOU IN.
WORLD DOMINATION. THE THOUGHT IS SO PLEASING, I'D SMILE IF I COULD.
IF ONLY WE COULD COMMUNICATE. IF ONLY I COULD LEARN YOUR SECRETS BEFORE IT'S TOO LATE.
PERHAPS A TELEPATHIC COMMUNICATION IS POSSIBLE. OUR TWO BRAINS ARE SO ADVANCED, I...
I CAN'T CONCENTRATE. MY DINNER IS LATE.
AND WHEN DR. CRUEL HUNGERS...
HE
MUST
EAT!
GREAT. THIRD PERSON... AGAIN.
GET MY DINNER! I'M FAMISHED! AND THIS TIME, REMEMBER THE STRAW!
YEAH, YEAH.
IF I DON'T GET A RAISE SOON, I'M OUTTA HERE.

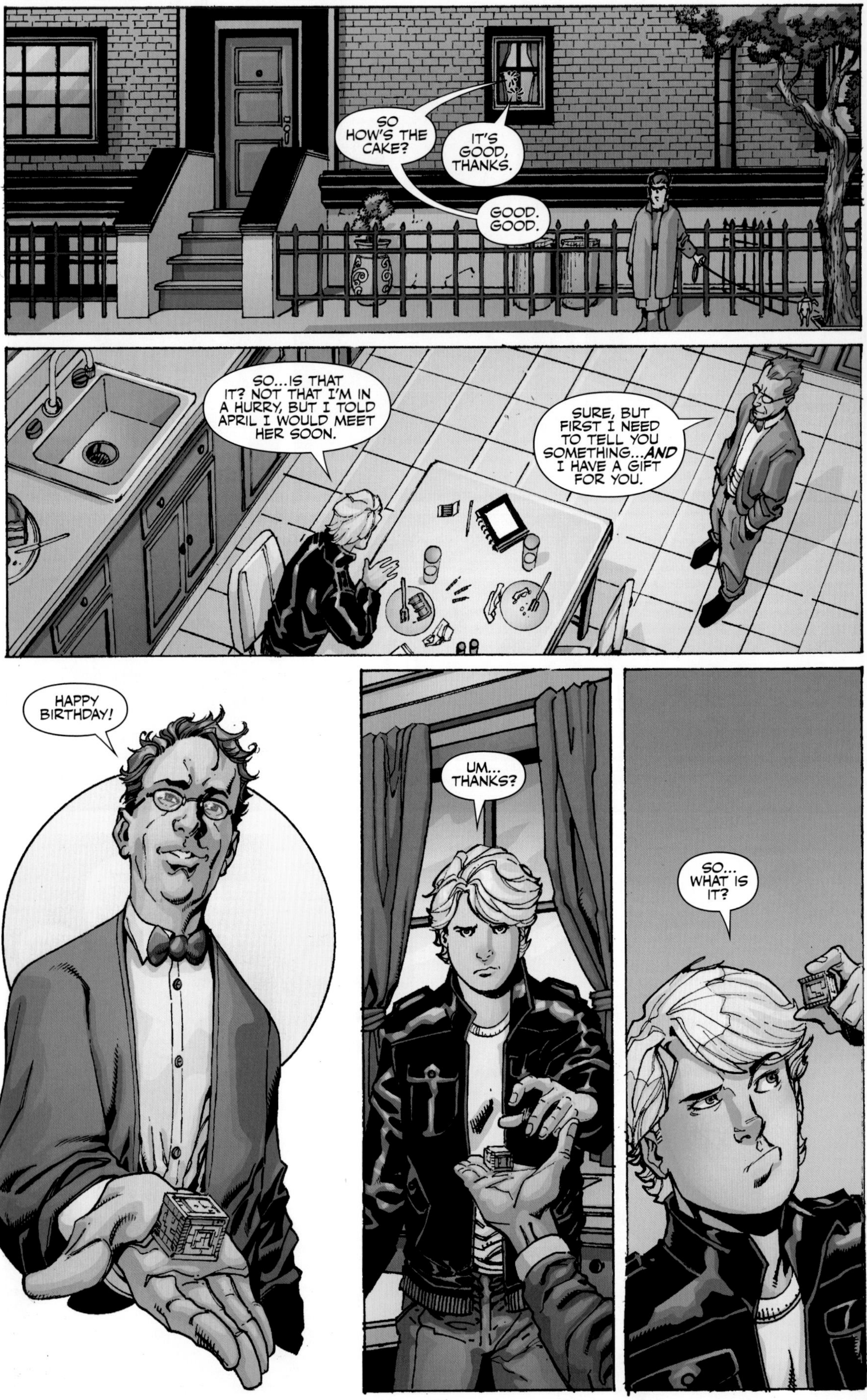
SO HOW'S THE CAKE?
IT'S GOOD, THANKS.
GOOD. GOOD.
SO...IS THAT IT? NOT THAT I'M IN A HURRY, BUT I TOLD APRIL I WOULD MEET HER SOON.
SURE, BUT FIRST I NEED TO TELL YOU SOMETHING...AND I HAVE A GIFT FOR YOU.
HAPPY BIRTHDAY!
UM... THANKS?
SO... WHAT IS IT?

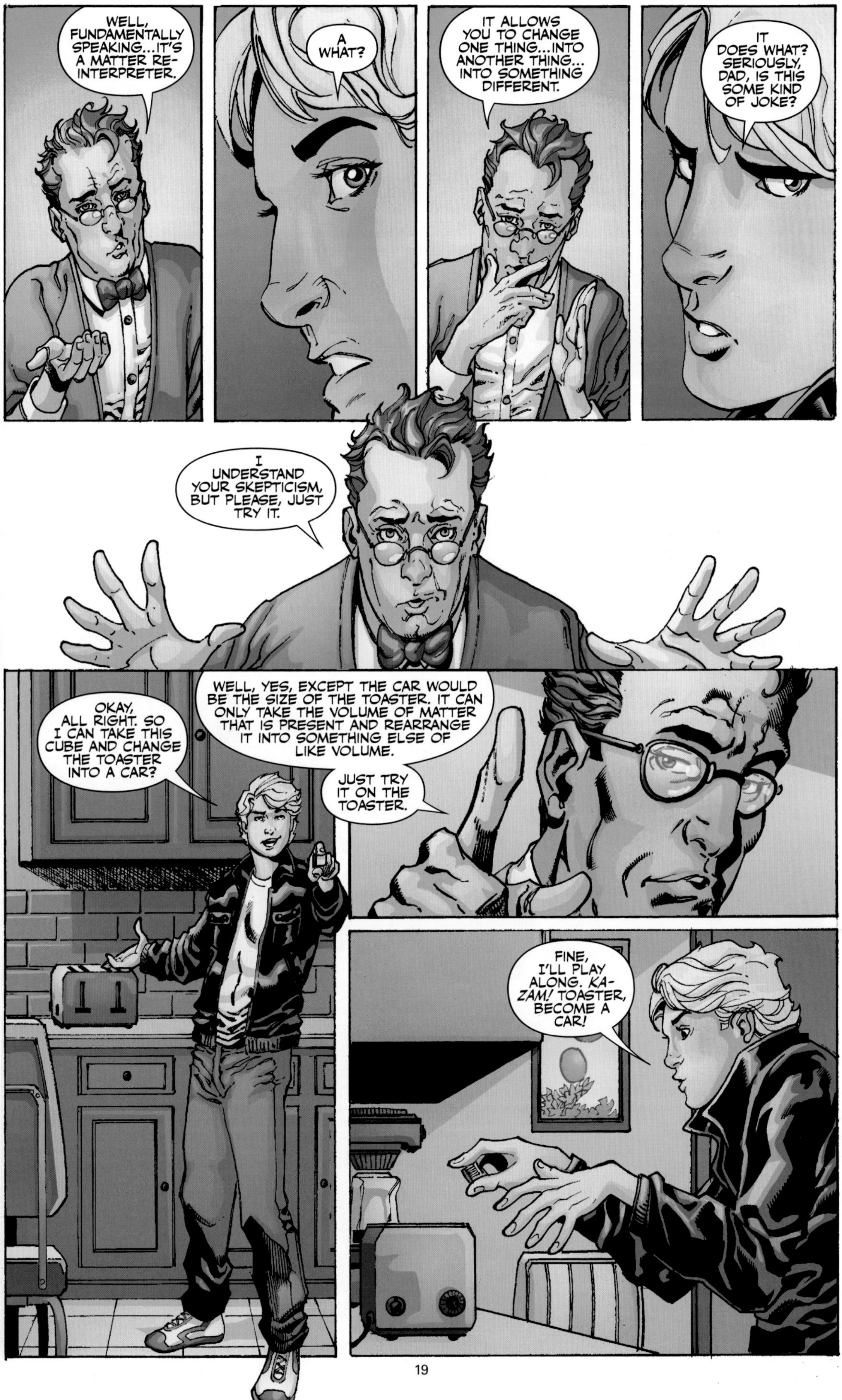
WELL, FUNDAMENTALLY SPEAKING...IT'S A MATTER RE-INTERPRETER.
A WHAT?
IT ALLOWS YOU TO CHANGE ONE THING...INTO ANOTHER THING... INTO SOMETHING DIFFERENT.
IT DOES WHAT? SERIOUSLY, DAD, IS THIS SOME KIND OF JOKE?
I UNDERSTAND YOUR SKEPTICISM, BUT PLEASE, JUST TRY IT.
OKAY, ALL RIGHT. SO I CAN TAKE THIS CUBE AND CHANGE THE TOASTER INTO A CAR?
WELL, YES, EXCEPT THE CAR WOULD BE THE SIZE OF THE TOASTER. IT CAN ONLY TAKE THE VOLUME OF MATTER THAT IS PRESENT AND REARRANGE IT INTO SOMETHING ELSE OF LIKE VOLUME.
JUST TRY IT ON THE TOASTER.
FINE, I'LL PLAY ALONG. *KA-ZAM!* TOASTER, BECOME A CAR!

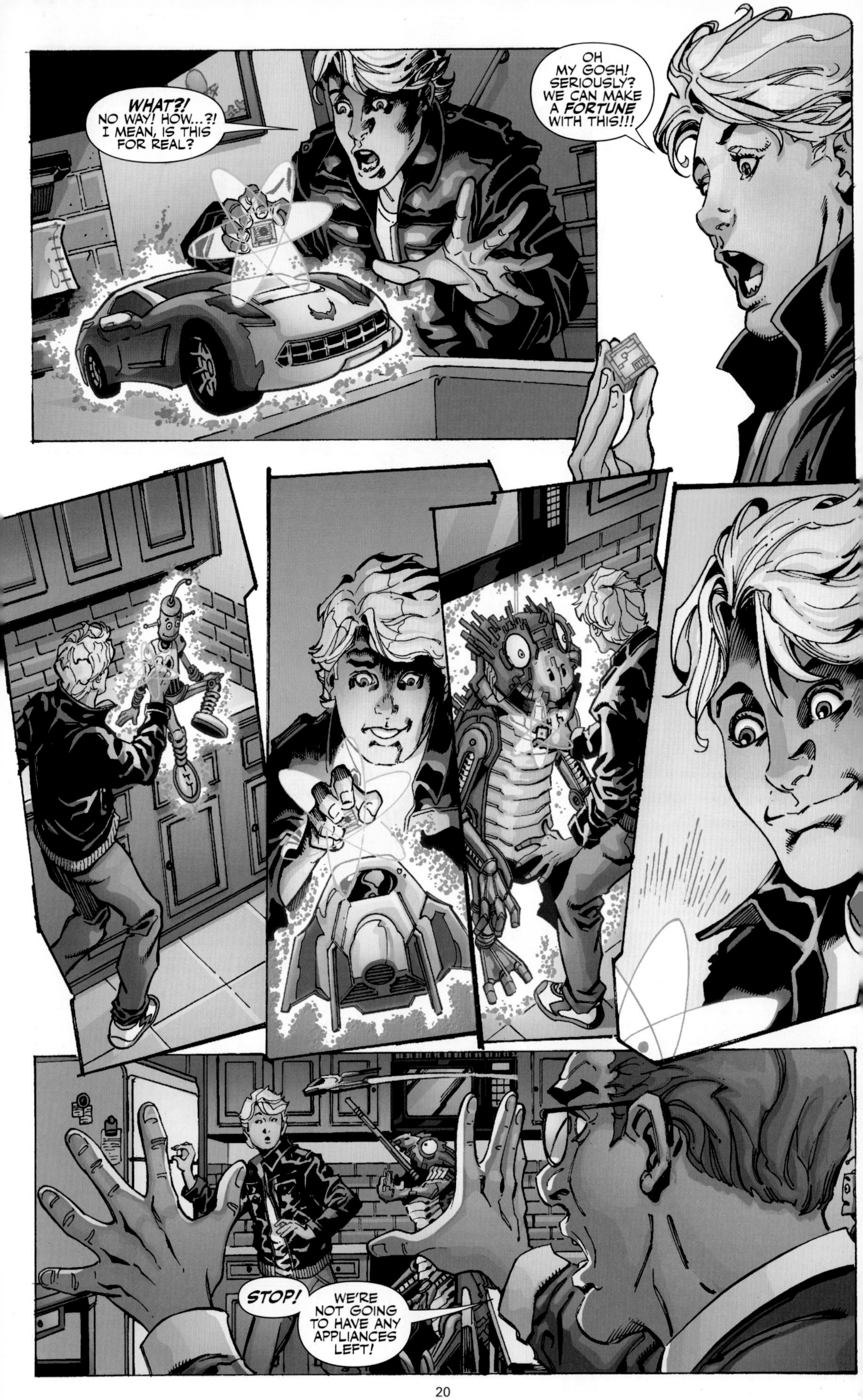
WHAT?! NO WAY! HOW...?! I MEAN, IS THIS FOR REAL?
OH MY GOSH! SERIOUSLY? WE CAN MAKE A FORTUNE WITH THIS!!!
STOP!
WE'RE NOT GOING TO HAVE ANY APPLIANCES LEFT!

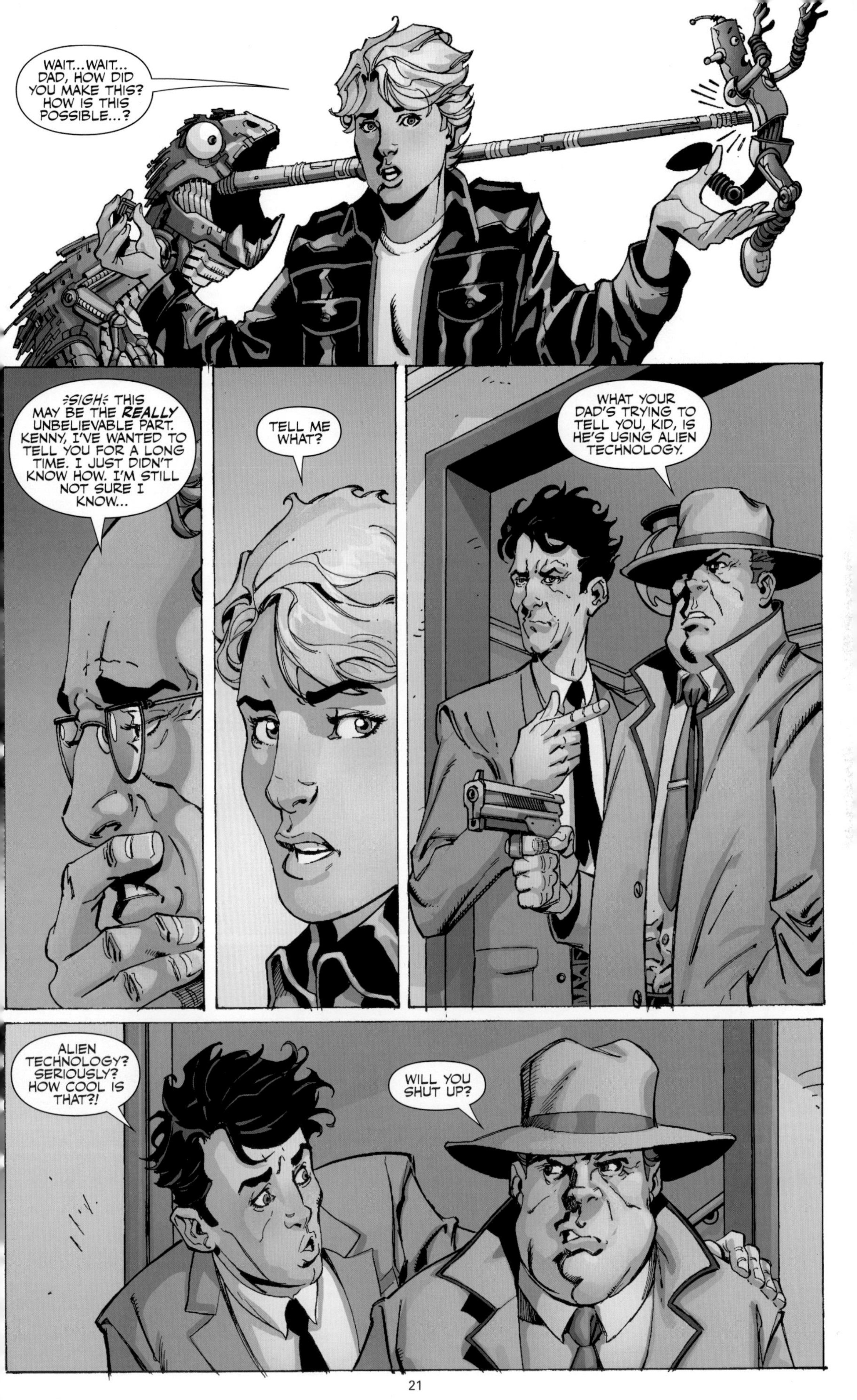
WAIT...WAIT... DAD, HOW DID YOU MAKE THIS? HOW IS THIS POSSIBLE...?
SIGH THIS MAY BE THE REALLY UNBELIEVABLE PART. KENNY, I'VE WANTED TO TELL YOU FOR A LONG TIME. I JUST DIDN'T KNOW HOW. I'M STILL NOT SURE I KNOW...
TELL ME WHAT?
WHAT YOUR DAD'S TRYING TO TELL YOU, KID, IS HE'S USING ALIEN TECHNOLOGY.
ALIEN TECHNOLOGY? SERIOUSLY? HOW COOL IS THAT?!
WILL YOU SHUT UP?

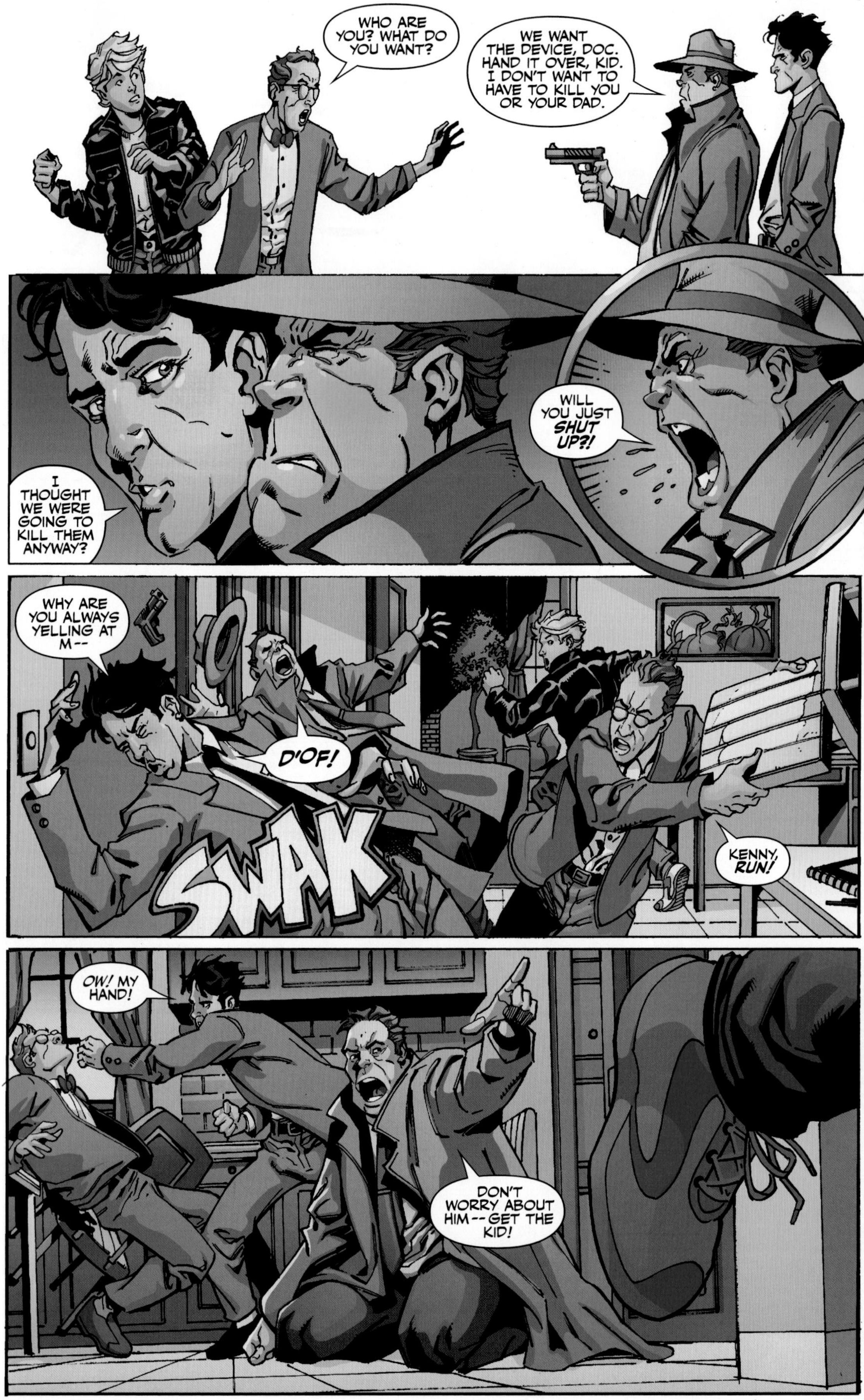

WHO ARE YOU? WHAT DO YOU WANT?
WE WANT THE DEVICE, DOC. HAND IT OVER, KID. I DON'T WANT TO HAVE TO KILL YOU OR YOUR DAD.
I THOUGHT WE WERE GOING TO KILL THEM ANYWAY?
WILL YOU JUST *SHUT UP?!*
WHY ARE YOU ALWAYS YELLING AT M--
D'OF!
SWAK
KENNY, *RUN!*
OW! MY HAND!
DON'T WORRY ABOUT HIM--GET THE KID!

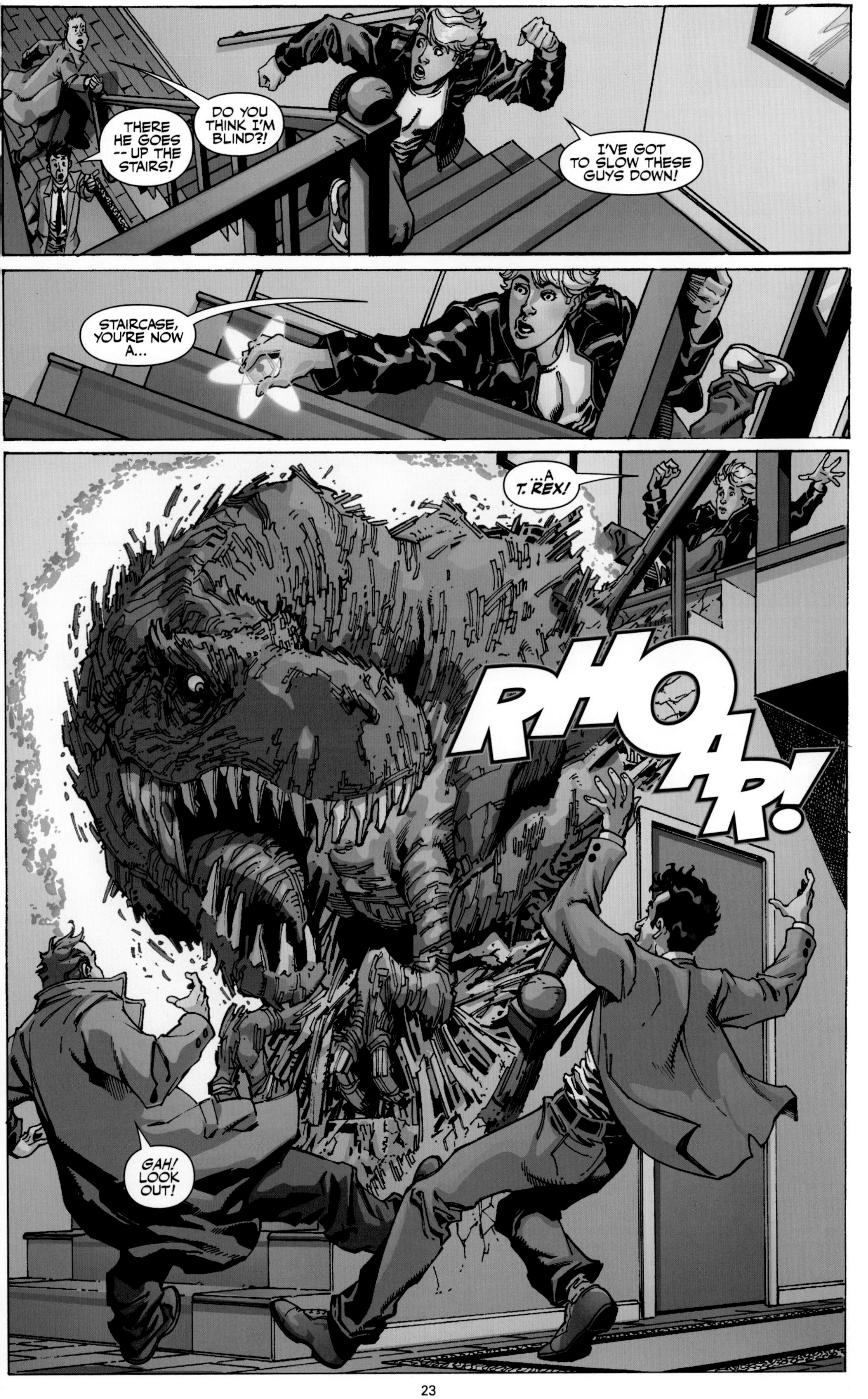

THERE HE GOES --UP THE STAIRS!
DO YOU THINK I'M BLIND?!
I'VE GOT TO SLOW THESE GUYS DOWN!
STAIRCASE, YOU'RE NOW A...
...A T. REX!
RHOAR!
GAH! LOOK OUT!

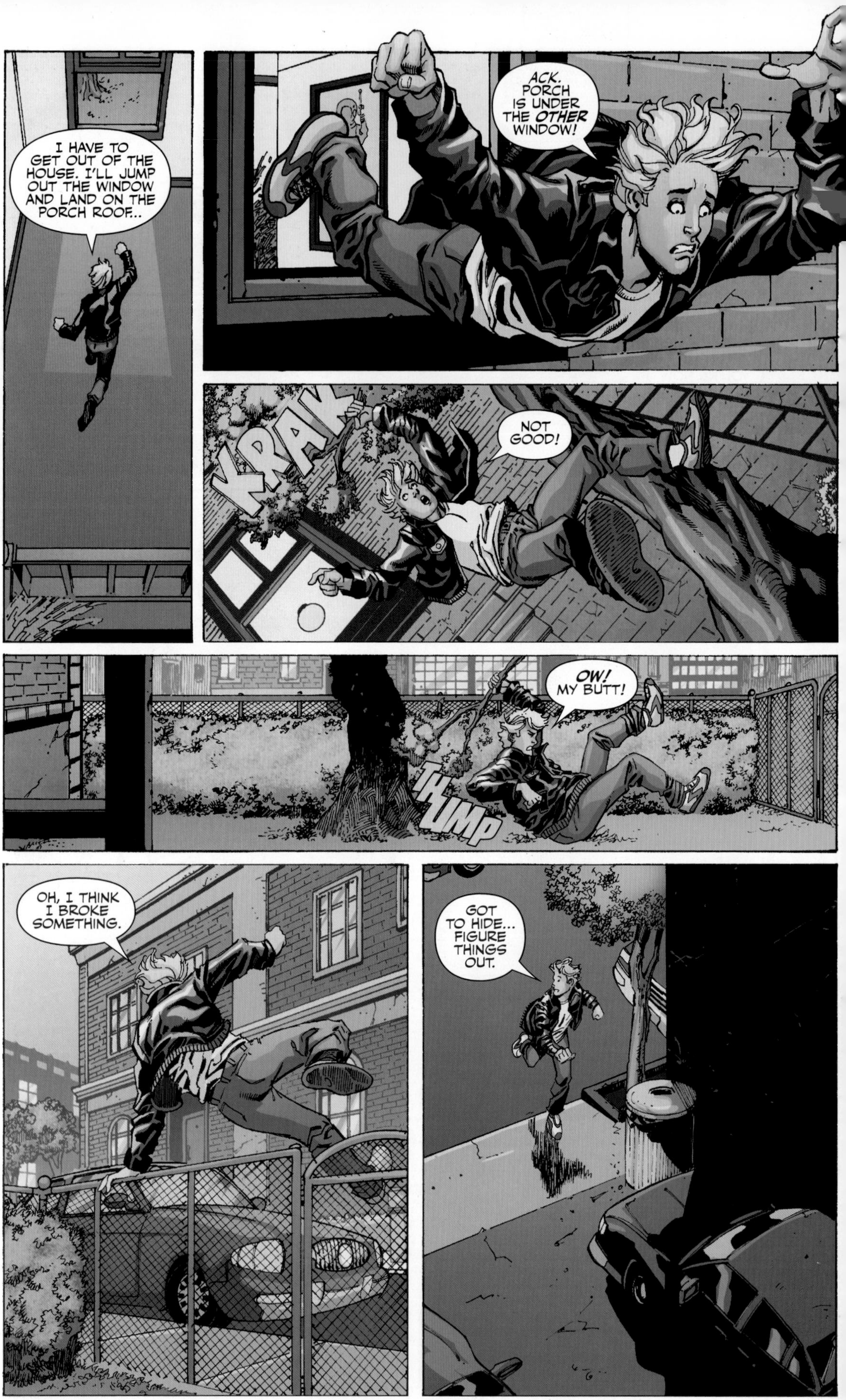
I HAVE TO GET OUT OF THE HOUSE. I'LL JUMP OUT THE WINDOW AND LAND ON THE PORCH ROOF...
ACK. PORCH IS UNDER THE *OTHER* WINDOW!
KRAK
NOT GOOD!
OW! MY BUTT!
THUMP
OH, I THINK I BROKE SOMETHING.
GOT TO HIDE... FIGURE THINGS OUT.

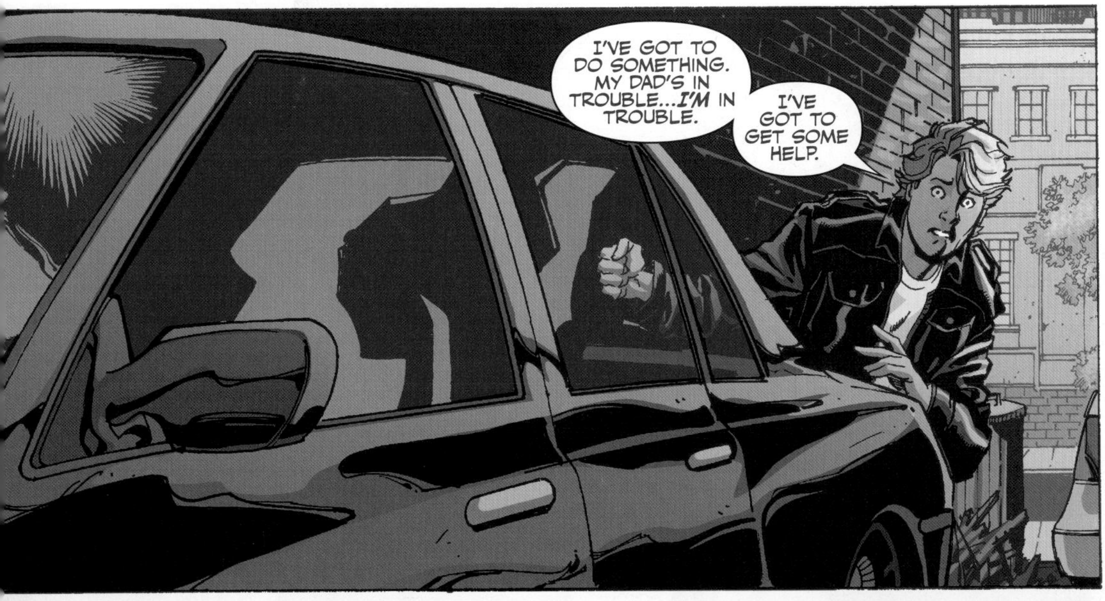
I'VE GOT TO DO SOMETHING. MY DAD'S IN TROUBLE...*I'M* IN TROUBLE.
I'VE GOT TO GET SOME HELP.

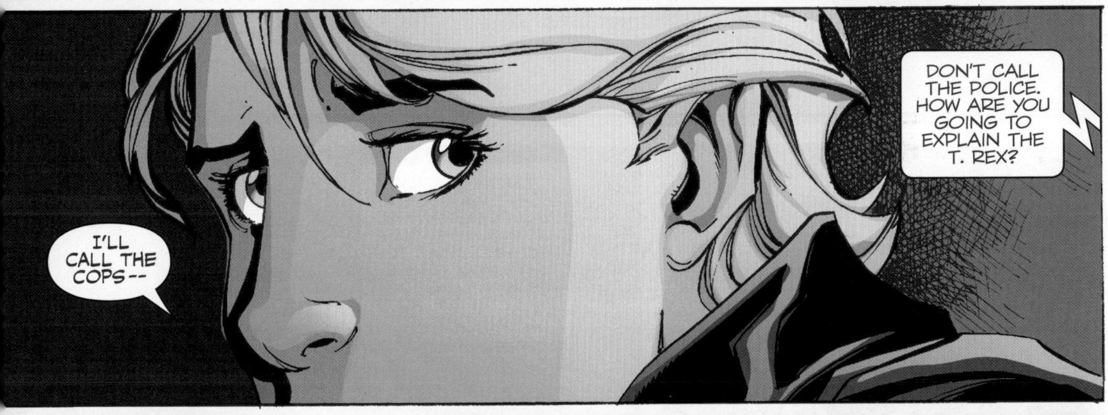
I'LL CALL THE COPS--
DON'T CALL THE POLICE. HOW ARE YOU GOING TO EXPLAIN THE T. REX?

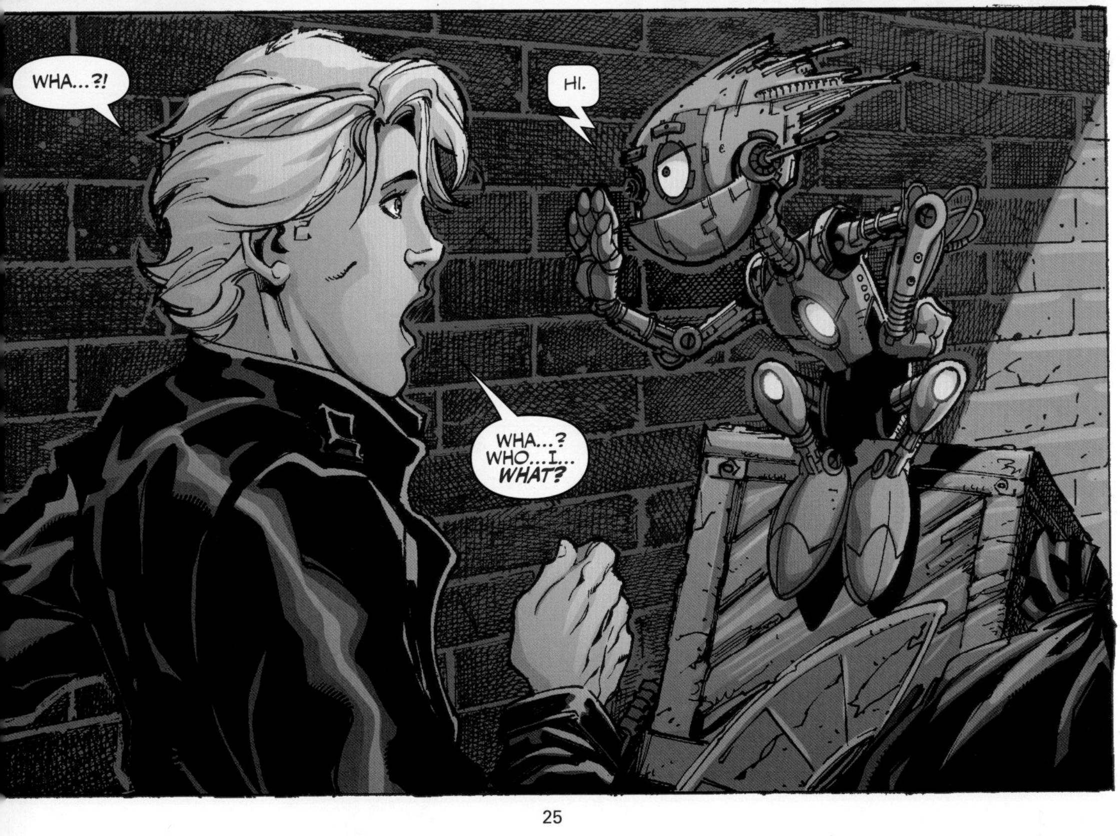
WHA...?!
HI.
WHA...? WHO...I... *WHAT?*

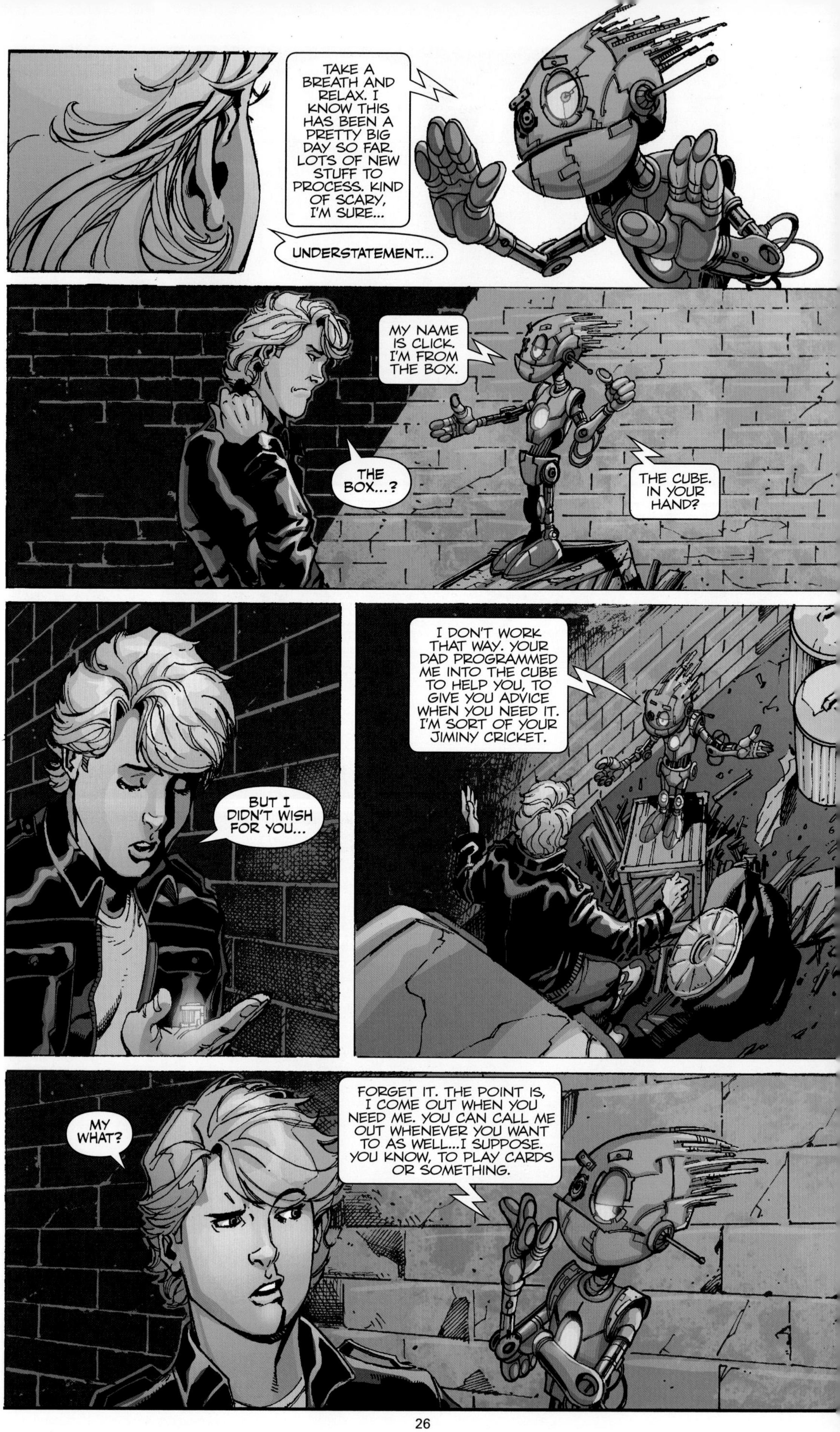
TAKE A BREATH AND RELAX. I KNOW THIS HAS BEEN A PRETTY BIG DAY SO FAR. LOTS OF NEW STUFF TO PROCESS. KIND OF SCARY, I'M SURE...
UNDERSTATEMENT...
MY NAME IS CLICK. I'M FROM THE BOX.
THE BOX...?
THE CUBE. IN YOUR HAND?
BUT I DIDN'T WISH FOR YOU...
I DON'T WORK THAT WAY. YOUR DAD PROGRAMMED ME INTO THE CUBE TO HELP YOU, TO GIVE YOU ADVICE WHEN YOU NEED IT. I'M SORT OF YOUR JIMINY CRICKET.
MY WHAT?
FORGET IT. THE POINT IS, I COME OUT WHEN YOU NEED ME. YOU CAN CALL ME OUT WHENEVER YOU WANT TO AS WELL...I SUPPOSE. YOU KNOW, TO PLAY CARDS OR SOMETHING.

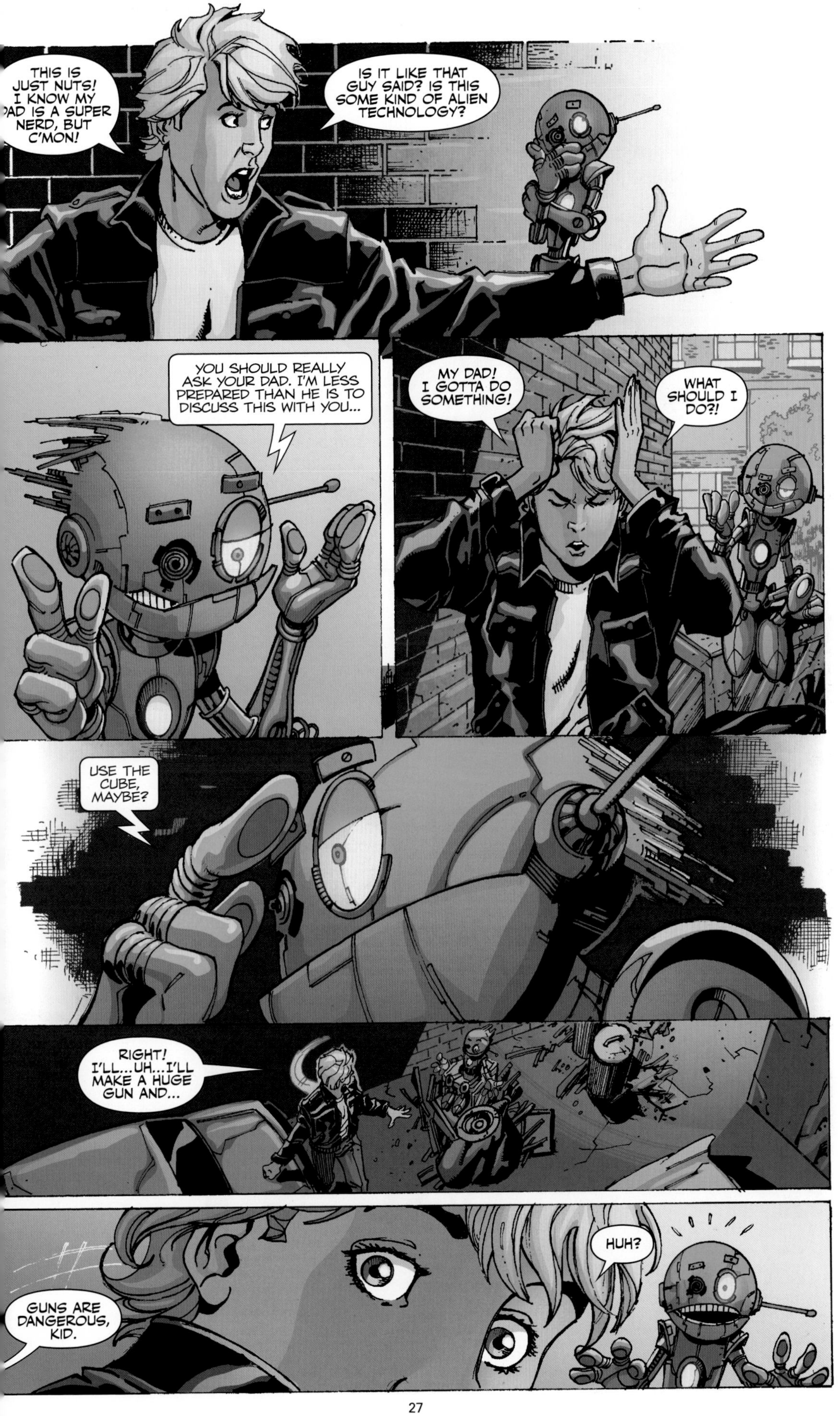
THIS IS JUST NUTS! I KNOW MY DAD IS A SUPER NERD, BUT C'MON!
IS IT LIKE THAT GUY SAID? IS THIS SOME KIND OF ALIEN TECHNOLOGY?
YOU SHOULD REALLY ASK YOUR DAD. I'M LESS PREPARED THAN HE IS TO DISCUSS THIS WITH YOU...
MY DAD! I GOTTA DO SOMETHING!
WHAT SHOULD I DO?!
USE THE CUBE, MAYBE?
RIGHT! I'LL...UH...I'LL MAKE A HUGE GUN AND...
HUH?
GUNS ARE DANGEROUS, KID.

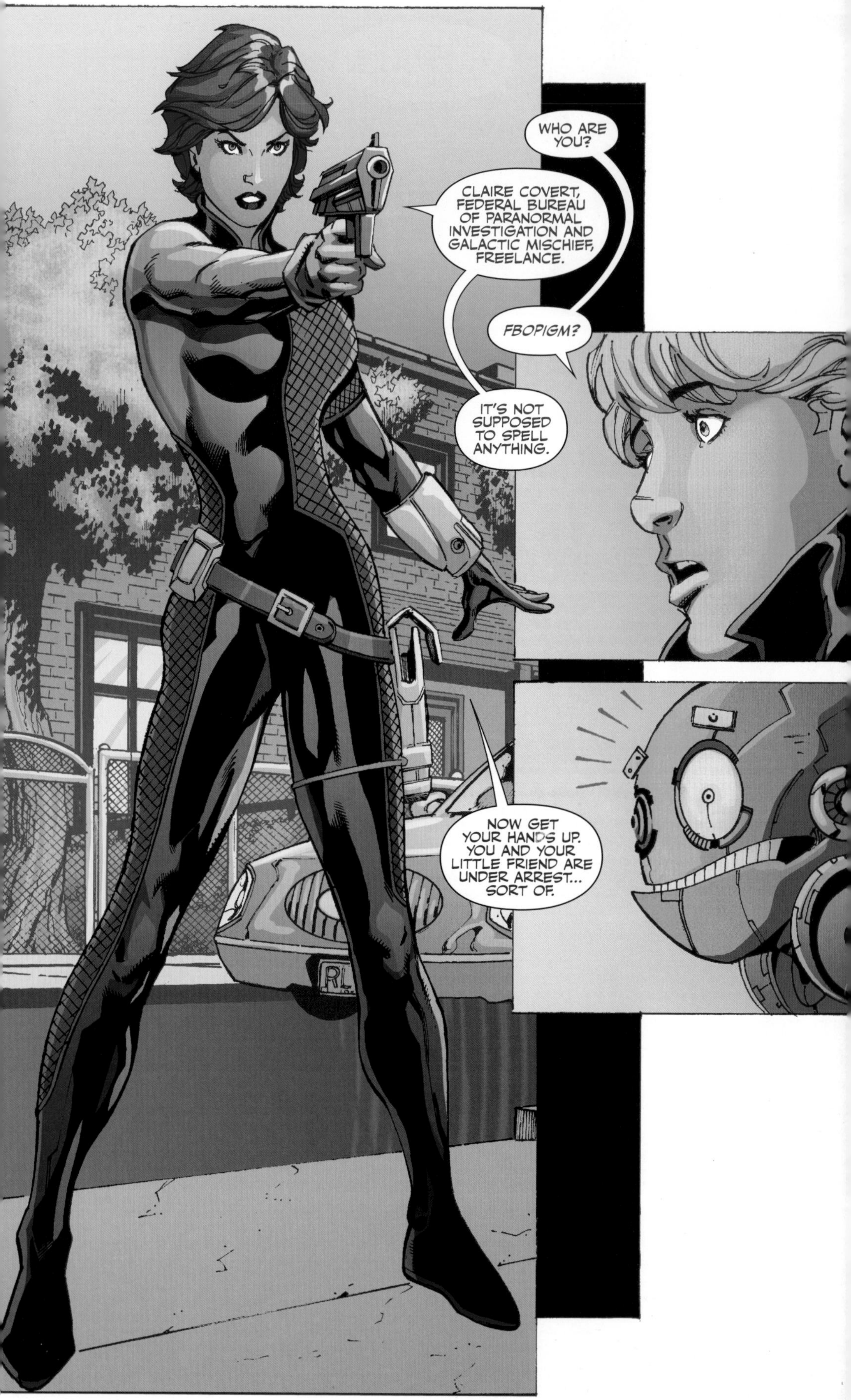
WHO ARE YOU?
CLAIRE COVERT, FEDERAL BUREAU OF PARANORMAL INVESTIGATION AND GALACTIC MISCHIEF, FREELANCE.
FBOPIGM?
IT'S NOT SUPPOSED TO SPELL ANYTHING.
NOW GET YOUR HANDS UP. YOU AND YOUR LITTLE FRIEND ARE UNDER ARREST... SORT OF.
RL

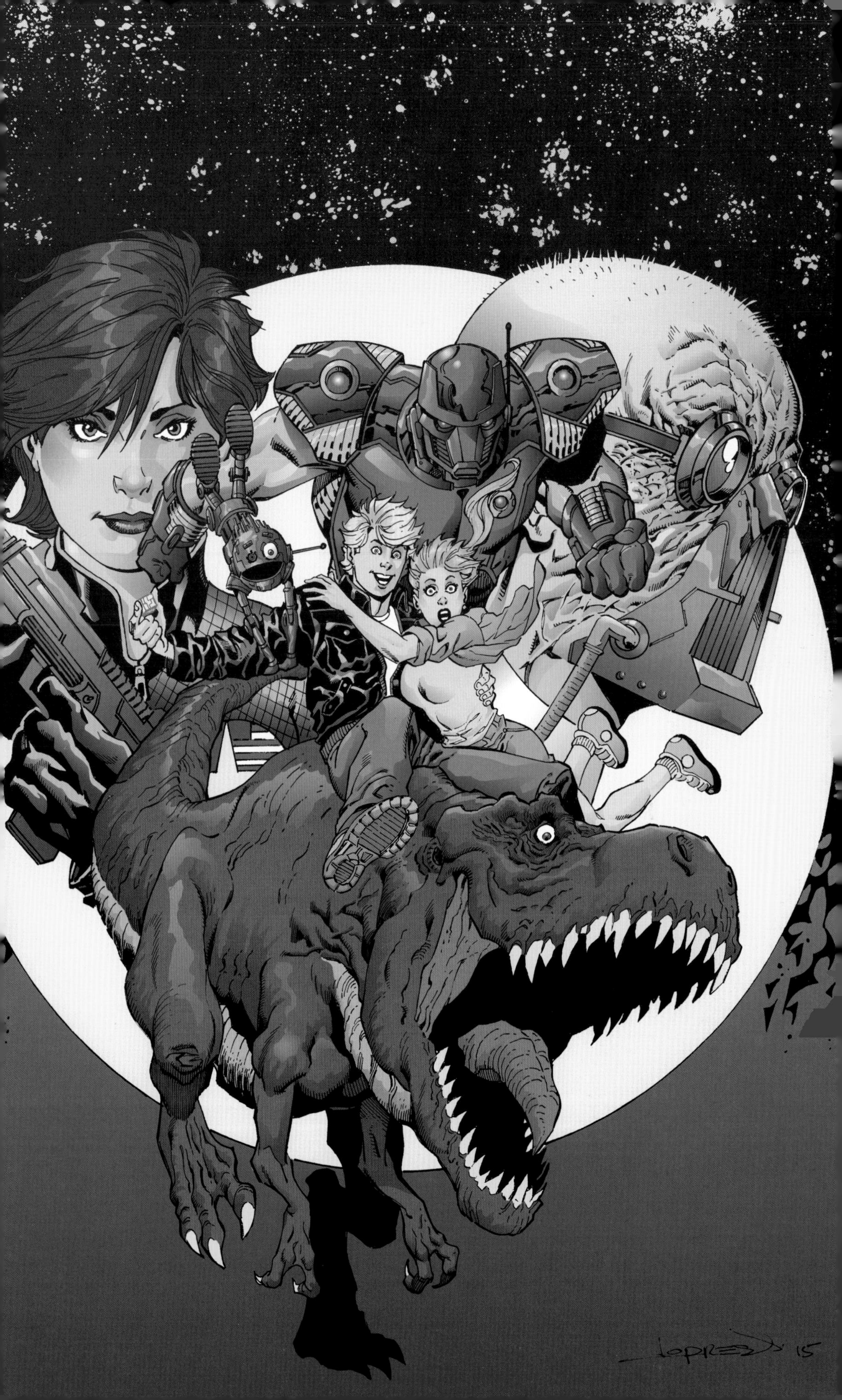

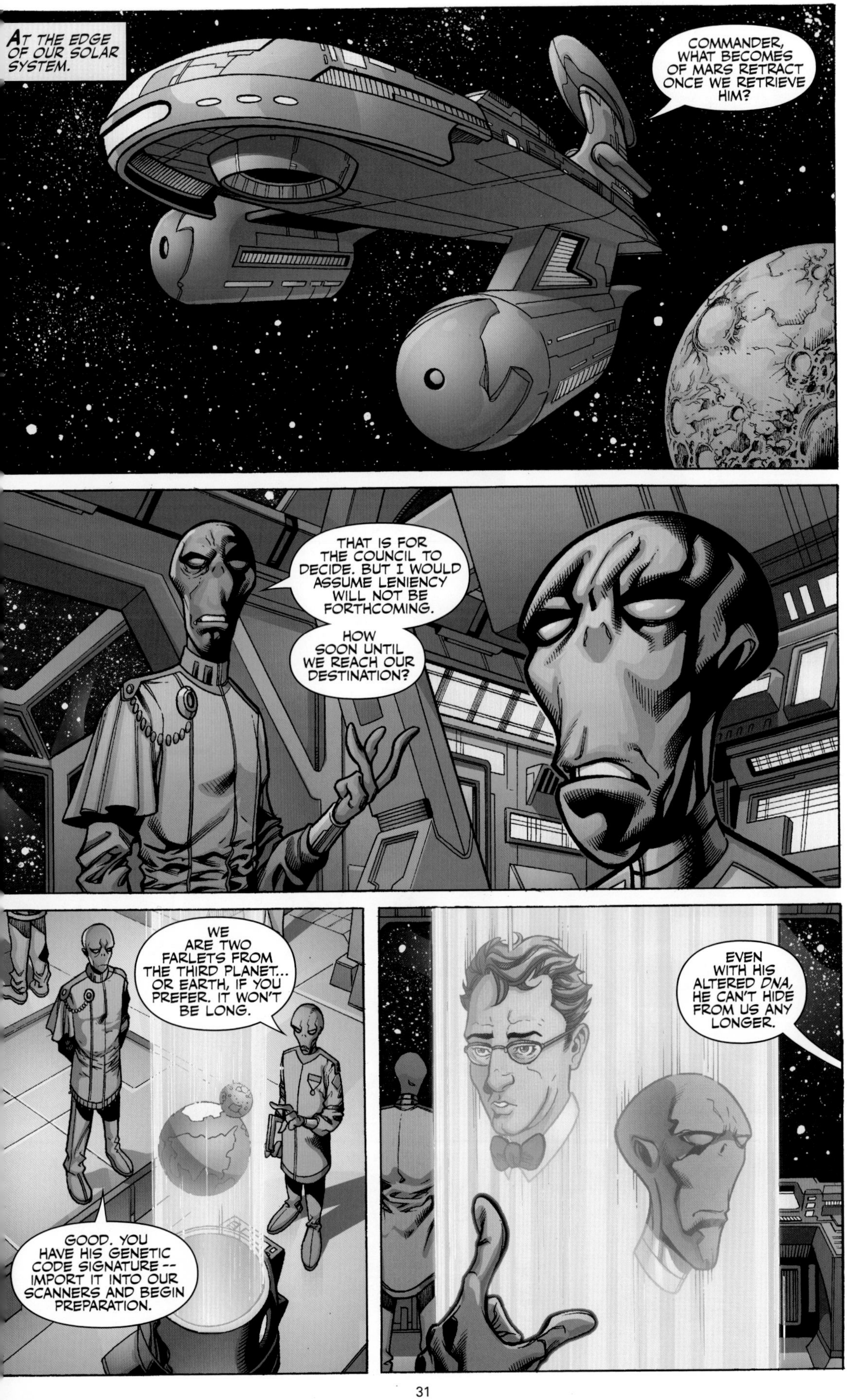
AT THE EDGE OF OUR SOLAR SYSTEM.
COMMANDER, WHAT BECOMES OF MARS RETRACT ONCE WE RETRIEVE HIM?
THAT IS FOR THE COUNCIL TO DECIDE. BUT I WOULD ASSUME LENIENCY WILL NOT BE FORTHCOMING.
HOW SOON UNTIL WE REACH OUR DESTINATION?
WE ARE TWO FARLETS FROM THE THIRD PLANET... OR EARTH, IF YOU PREFER. IT WON'T BE LONG.
GOOD. YOU HAVE HIS GENETIC CODE SIGNATURE -- IMPORT IT INTO OUR SCANNERS AND BEGIN PREPARATION.
EVEN WITH HIS ALTERED *DNA*, HE CAN'T HIDE FROM US ANY LONGER.

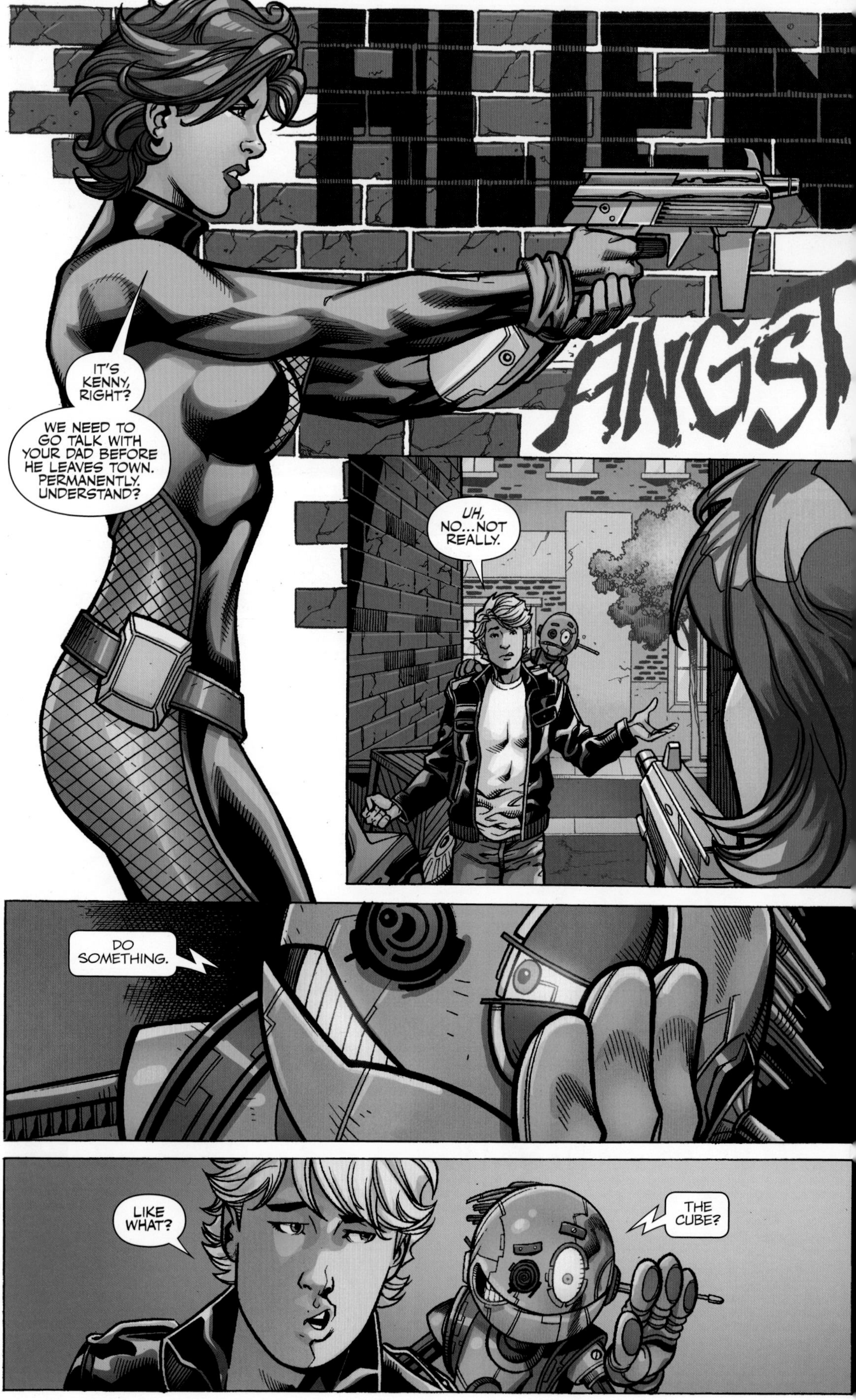
ALIEN
ANGST
IT'S KENNY, RIGHT?
WE NEED TO GO TALK WITH YOUR DAD BEFORE HE LEAVES TOWN. PERMANENTLY. UNDERSTAND?
UH, NO...NOT REALLY.
DO SOMETHING.
LIKE WHAT?
THE CUBE?

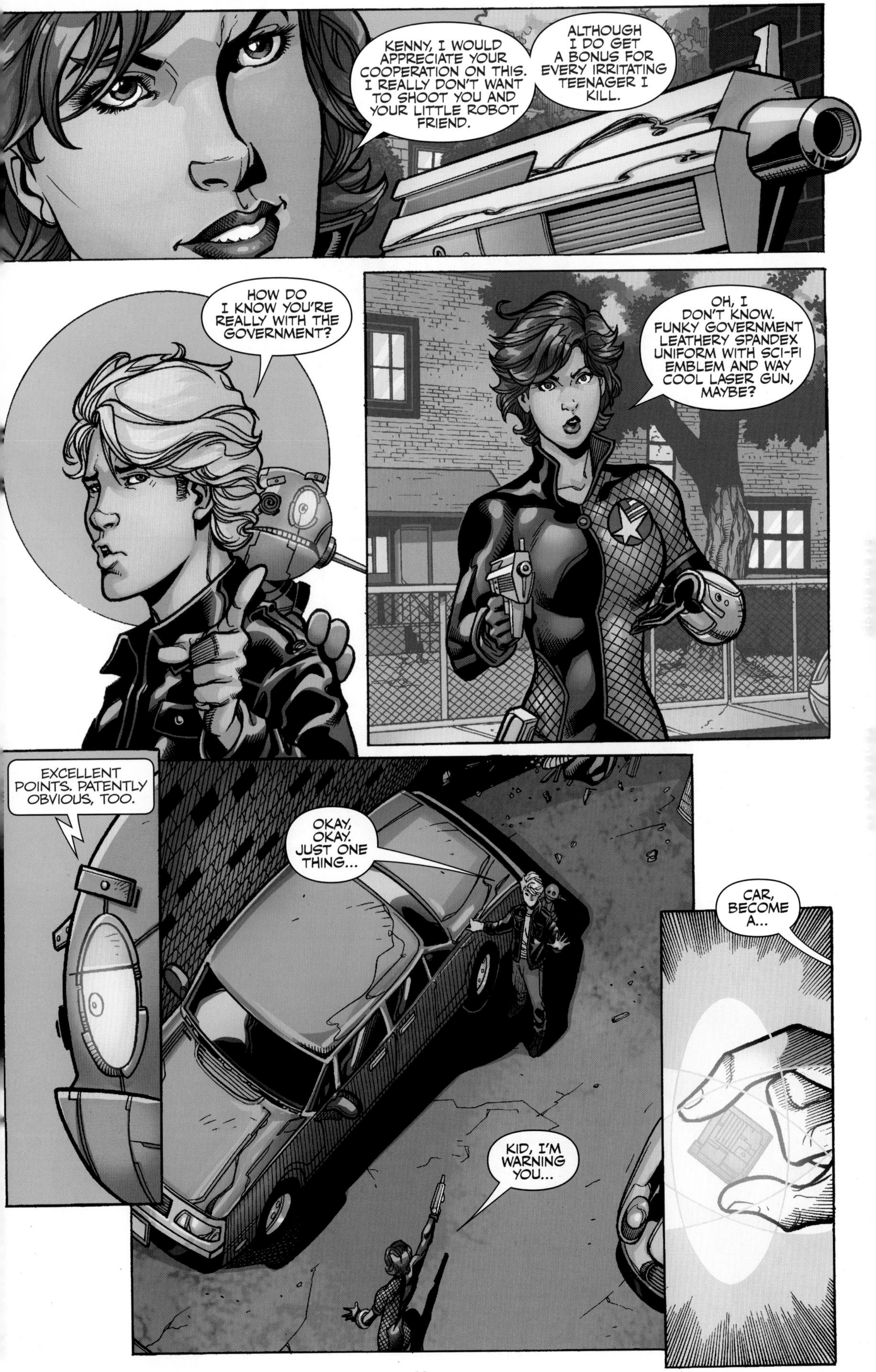

KENNY, I WOULD APPRECIATE YOUR COOPERATION ON THIS. I REALLY DON'T WANT TO SHOOT YOU AND YOUR LITTLE ROBOT FRIEND.
ALTHOUGH I DO GET A BONUS FOR EVERY IRRITATING TEENAGER I KILL.
HOW DO I KNOW YOU'RE REALLY WITH THE GOVERNMENT?
OH, I DON'T KNOW. FUNKY GOVERNMENT LEATHERY SPANDEX UNIFORM WITH SCI-FI EMBLEM AND WAY COOL LASER GUN, MAYBE?
EXCELLENT POINTS. PATENTLY OBVIOUS, TOO.
OKAY, OKAY. JUST ONE THING...
KID, I'M WARNING YOU...
CAR, BECOME A...

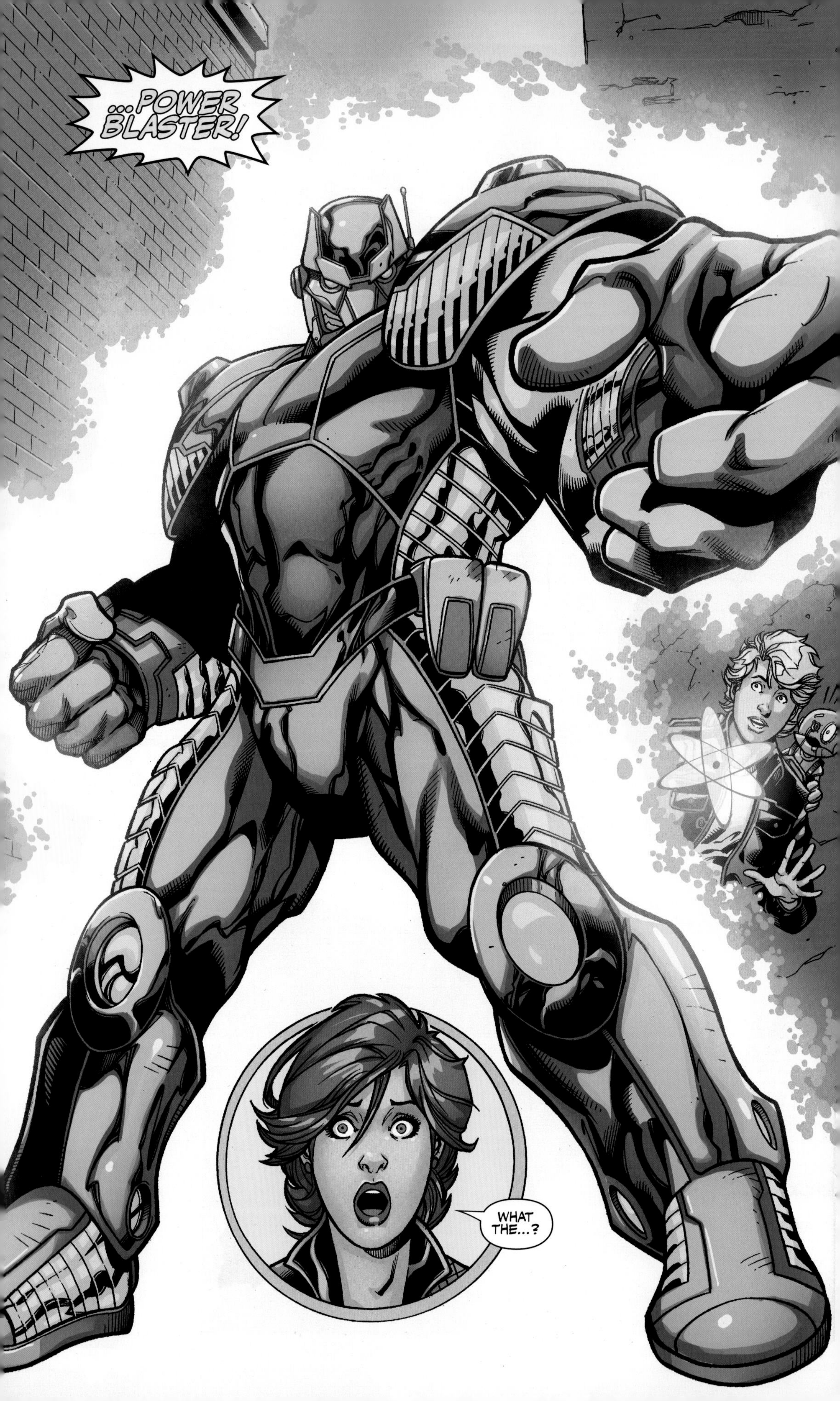
...POWER BLASTER!
WHAT THE...?

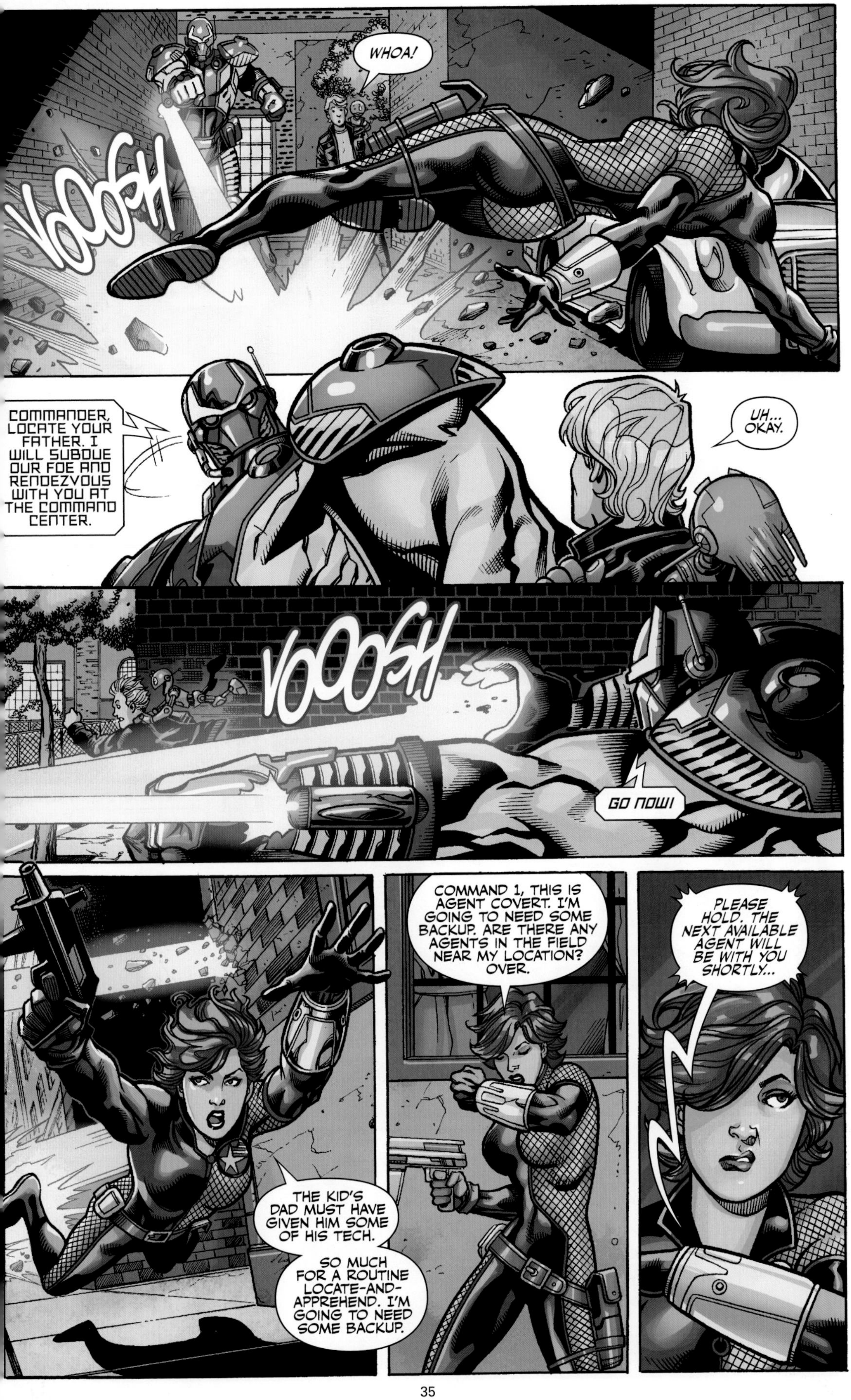
WHOA!
VOOOSH
COMMANDER, LOCATE YOUR FATHER. I WILL SUBDUE OUR FOE AND RENDEZVOUS WITH YOU AT THE COMMAND CENTER.
UH... OKAY.
VOOOSH
GO NOW!
THE KID'S DAD MUST HAVE GIVEN HIM SOME OF HIS TECH.
SO MUCH FOR A ROUTINE LOCATE-AND-APPREHEND. I'M GOING TO NEED SOME BACKUP.
COMMAND 1, THIS IS AGENT COVERT. I'M GOING TO NEED SOME BACKUP. ARE THERE ANY AGENTS IN THE FIELD NEAR MY LOCATION? OVER.
PLEASE HOLD. THE NEXT AVAILABLE AGENT WILL BE WITH YOU SHORTLY...

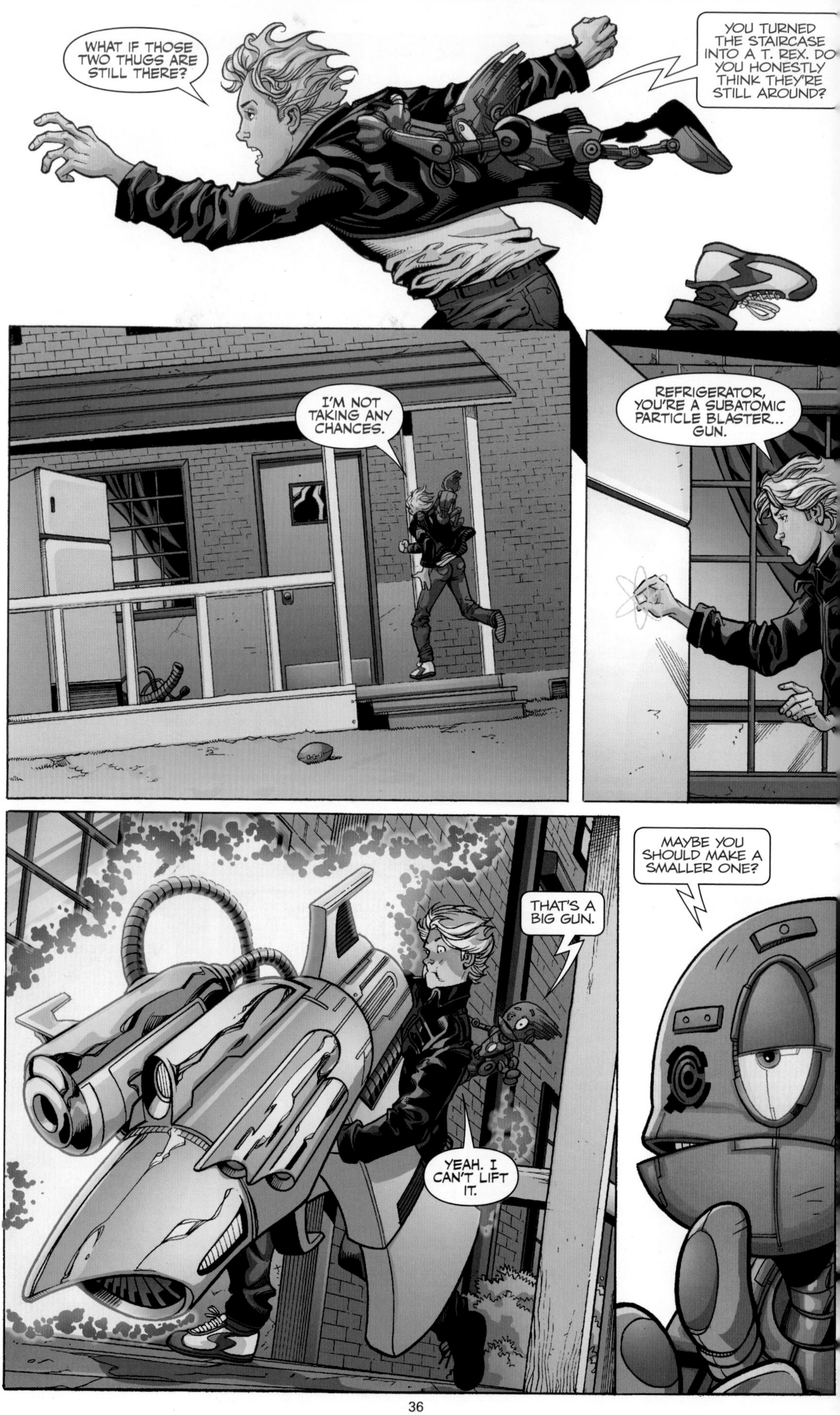
WHAT IF THOSE TWO THUGS ARE STILL THERE?
YOU TURNED THE STAIRCASE INTO A T. REX. DO YOU HONESTLY THINK THEY'RE STILL AROUND?
I'M NOT TAKING ANY CHANCES.
REFRIGERATOR, YOU'RE A SUBATOMIC PARTICLE BLASTER... GUN.
THAT'S A BIG GUN.
YEAH. I CAN'T LIFT IT.
MAYBE YOU SHOULD MAKE A SMALLER ONE?

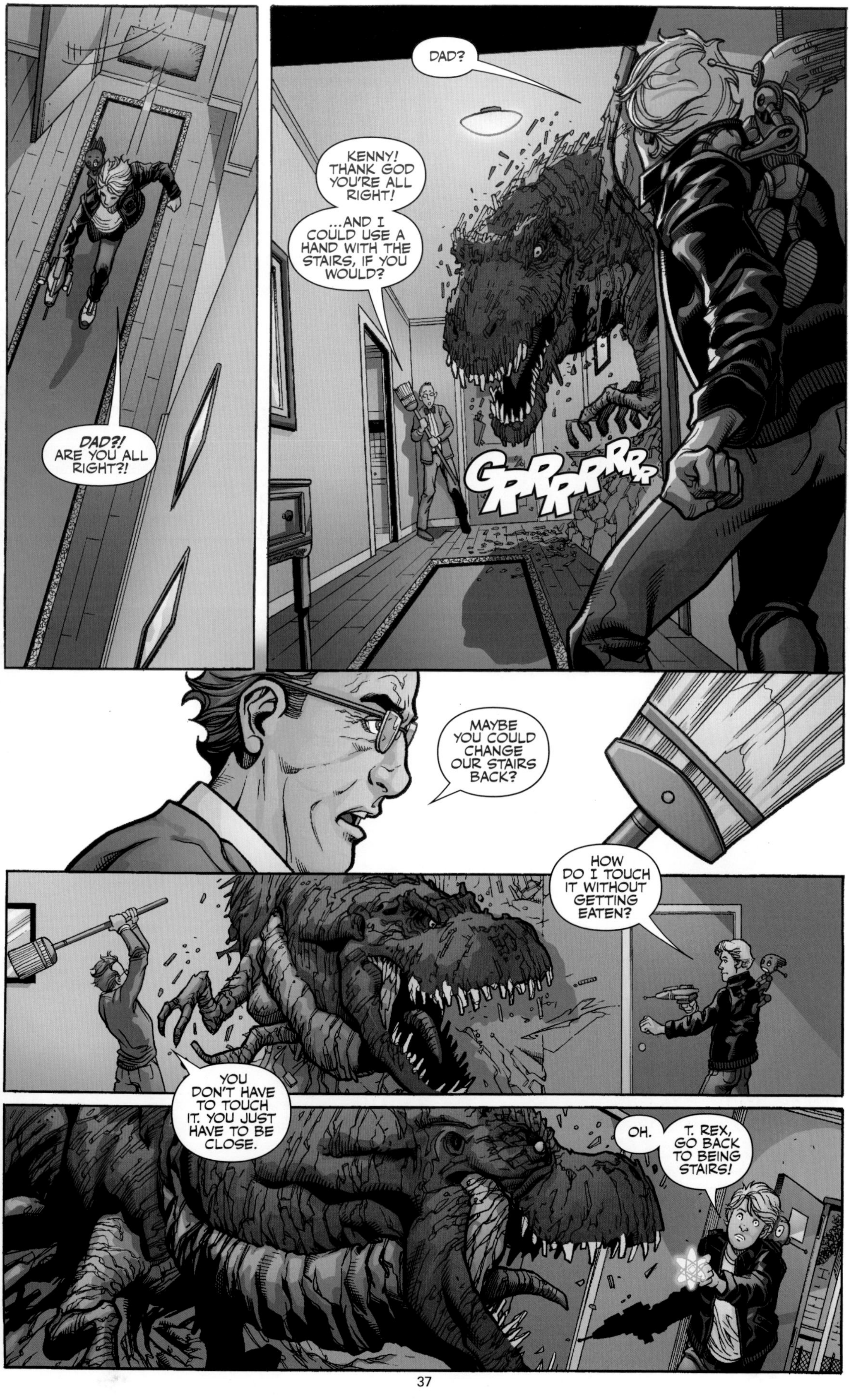
DAD?! ARE YOU ALL RIGHT?!
DAD?
KENNY! THANK GOD YOU'RE ALL RIGHT!
...AND I COULD USE A HAND WITH THE STAIRS, IF YOU WOULD?
GRRRRRRRR
MAYBE YOU COULD CHANGE OUR STAIRS BACK?
HOW DO I TOUCH IT WITHOUT GETTING EATEN?
YOU DON'T HAVE TO TOUCH IT. YOU JUST HAVE TO BE CLOSE.
OH.
T. REX, GO BACK TO BEING STAIRS!

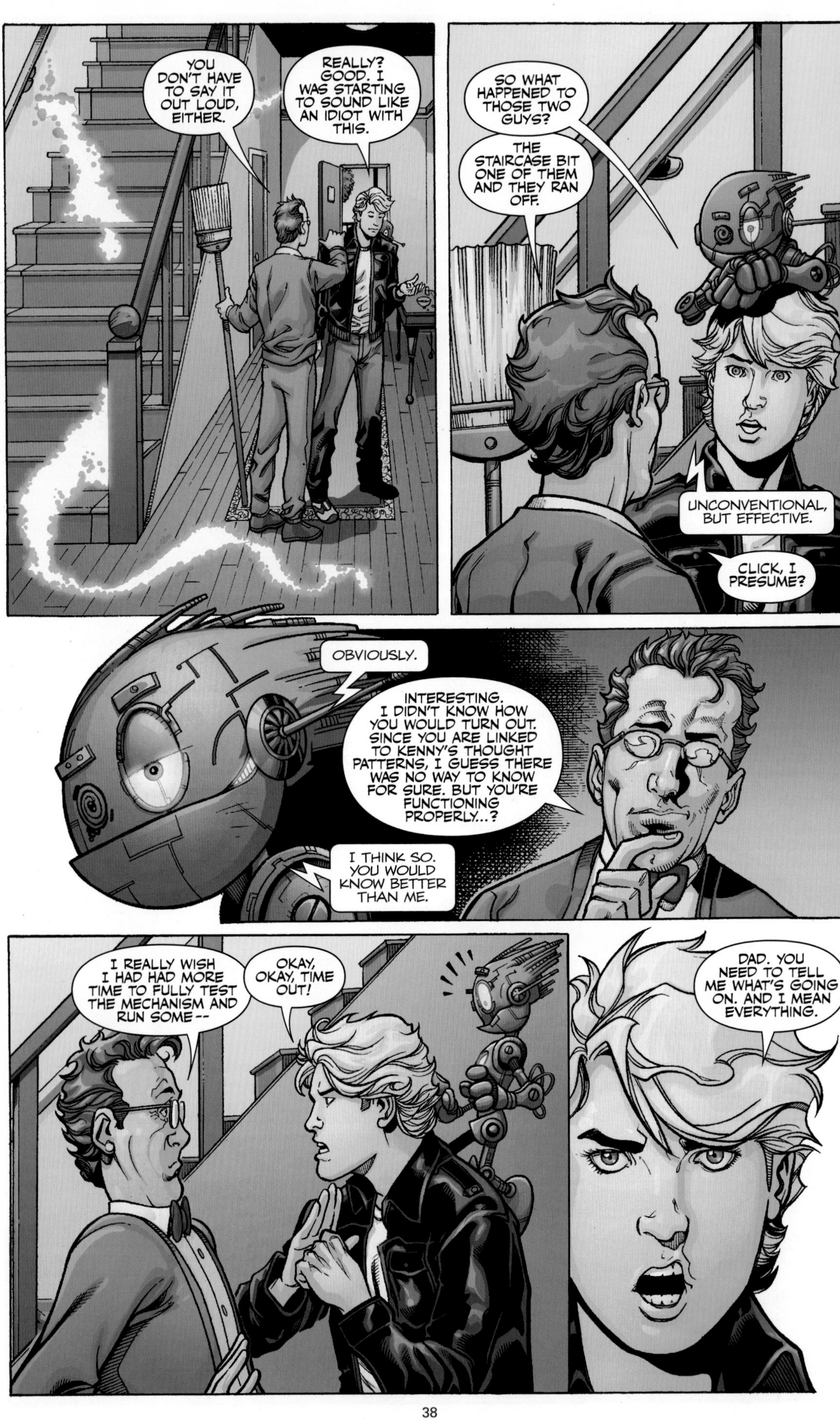
YOU DON'T HAVE TO SAY IT OUT LOUD, EITHER.
REALLY? GOOD. I WAS STARTING TO SOUND LIKE AN IDIOT WITH THIS.
SO WHAT HAPPENED TO THOSE TWO GUYS?
THE STAIRCASE BIT ONE OF THEM AND THEY RAN OFF.
UNCONVENTIONAL, BUT EFFECTIVE.
CLICK, I PRESUME?
OBVIOUSLY.
INTERESTING. I DIDN'T KNOW HOW YOU WOULD TURN OUT. SINCE YOU ARE LINKED TO KENNY'S THOUGHT PATTERNS, I GUESS THERE WAS NO WAY TO KNOW FOR SURE. BUT YOU'RE FUNCTIONING PROPERLY...?
I THINK SO. YOU WOULD KNOW BETTER THAN ME.
I REALLY WISH I HAD HAD MORE TIME TO FULLY TEST THE MECHANISM AND RUN SOME--
OKAY, OKAY, TIME OUT!
DAD. YOU NEED TO TELL ME WHAT'S GOING ON. AND I MEAN EVERYTHING.

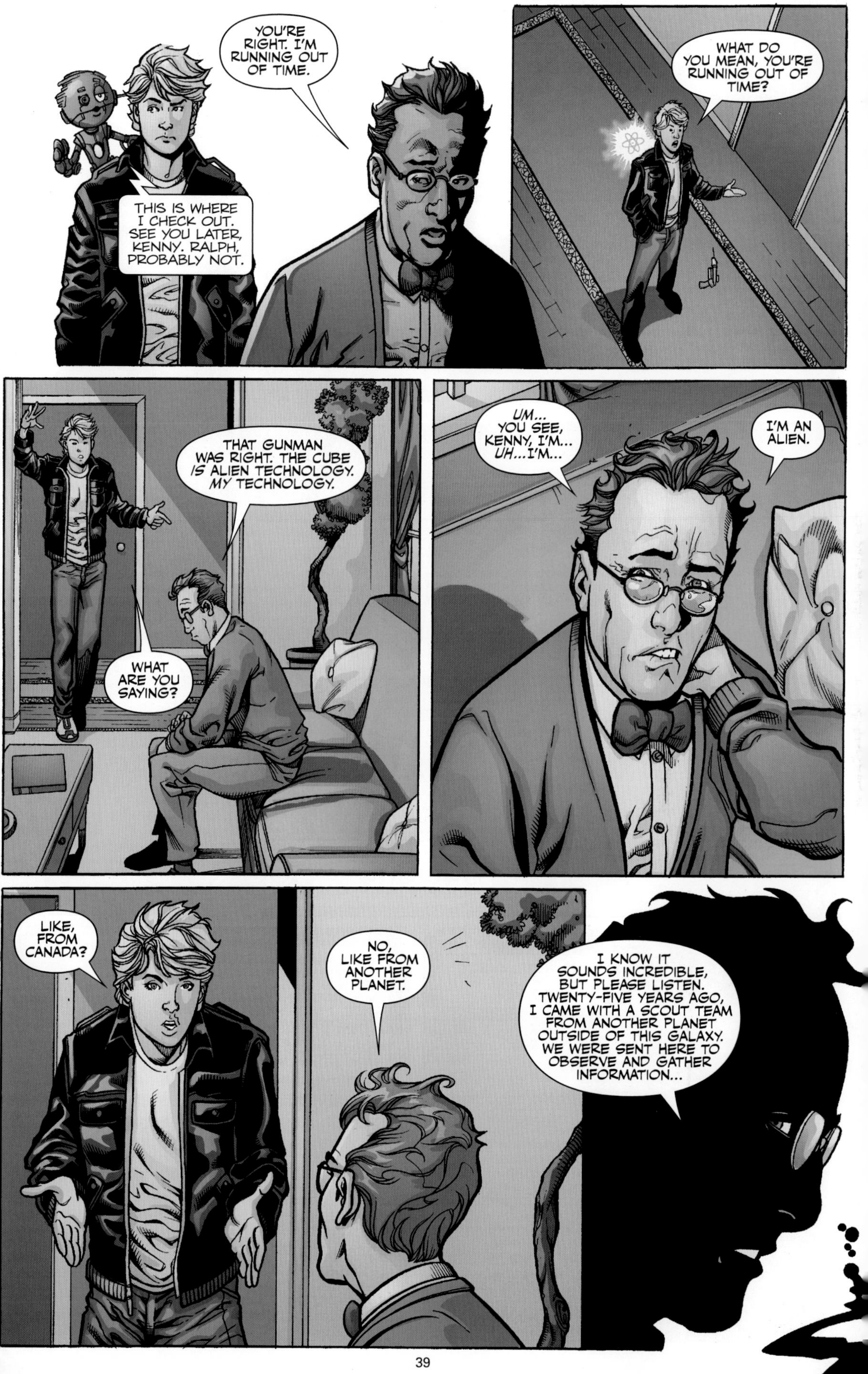

YOU'RE RIGHT. I'M RUNNING OUT OF TIME.
THIS IS WHERE I CHECK OUT. SEE YOU LATER, KENNY. RALPH, PROBABLY NOT.
WHAT DO YOU MEAN, YOU'RE RUNNING OUT OF TIME?
THAT GUNMAN WAS RIGHT. THE CUBE *IS* ALIEN TECHNOLOGY. *MY* TECHNOLOGY.
WHAT ARE YOU SAYING?
UM... YOU SEE, KENNY, I'M... *UH*...I'M...
I'M AN ALIEN.
LIKE, FROM CANADA?
NO, LIKE FROM ANOTHER PLANET.
I KNOW IT SOUNDS INCREDIBLE, BUT PLEASE LISTEN. TWENTY-FIVE YEARS AGO, I CAME WITH A SCOUT TEAM FROM ANOTHER PLANET OUTSIDE OF THIS GALAXY. WE WERE SENT HERE TO OBSERVE AND GATHER INFORMATION...

"OUR HOME PLANET WAS DEVASTATED BY CIVIL WAR. WE HAD TO LOCATE A PLANET THAT COULD SUSTAIN OUR RACE. EARTH APPEARED TO BE THE CLOSEST AND BEST CHOICE."

SO WHAT ABOUT MOM? SHE WAS AN ALIEN TOO?

"NO. WE ABDUCTED SEVERAL HUMANS TO DO SHORT-TERM STUDIES ON. YOUR MOTHER WAS ONE OF THEM.

"BEING THE SHIP'S SCIENCE OFFICER, IT FELL UPON ME TO PERFORM THE TESTS AND PROBABLE DISSECTION.

"BUT, INEXPLICABLY, I FELL IN LOVE WITH YOUR MOTHER.

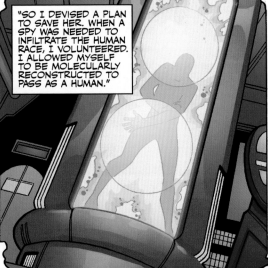

"SO I DEVISED A PLAN TO SAVE HER. WHEN A SPY WAS NEEDED TO INFILTRATE THE HUMAN RACE, I VOLUNTEERED. I ALLOWED MYSELF TO BE MOLECULARLY RECONSTRUCTED TO PASS AS A HUMAN."

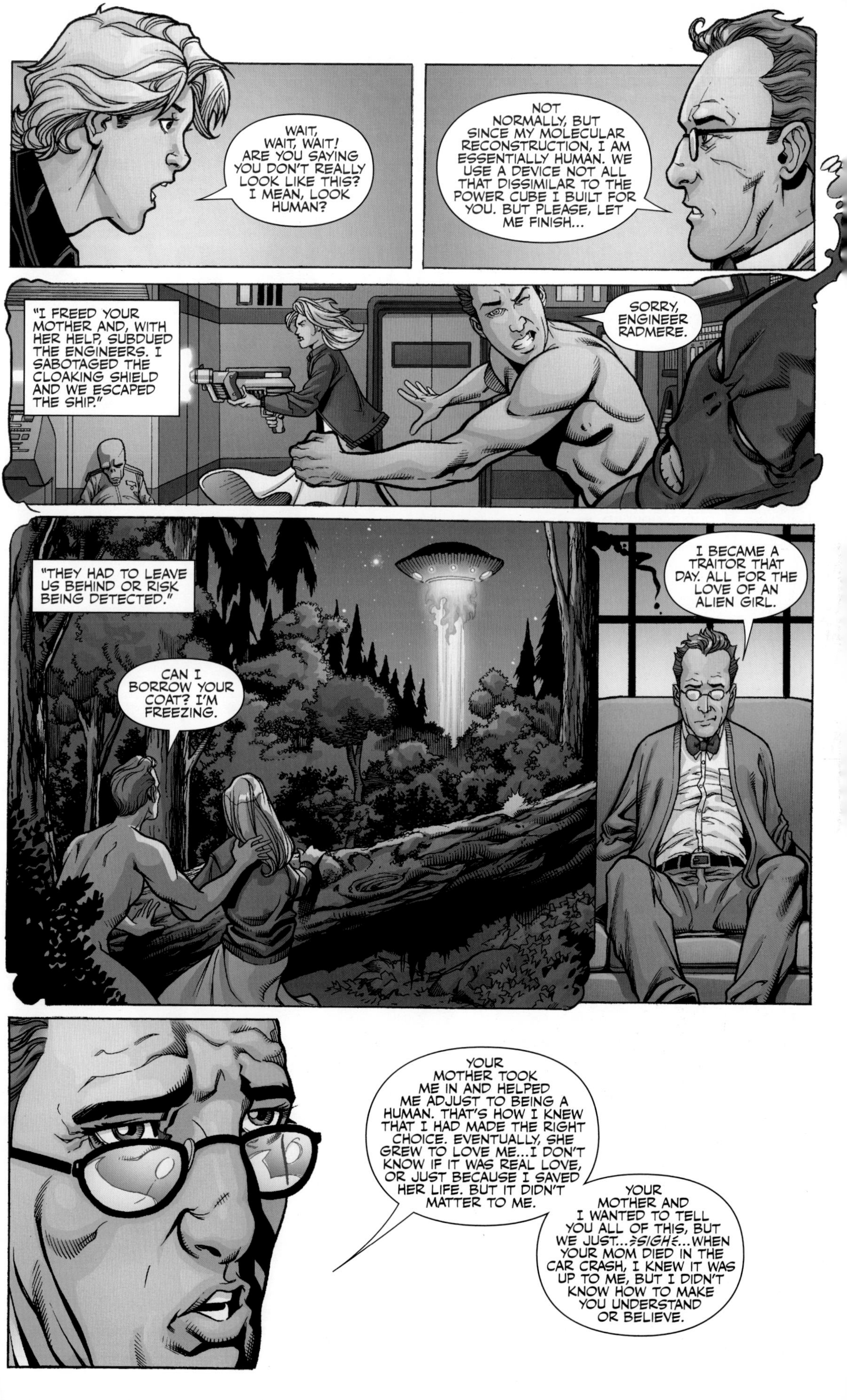
WAIT, WAIT, WAIT! ARE YOU SAYING YOU DON'T REALLY LOOK LIKE THIS? I MEAN, LOOK HUMAN?
NOT NORMALLY, BUT SINCE MY MOLECULAR RECONSTRUCTION, I AM ESSENTIALLY HUMAN. WE USE A DEVICE NOT ALL THAT DISSIMILAR TO THE POWER CUBE I BUILT FOR YOU. BUT PLEASE, LET ME FINISH...
"I FREED YOUR MOTHER AND, WITH HER HELP, SUBDUED THE ENGINEERS. I SABOTAGED THE CLOAKING SHIELD AND WE ESCAPED THE SHIP."
SORRY, ENGINEER RADMERE.
"THEY HAD TO LEAVE US BEHIND OR RISK BEING DETECTED."
CAN I BORROW YOUR COAT? I'M FREEZING.
I BECAME A TRAITOR THAT DAY. ALL FOR THE LOVE OF AN ALIEN GIRL.
YOUR MOTHER TOOK ME IN AND HELPED ME ADJUST TO BEING A HUMAN. THAT'S HOW I KNEW THAT I HAD MADE THE RIGHT CHOICE. EVENTUALLY, SHE GREW TO LOVE ME...I DON'T KNOW IF IT WAS REAL LOVE, OR JUST BECAUSE I SAVED HER LIFE. BUT IT DIDN'T MATTER TO ME.
YOUR MOTHER AND I WANTED TO TELL YOU ALL OF THIS, BUT WE JUST...≥SIGH≤...WHEN YOUR MOM DIED IN THE CAR CRASH, I KNEW IT WAS UP TO ME, BUT I DIDN'T KNOW HOW TO MAKE YOU UNDERSTAND OR BELIEVE.

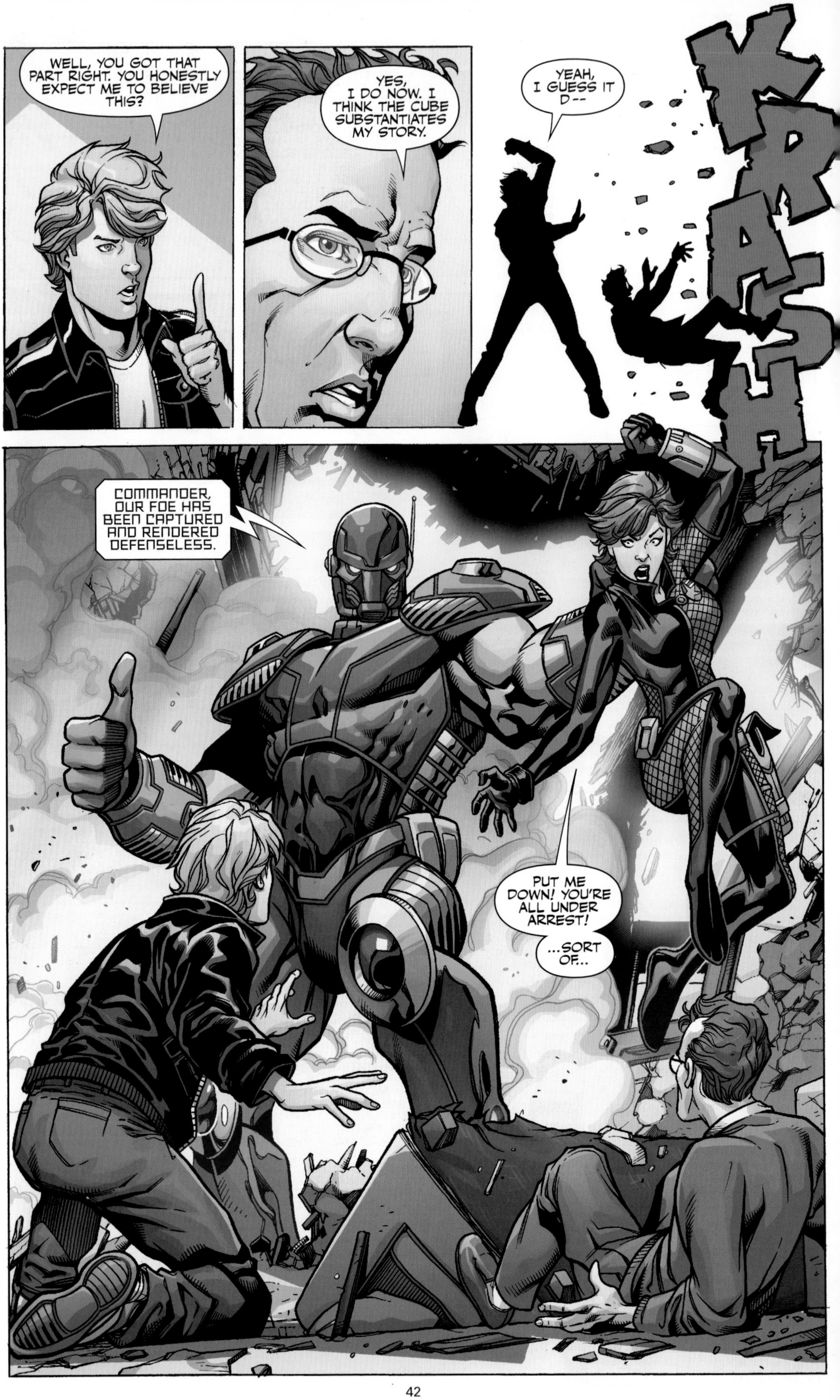

WELL, YOU GOT THAT PART RIGHT. YOU HONESTLY EXPECT ME TO BELIEVE THIS?
YES, I DO NOW. I THINK THE CUBE SUBSTANTIATES MY STORY.
YEAH, I GUESS IT D--
KRASH
COMMANDER, OUR FOE HAS BEEN CAPTURED AND RENDERED DEFENSELESS.
PUT ME DOWN! YOU'RE ALL UNDER ARREST!
...SORT OF...

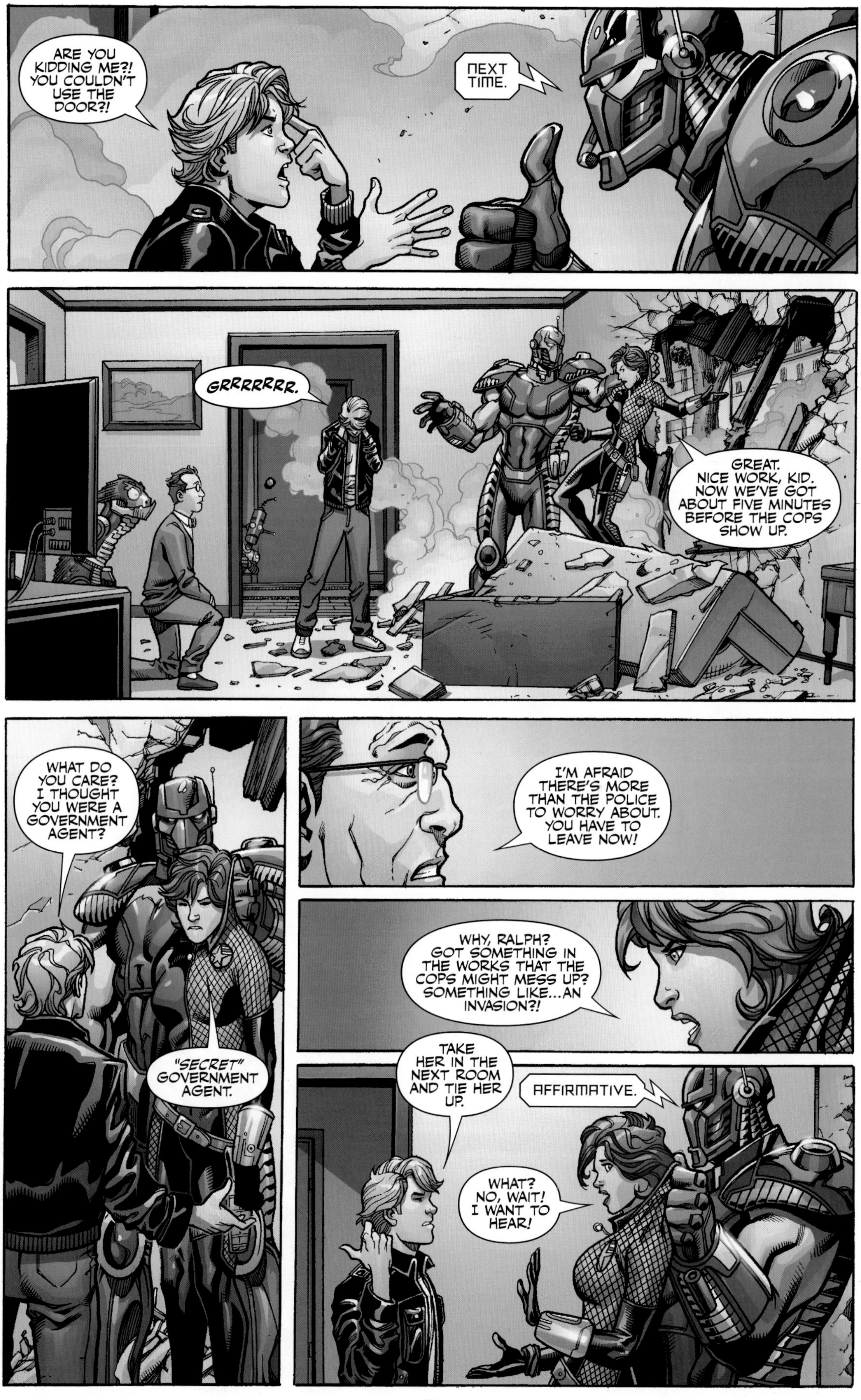
ARE YOU KIDDING ME?! YOU COULDN'T USE THE DOOR?!
NEXT TIME.
GRRRRRRR.
GREAT. NICE WORK, KID. NOW WE'VE GOT ABOUT FIVE MINUTES BEFORE THE COPS SHOW UP.
WHAT DO YOU CARE? I THOUGHT YOU WERE A GOVERNMENT AGENT?
"SECRET" GOVERNMENT AGENT.
I'M AFRAID THERE'S MORE THAN THE POLICE TO WORRY ABOUT. YOU HAVE TO LEAVE NOW!
WHY, RALPH? GOT SOMETHING IN THE WORKS THAT THE COPS MIGHT MESS UP? SOMETHING LIKE...AN INVASION?!
TAKE HER IN THE NEXT ROOM AND TIE HER UP.
AFFIRMATIVE.
WHAT? NO, WAIT! I WANT TO HEAR!

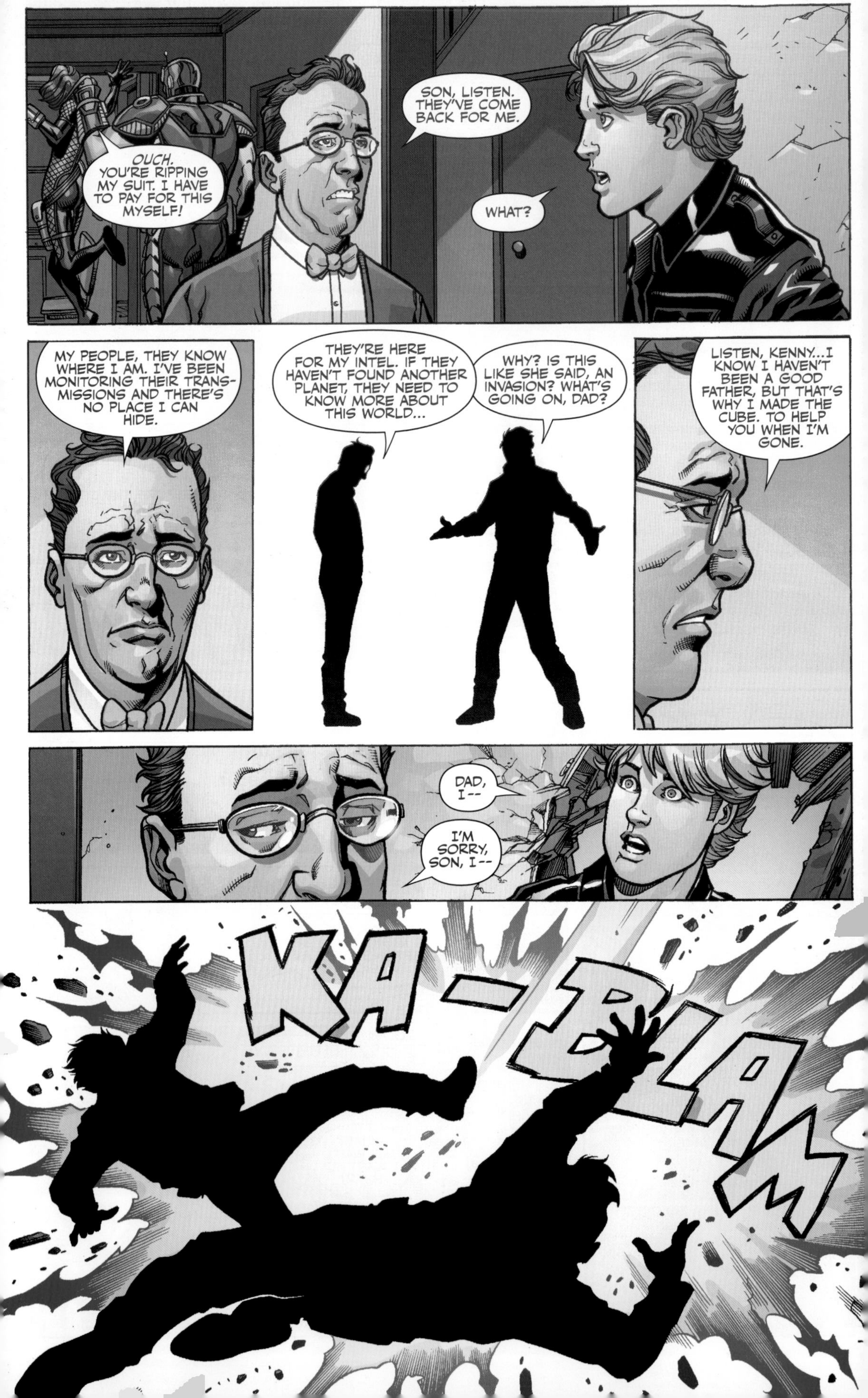

OUCH. YOU'RE RIPPING MY SUIT. I HAVE TO PAY FOR THIS MYSELF!
SON, LISTEN. THEY'VE COME BACK FOR ME.
WHAT?
MY PEOPLE, THEY KNOW WHERE I AM. I'VE BEEN MONITORING THEIR TRANS-MISSIONS AND THERE'S NO PLACE I CAN HIDE.
THEY'RE HERE FOR MY INTEL. IF THEY HAVEN'T FOUND ANOTHER PLANET, THEY NEED TO KNOW MORE ABOUT THIS WORLD...
WHY? IS THIS LIKE SHE SAID, AN INVASION? WHAT'S GOING ON, DAD?
LISTEN, KENNY...I KNOW I HAVEN'T BEEN A GOOD FATHER, BUT THAT'S WHY I MADE THE CUBE. TO HELP YOU WHEN I'M GONE.
DAD, I--
I'M SORRY, SON, I--
KA-BLAM

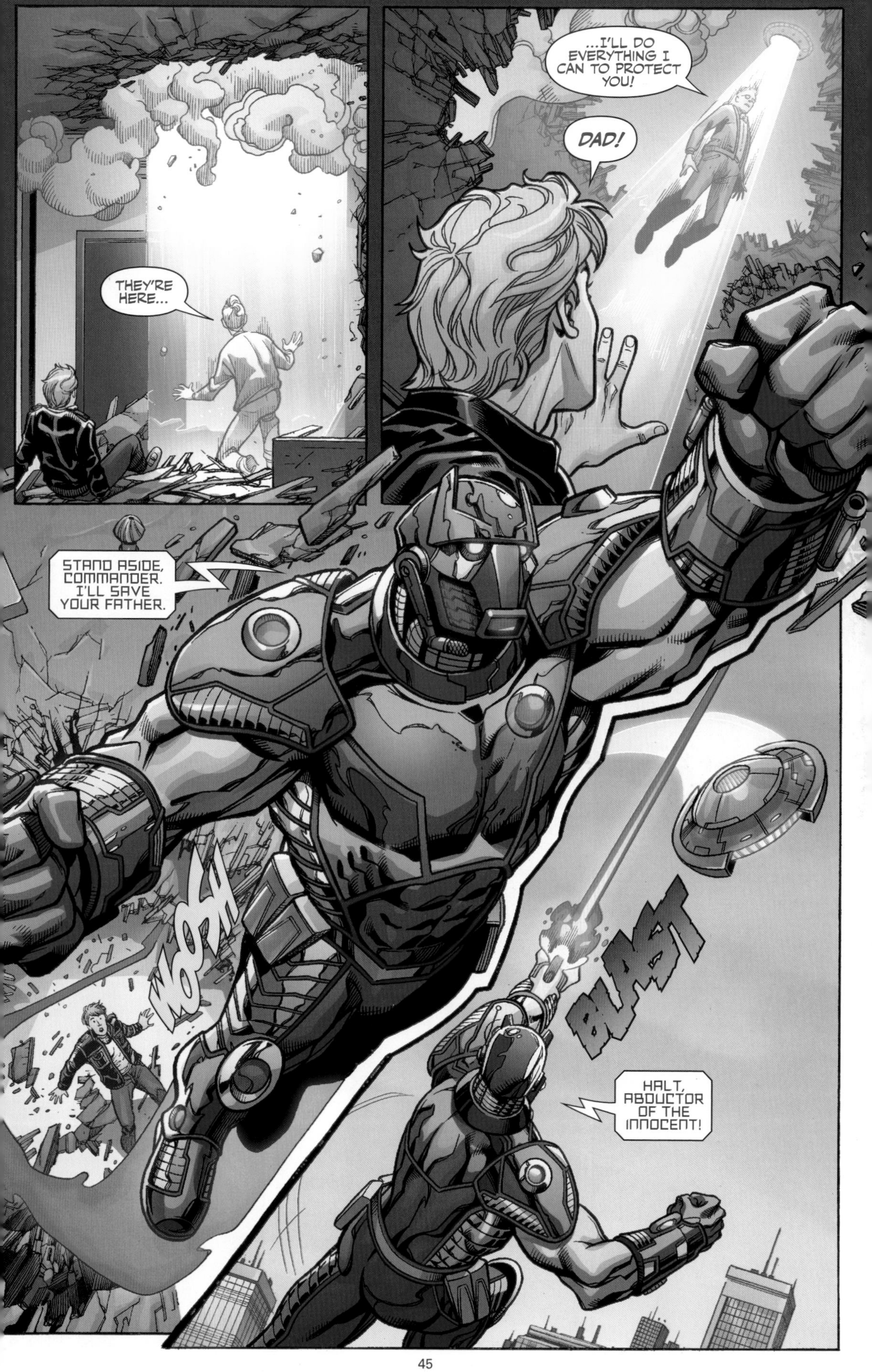
THEY'RE HERE...
...I'LL DO EVERYTHING I CAN TO PROTECT YOU!
DAD!
STAND ASIDE, COMMANDER. I'LL SAVE YOUR FATHER.
WOOSH
BLAST
HALT, ABDUCTOR OF THE INNOCENT!

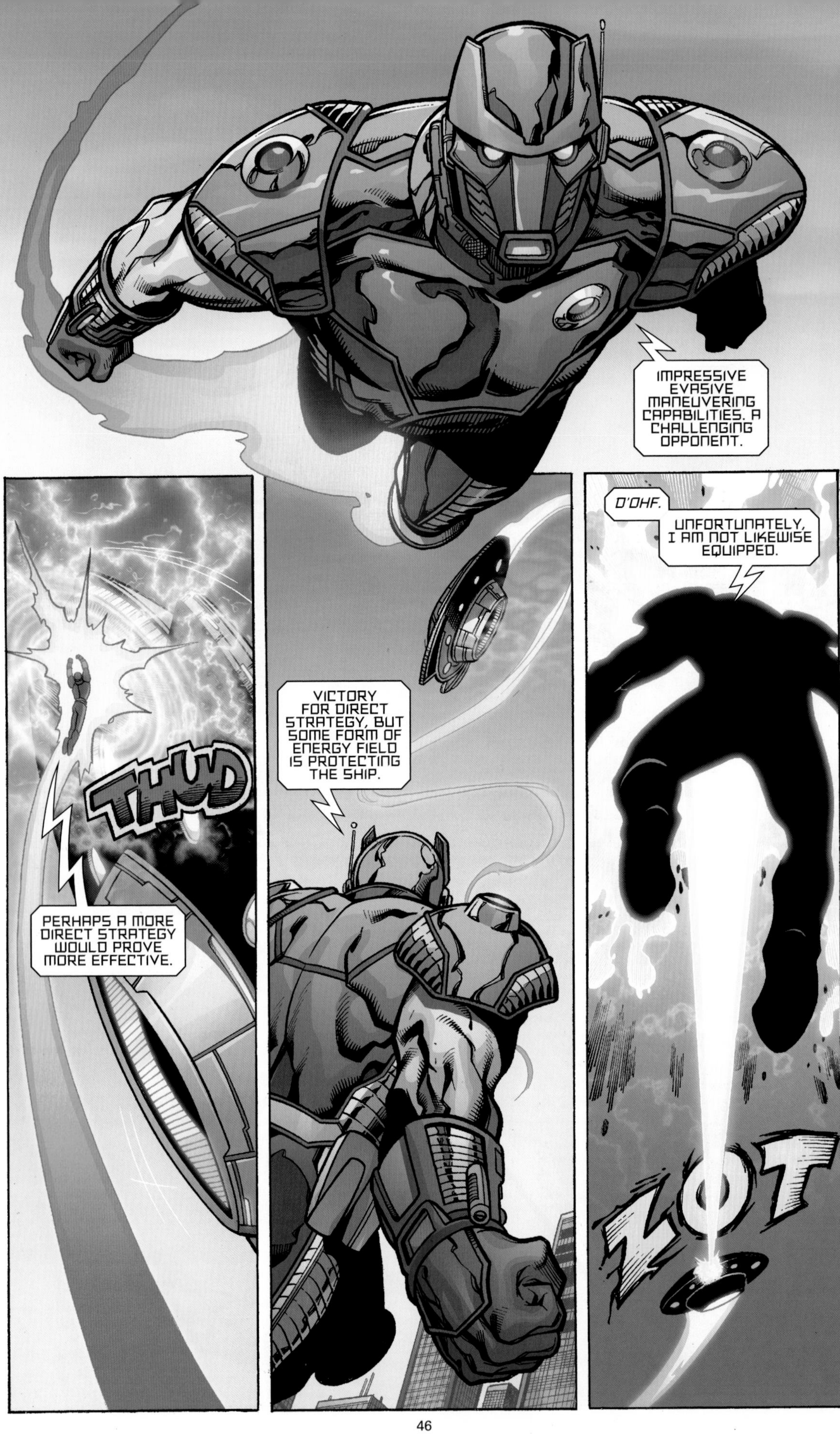
IMPRESSIVE EVASIVE MANEUVERING CAPABILITIES. A CHALLENGING OPPONENT.
THUD
PERHAPS A MORE DIRECT STRATEGY WOULD PROVE MORE EFFECTIVE.
VICTORY FOR DIRECT STRATEGY, BUT SOME FORM OF ENERGY FIELD IS PROTECTING THE SHIP.
D'OHF.
UNFORTUNATELY, I AM NOT LIKEWISE EQUIPPED.
ZOT

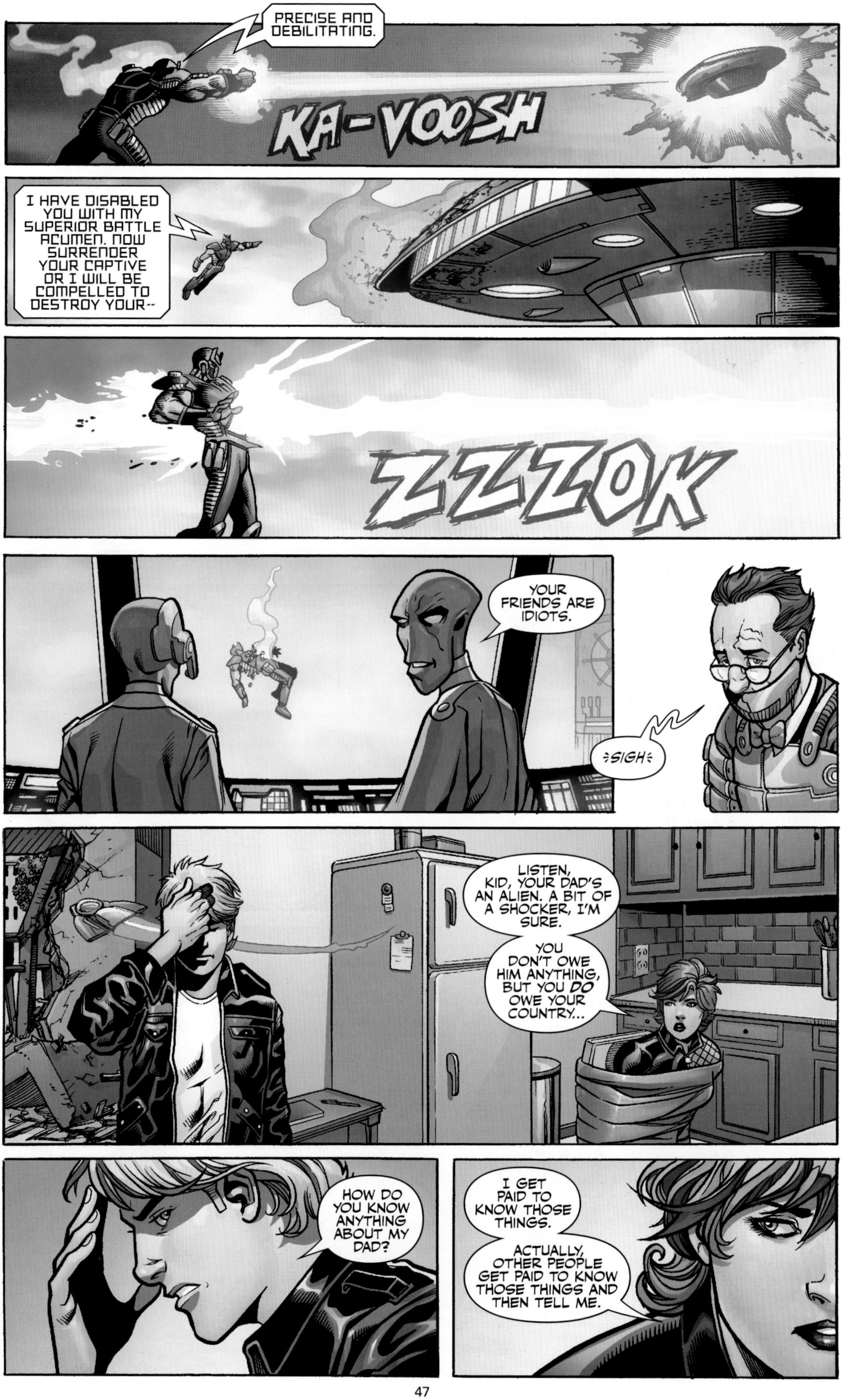
PRECISE AND DEBILITATING.
KA-VOOSH
I HAVE DISABLED YOU WITH MY SUPERIOR BATTLE ACUMEN. NOW SURRENDER YOUR CAPTIVE OR I WILL BE COMPELLED TO DESTROY YOUR--
ZZZOK
YOUR FRIENDS ARE IDIOTS.
SIGH
LISTEN, KID, YOUR DAD'S AN ALIEN. A BIT OF A SHOCKER, I'M SURE.
YOU DON'T OWE HIM ANYTHING, BUT YOU DO OWE YOUR COUNTRY...
HOW DO YOU KNOW ANYTHING ABOUT MY DAD?
I GET PAID TO KNOW THOSE THINGS.
ACTUALLY, OTHER PEOPLE GET PAID TO KNOW THOSE THINGS AND THEN TELL ME.

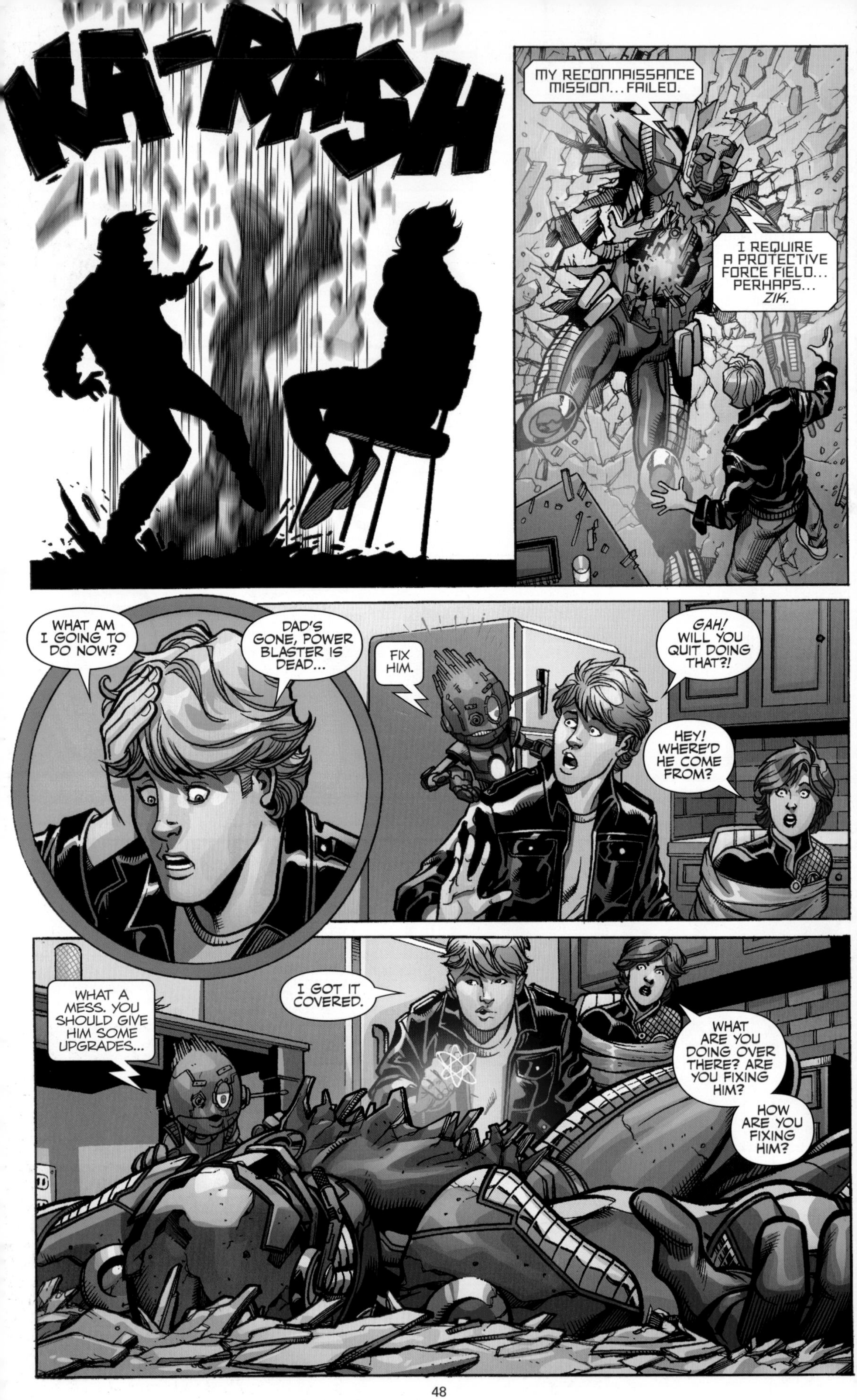
KA-RASH
MY RECONNAISSANCE MISSION... FAILED.
I REQUIRE A PROTECTIVE FORCE FIELD... PERHAPS... ZIK.
WHAT AM I GOING TO DO NOW?
DAD'S GONE, POWER BLASTER IS DEAD...
FIX HIM.
GAH! WILL YOU QUIT DOING THAT?!
HEY! WHERE'D HE COME FROM?
WHAT A MESS. YOU SHOULD GIVE HIM SOME UPGRADES...
I GOT IT COVERED.
WHAT ARE YOU DOING OVER THERE? ARE YOU FIXING HIM?
HOW ARE YOU FIXING HIM?

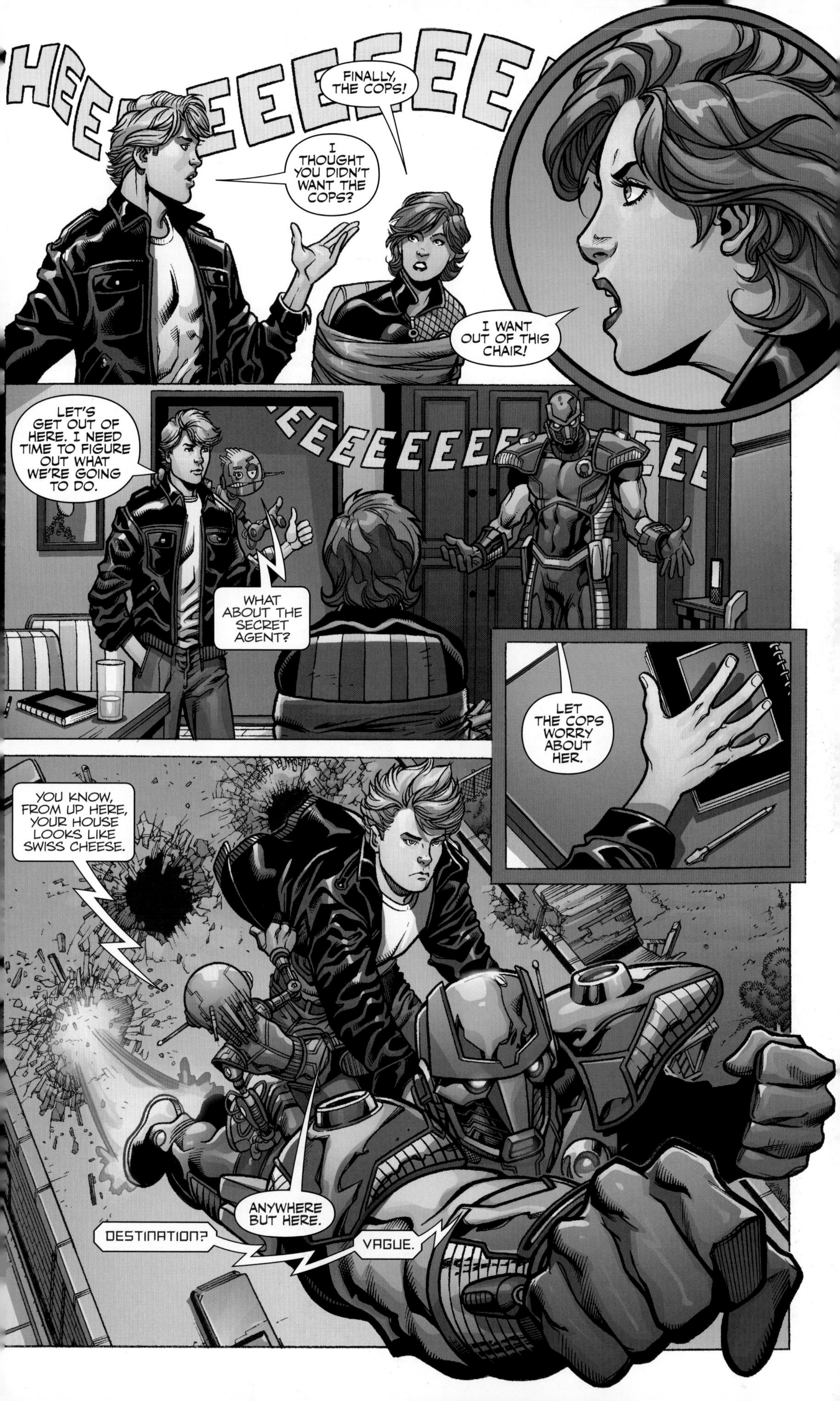
HEEEEEEEEEEE
FINALLY, THE COPS!
I THOUGHT YOU DIDN'T WANT THE COPS?
I WANT OUT OF THIS CHAIR!
EEEEEEEEEEEE
LET'S GET OUT OF HERE. I NEED TIME TO FIGURE OUT WHAT WE'RE GOING TO DO.
WHAT ABOUT THE SECRET AGENT?
LET THE COPS WORRY ABOUT HER.
YOU KNOW, FROM UP HERE, YOUR HOUSE LOOKS LIKE SWISS CHEESE.
DESTINATION?
ANYWHERE BUT HERE.
VAGUE.

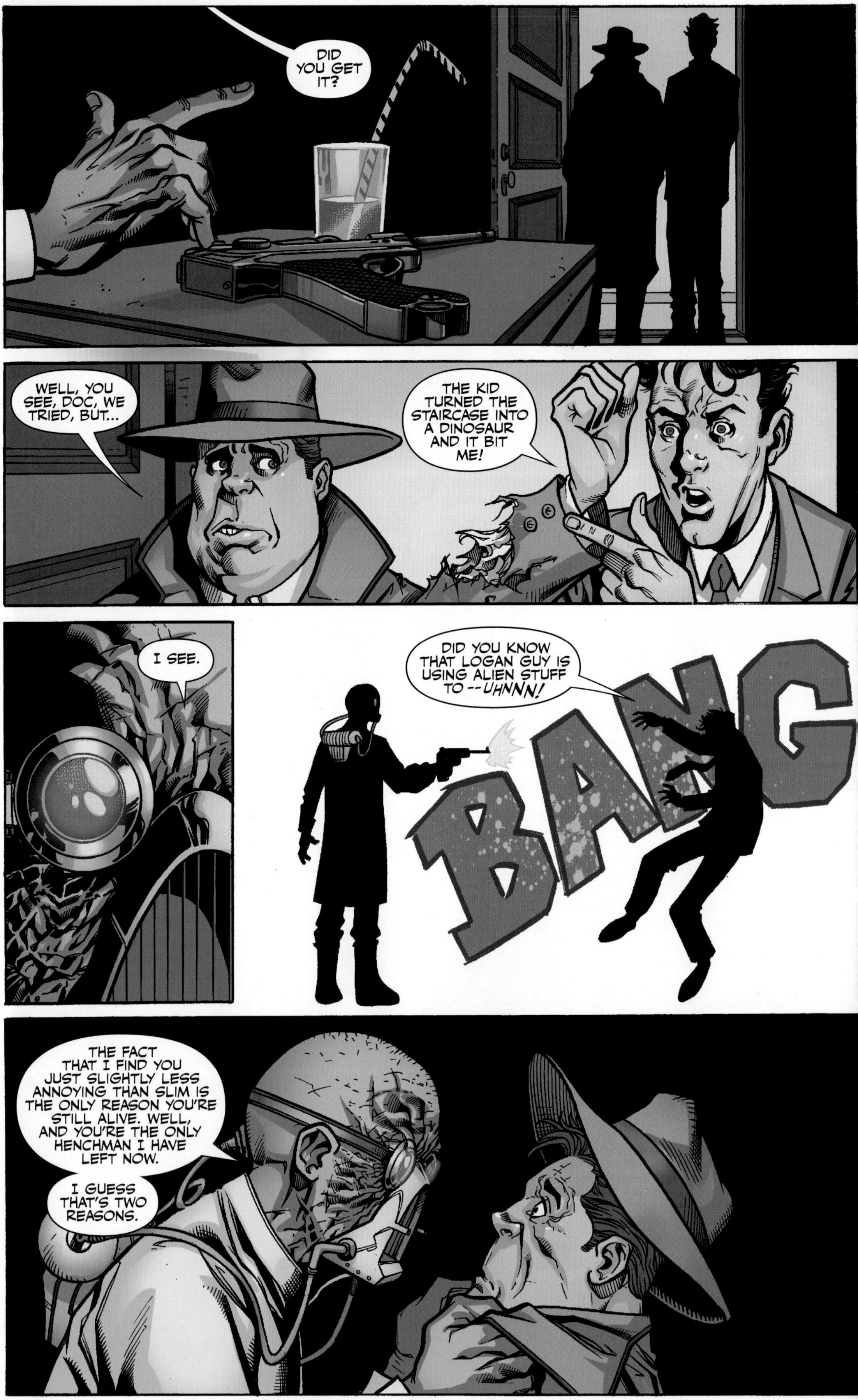

DID YOU GET IT?
WELL, YOU SEE, DOC, WE TRIED, BUT...
THE KID TURNED THE STAIRCASE INTO A DINOSAUR AND IT BIT ME!
I SEE.
DID YOU KNOW THAT LOGAN GUY IS USING ALIEN STUFF TO --UHNNN!
BANG
THE FACT THAT I FIND YOU JUST SLIGHTLY LESS ANNOYING THAN SLIM IS THE ONLY REASON YOU'RE STILL ALIVE. WELL, AND YOU'RE THE ONLY HENCHMAN I HAVE LEFT NOW.
I GUESS THAT'S TWO REASONS.

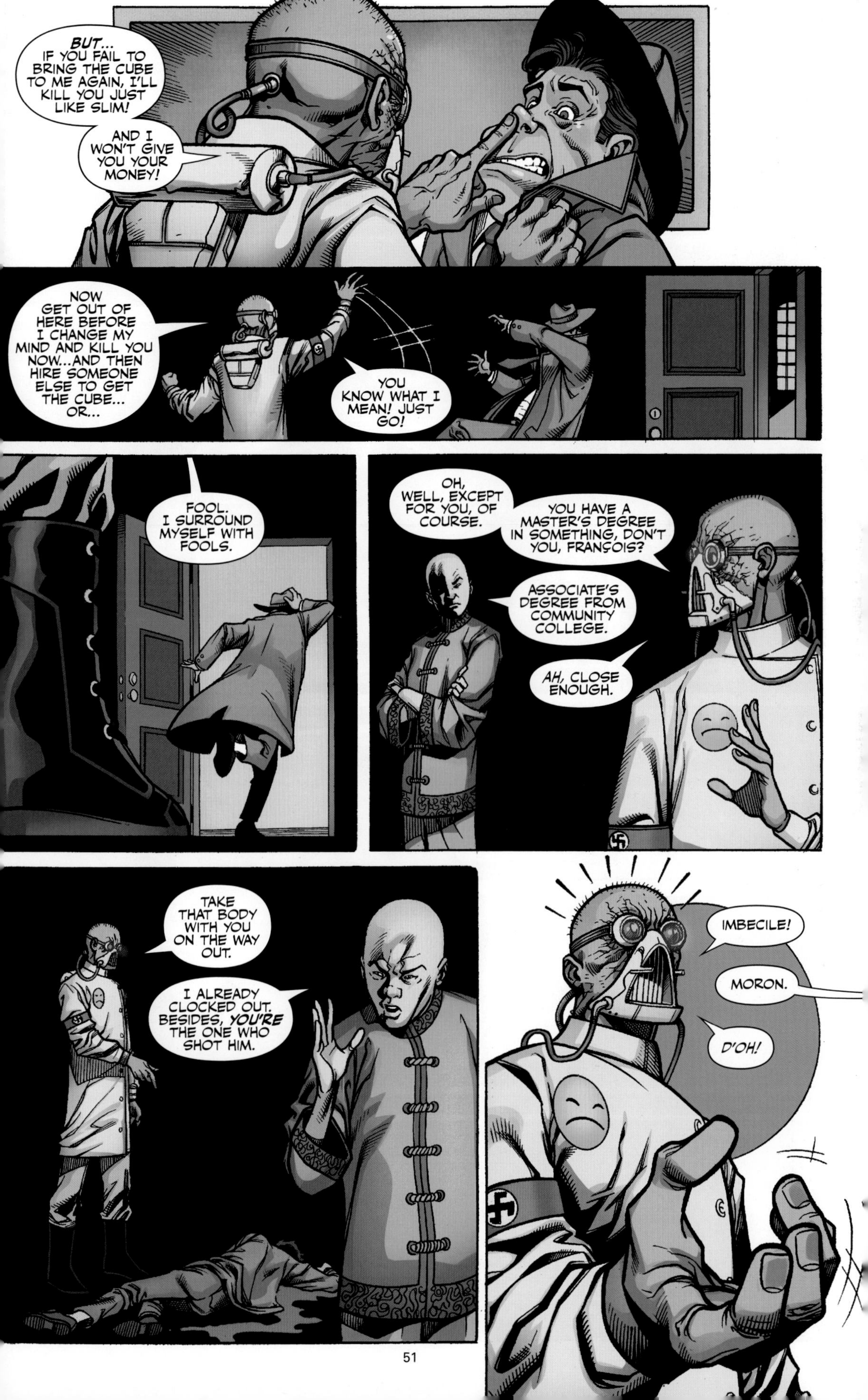
BUT... IF YOU FAIL TO BRING THE CUBE TO ME AGAIN, I'LL KILL YOU JUST LIKE SLIM!
AND I WON'T GIVE YOU YOUR MONEY!
NOW GET OUT OF HERE BEFORE I CHANGE MY MIND AND KILL YOU NOW...AND THEN HIRE SOMEONE ELSE TO GET THE CUBE... OR...
YOU KNOW WHAT I MEAN! JUST GO!
FOOL. I SURROUND MYSELF WITH FOOLS.
OH, WELL, EXCEPT FOR YOU, OF COURSE.
YOU HAVE A MASTER'S DEGREE IN SOMETHING, DON'T YOU, FRANÇOIS?
ASSOCIATE'S DEGREE FROM COMMUNITY COLLEGE.
AH, CLOSE ENOUGH.
TAKE THAT BODY WITH YOU ON THE WAY OUT.
I ALREADY CLOCKED OUT. BESIDES, YOU'RE THE ONE WHO SHOT HIM.
IMBECILE!
MORON.
D'OH!

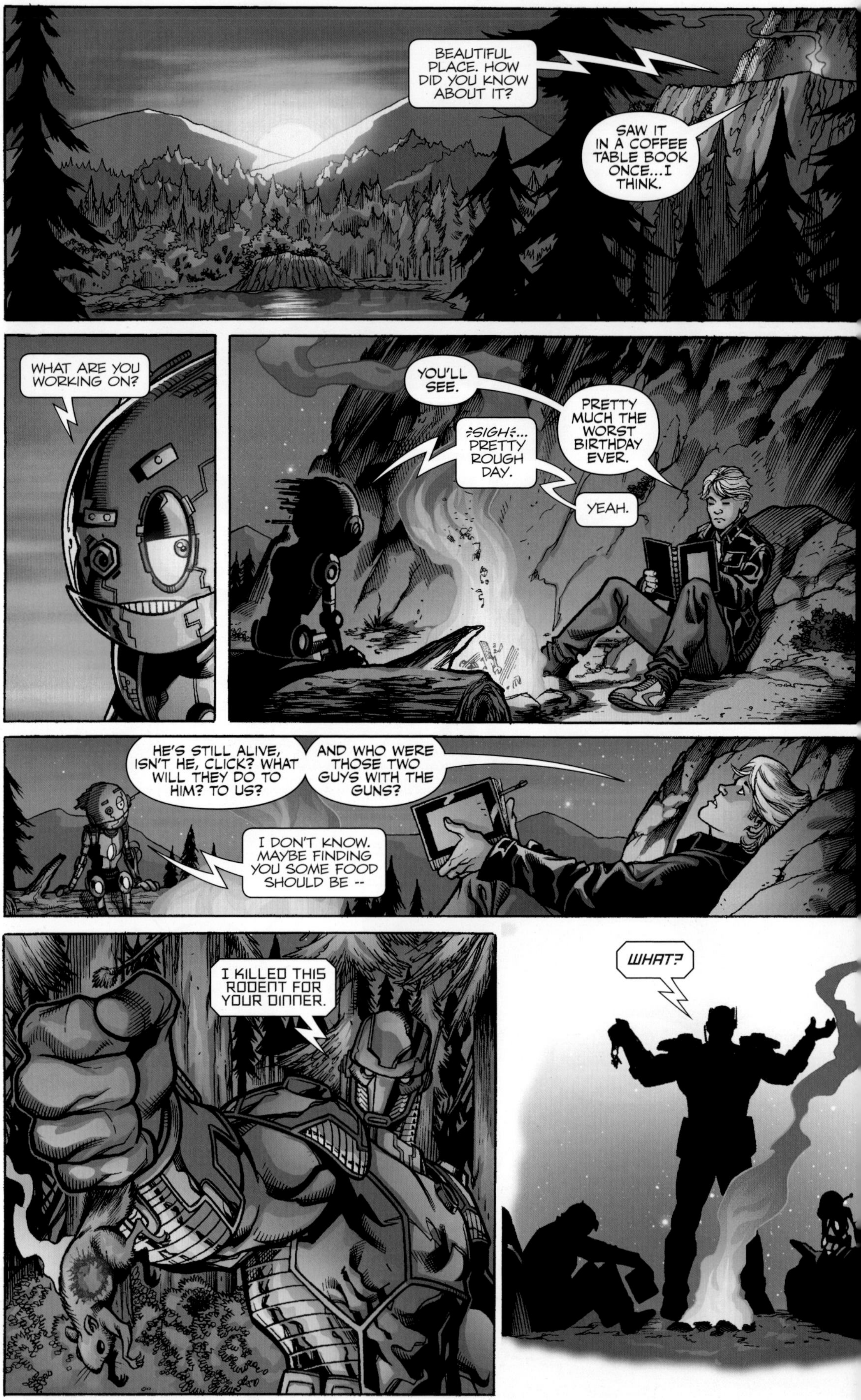
BEAUTIFUL PLACE. HOW DID YOU KNOW ABOUT IT?
SAW IT IN A COFFEE TABLE BOOK ONCE...I THINK.
WHAT ARE YOU WORKING ON?
YOU'LL SEE.
PRETTY MUCH THE WORST BIRTHDAY EVER.
SIGH... PRETTY ROUGH DAY.
YEAH.
HE'S STILL ALIVE, ISN'T HE, CLICK? WHAT WILL THEY DO TO HIM? TO US?
AND WHO WERE THOSE TWO GUYS WITH THE GUNS?
I DON'T KNOW. MAYBE FINDING YOU SOME FOOD SHOULD BE --
I KILLED THIS RODENT FOR YOUR DINNER.
WHAT?

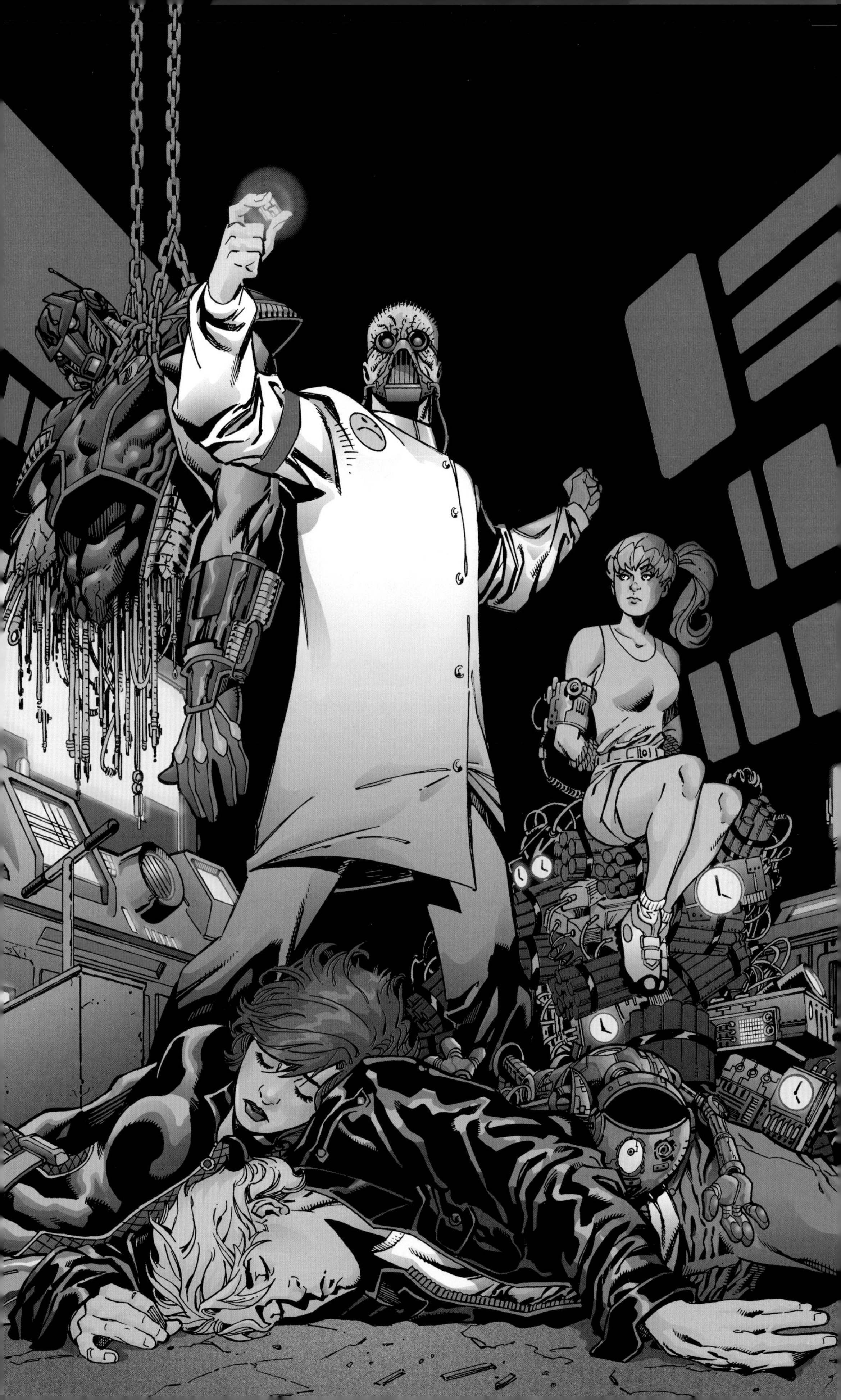

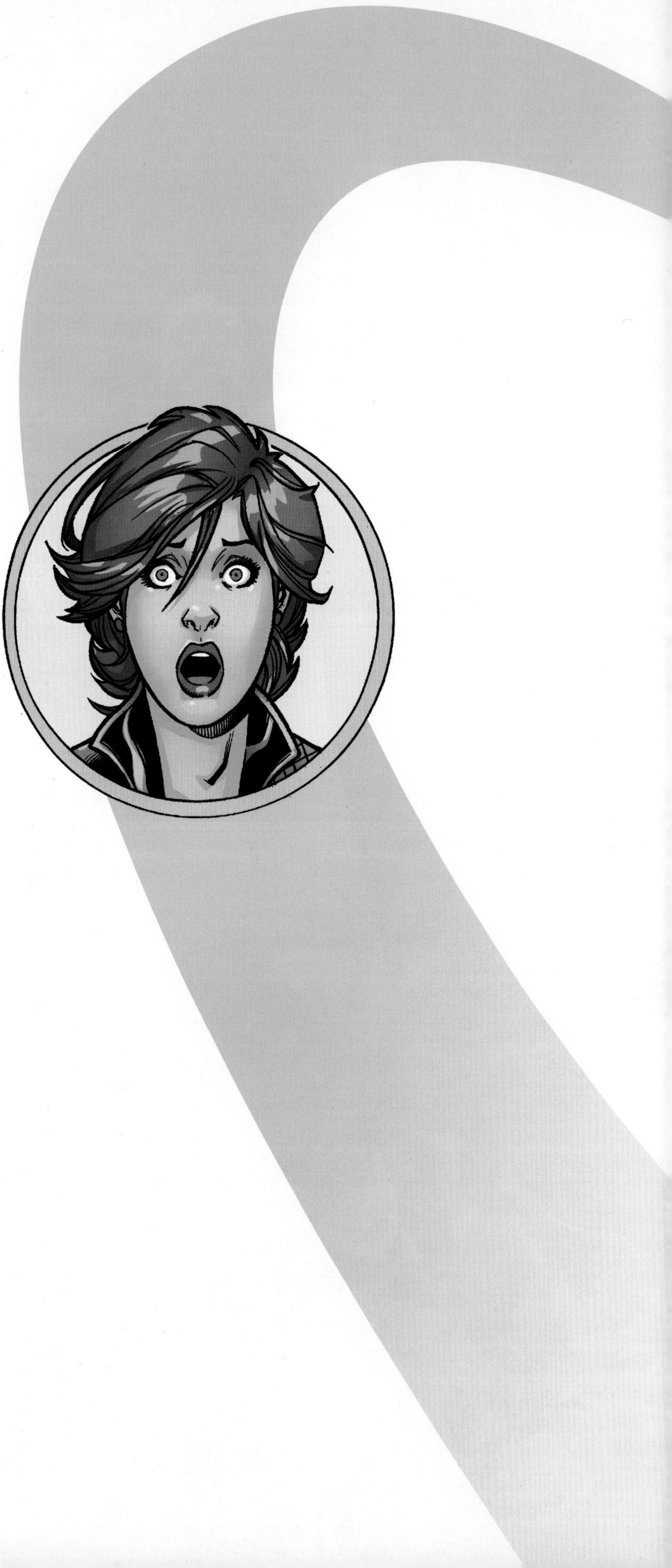

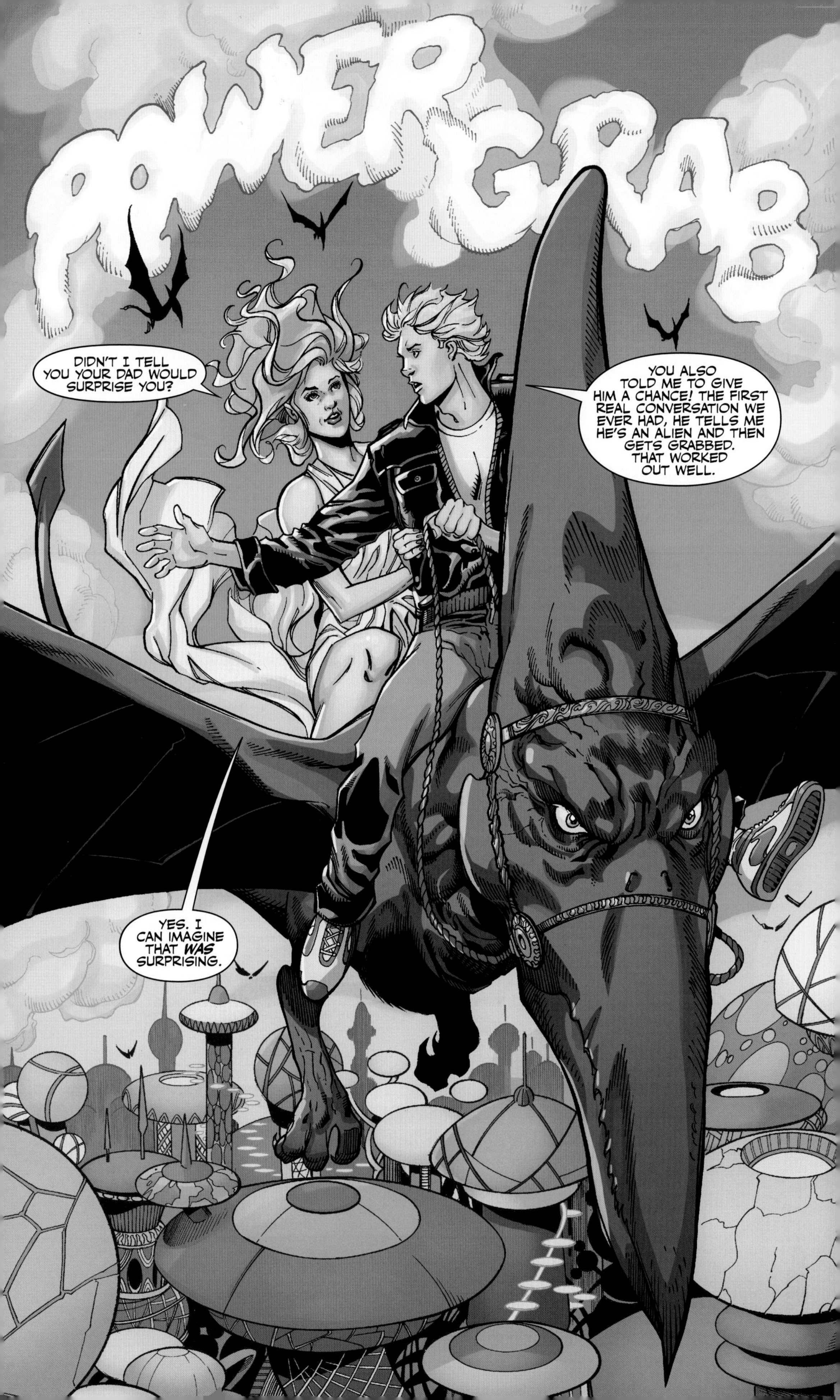
POWER GRAB
DIDN'T I TELL YOU YOUR DAD WOULD SURPRISE YOU?
YOU ALSO TOLD ME TO GIVE HIM A CHANCE! THE FIRST REAL CONVERSATION WE EVER HAD, HE TELLS ME HE'S AN ALIEN AND THEN GETS GRABBED. THAT WORKED OUT WELL.
YES. I CAN IMAGINE THAT *WAS* SURPRISING.

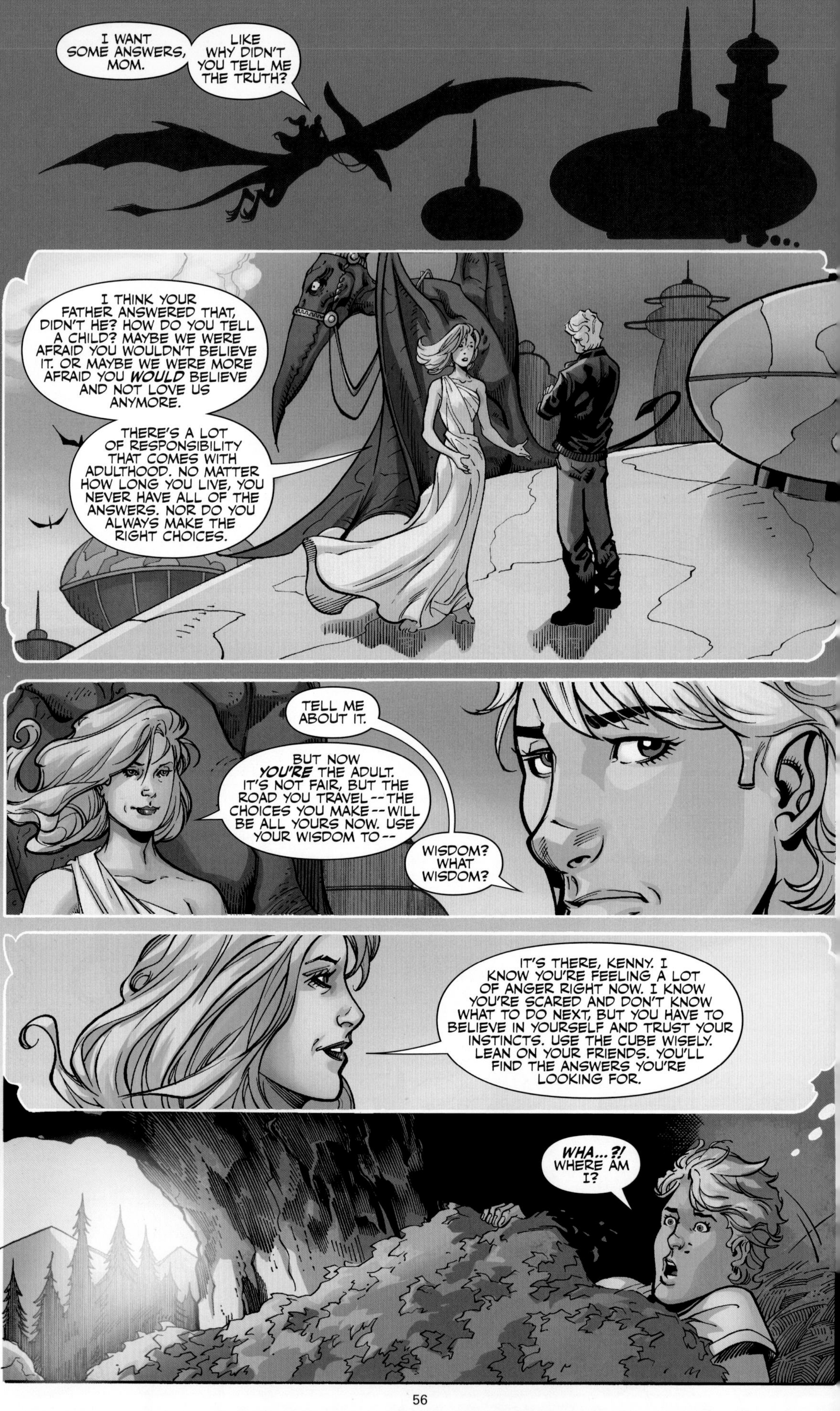

I WANT SOME ANSWERS, MOM.
LIKE WHY DIDN'T YOU TELL ME THE TRUTH?
I THINK YOUR FATHER ANSWERED THAT, DIDN'T HE? HOW DO YOU TELL A CHILD? MAYBE WE WERE AFRAID YOU WOULDN'T BELIEVE IT. OR MAYBE WE WERE MORE AFRAID YOU *WOULD* BELIEVE AND NOT LOVE US ANYMORE.
THERE'S A LOT OF RESPONSIBILITY THAT COMES WITH ADULTHOOD. NO MATTER HOW LONG YOU LIVE, YOU NEVER HAVE ALL OF THE ANSWERS. NOR DO YOU ALWAYS MAKE THE RIGHT CHOICES.
TELL ME ABOUT IT.
BUT NOW *YOU'RE* THE ADULT. IT'S NOT FAIR, BUT THE ROAD YOU TRAVEL--THE CHOICES YOU MAKE--WILL BE ALL YOURS NOW. USE YOUR WISDOM TO--
WISDOM? WHAT WISDOM?
IT'S THERE, KENNY. I KNOW YOU'RE FEELING A LOT OF ANGER RIGHT NOW. I KNOW YOU'RE SCARED AND DON'T KNOW WHAT TO DO NEXT, BUT YOU HAVE TO BELIEVE IN YOURSELF AND TRUST YOUR INSTINCTS. USE THE CUBE WISELY. LEAN ON YOUR FRIENDS. YOU'LL FIND THE ANSWERS YOU'RE LOOKING FOR.
WHA...?! WHERE AM I?

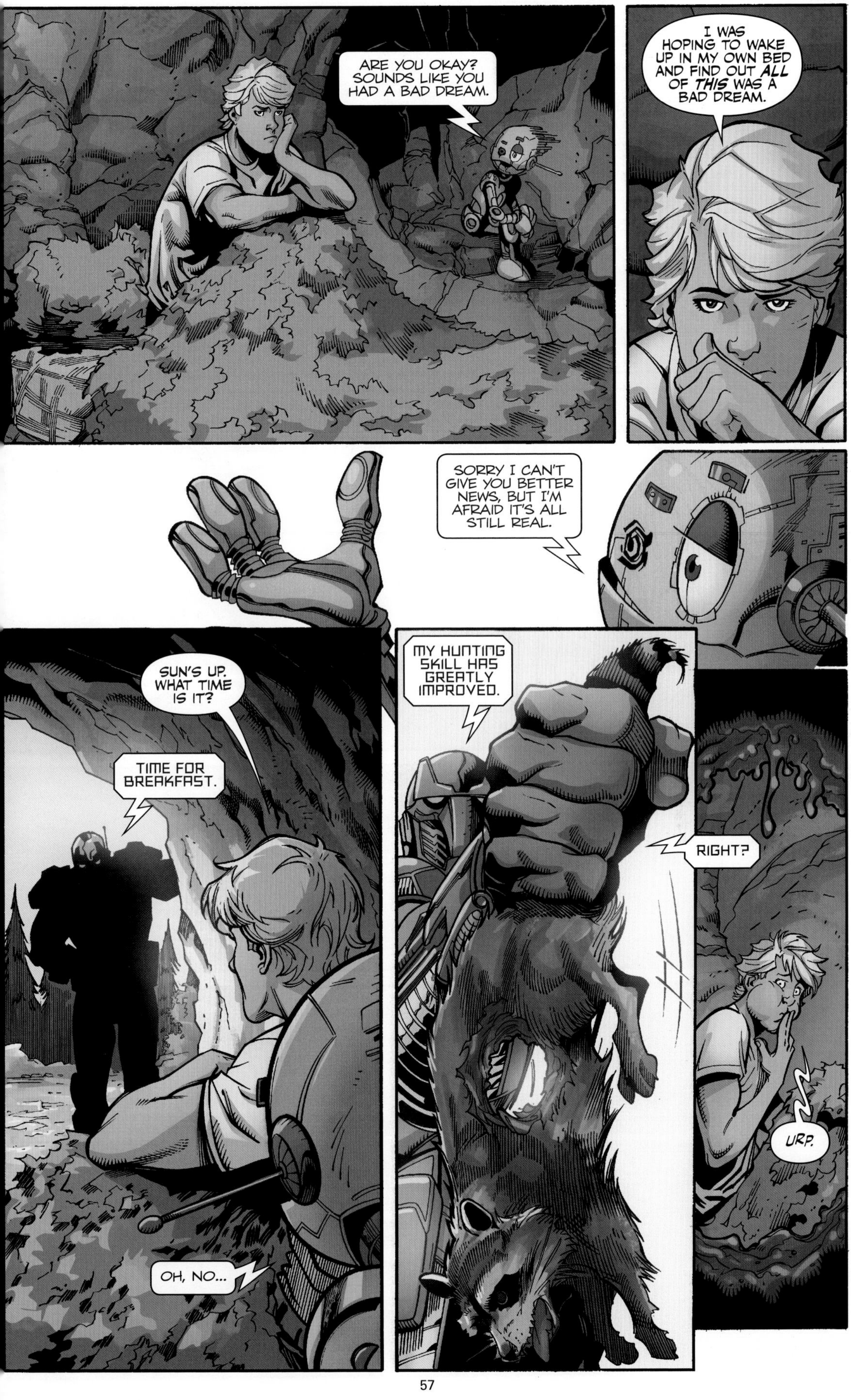
ARE YOU OKAY? SOUNDS LIKE YOU HAD A BAD DREAM.
I WAS HOPING TO WAKE UP IN MY OWN BED AND FIND OUT ALL OF THIS WAS A BAD DREAM.
SORRY I CAN'T GIVE YOU BETTER NEWS, BUT I'M AFRAID IT'S ALL STILL REAL.
SUN'S UP. WHAT TIME IS IT?
TIME FOR BREAKFAST.
OH, NO...
MY HUNTING SKILL HAS GREATLY IMPROVED.
RIGHT?
URP.

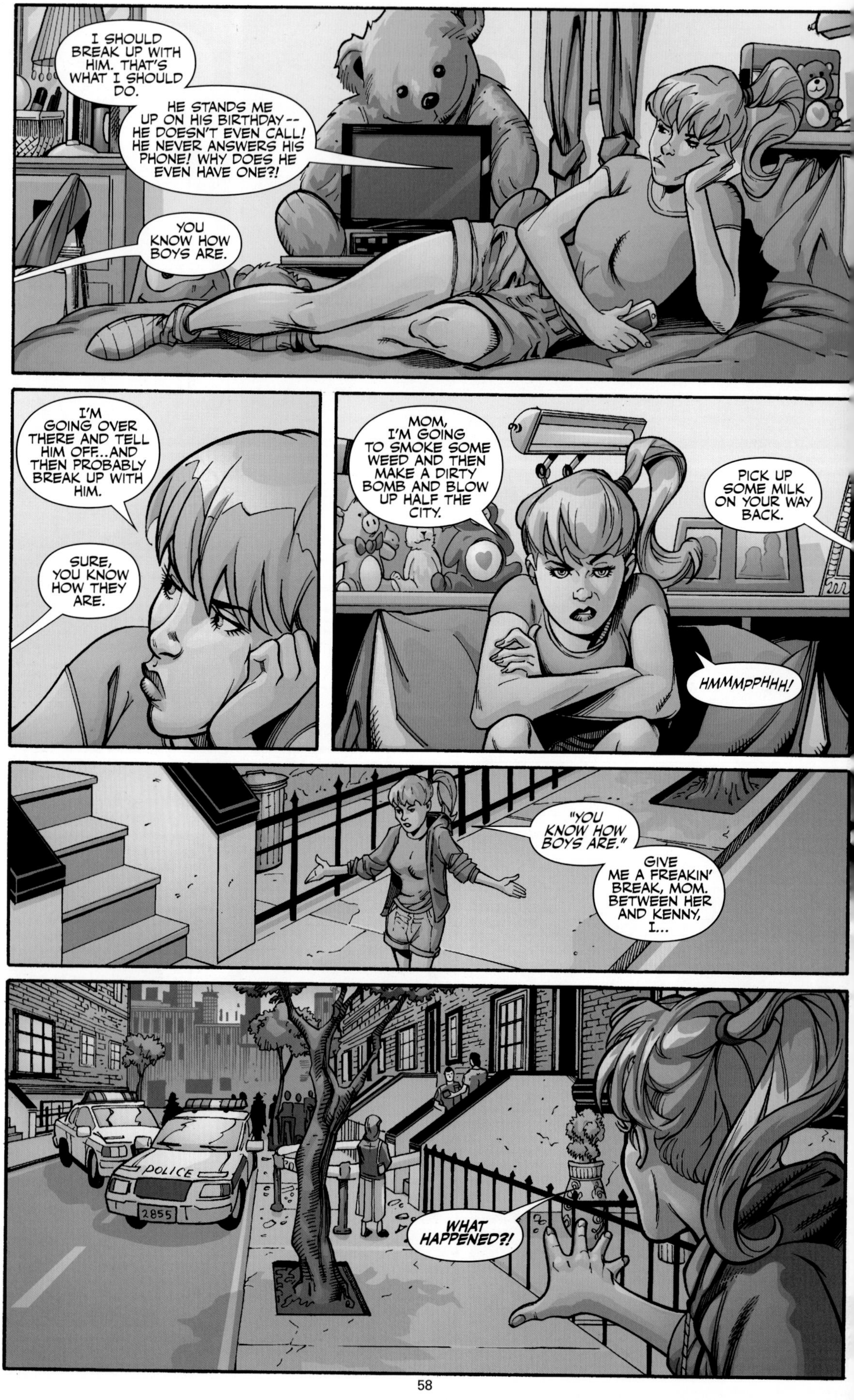
I SHOULD BREAK UP WITH HIM. THAT'S WHAT I SHOULD DO.
HE STANDS ME UP ON HIS BIRTHDAY-- HE DOESN'T EVEN CALL! HE NEVER ANSWERS HIS PHONE! WHY DOES HE EVEN HAVE ONE?!
YOU KNOW HOW BOYS ARE.
I'M GOING OVER THERE AND TELL HIM OFF...AND THEN PROBABLY BREAK UP WITH HIM.
SURE, YOU KNOW HOW THEY ARE.
MOM, I'M GOING TO SMOKE SOME WEED AND THEN MAKE A DIRTY BOMB AND BLOW UP HALF THE CITY.
PICK UP SOME MILK ON YOUR WAY BACK.
HMMMPPHHH!
"YOU KNOW HOW BOYS ARE."
GIVE ME A FREAKIN' BREAK, MOM. BETWEEN HER AND KENNY, I...
POLICE
2855
WHAT HAPPENED?!

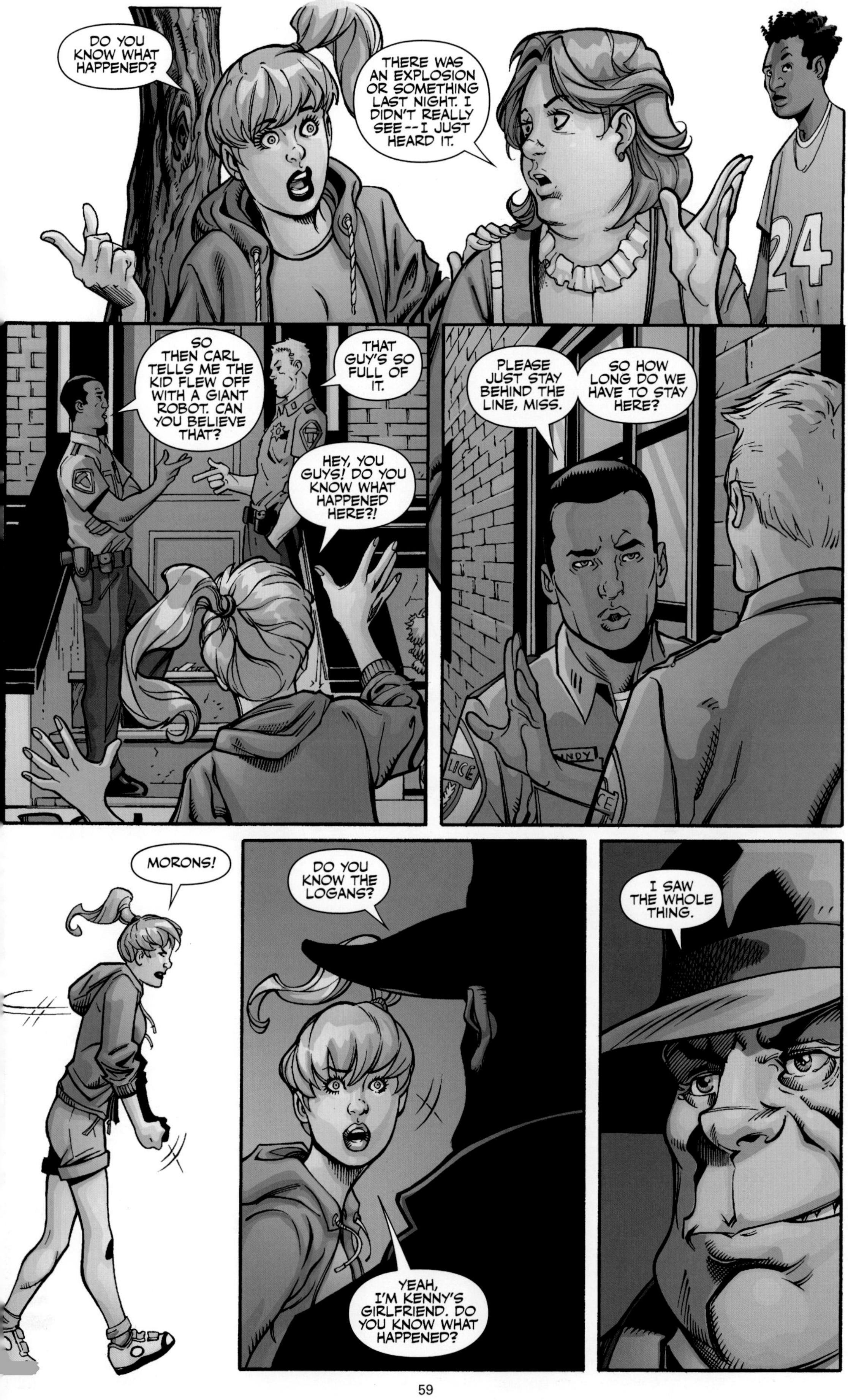

DO YOU KNOW WHAT HAPPENED?
THERE WAS AN EXPLOSION OR SOMETHING LAST NIGHT. I DIDN'T REALLY SEE--I JUST HEARD IT.
SO THEN CARL TELLS ME THE KID FLEW OFF WITH A GIANT ROBOT. CAN YOU BELIEVE THAT?
THAT GUY'S SO FULL OF IT.
HEY, YOU GUYS! DO YOU KNOW WHAT HAPPENED HERE?!
PLEASE JUST STAY BEHIND THE LINE, MISS.
SO HOW LONG DO WE HAVE TO STAY HERE?
24
MORONS!
DO YOU KNOW THE LOGANS?
YEAH, I'M KENNY'S GIRLFRIEND. DO YOU KNOW WHAT HAPPENED?
I SAW THE WHOLE THING.

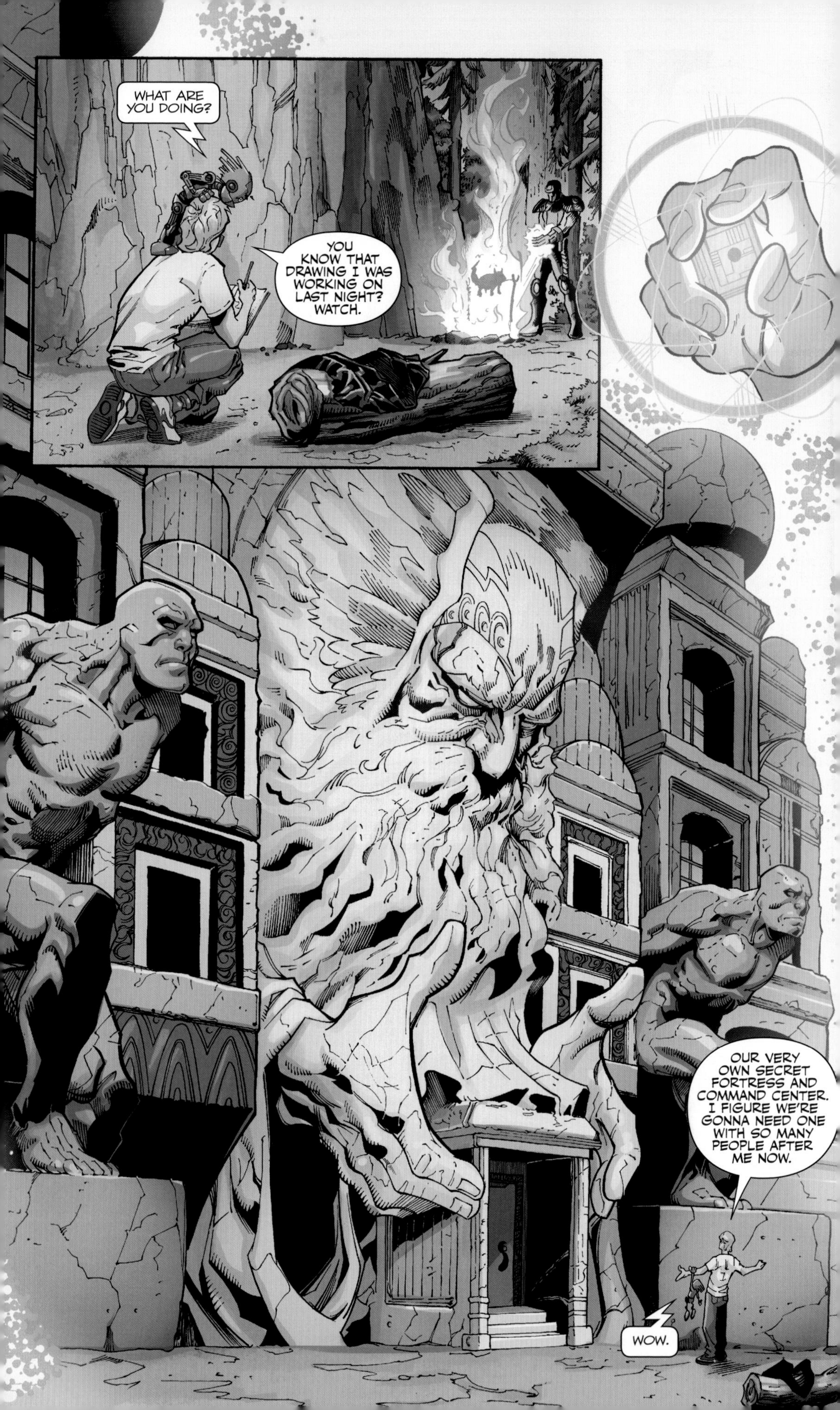
WHAT ARE YOU DOING?
YOU KNOW THAT DRAWING I WAS WORKING ON LAST NIGHT? WATCH.
OUR VERY OWN SECRET FORTRESS AND COMMAND CENTER. I FIGURE WE'RE GONNA NEED ONE WITH SO MANY PEOPLE AFTER ME NOW.
WOW.

PRETTY IMPRESSIVE BUT NOT EXACTLY DISCREET. YOU DID SAY "SECRET"?

GO BIG OR GO HOME, RIGHT? BESIDES, WE'RE IN THE MIDDLE OF NOWHERE. WHO'S GONNA SEE IT?

LET'S GO INSIDE AND CHECK IT OUT.

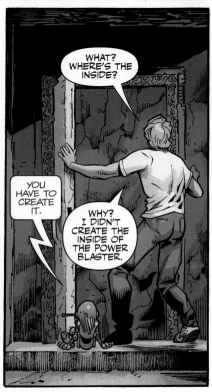

WHAT? WHERE'S THE INSIDE?

YOU HAVE TO CREATE IT.

WHY? I DIDN'T CREATE THE INSIDE OF THE POWER BLASTER.

THE CUBE IS A MANUFACTURER. GUNS, ROBOTS, DINOSAURS -- THEY'RE ALL ESSENTIALLY SINGLE FUNCTIONING MECHANISMS THAT FOLLOW STANDARD OPERATING GUIDELINES. THE INSIDE OF A HOUSE IS MORE OF A CREATIVE DESIGN OR ARTISTIC IMPRESSION. YOU HAVE TO HAVE A CLEAR IMAGE OF IT FOR THE CUBE TO EXTRAPOLATE IT.

SO I HAVE TO DESIGN THE WHOLE INSIDE BEFORE WE CAN USE IT? THAT SUCKS.

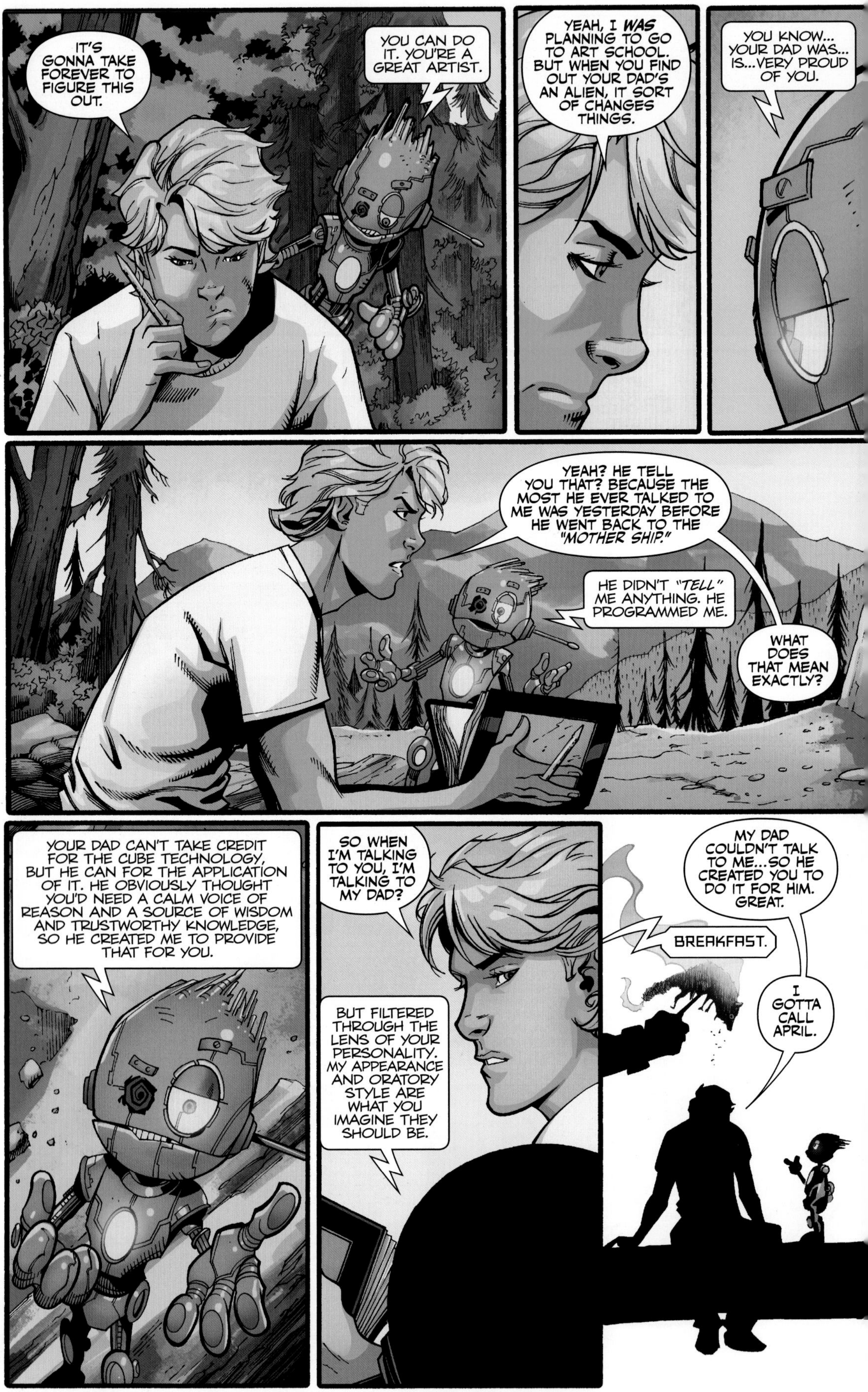
IT'S GONNA TAKE FOREVER TO FIGURE THIS OUT.
YOU CAN DO IT. YOU'RE A GREAT ARTIST.
YEAH, I WAS PLANNING TO GO TO ART SCHOOL. BUT WHEN YOU FIND OUT YOUR DAD'S AN ALIEN, IT SORT OF CHANGES THINGS.
YOU KNOW... YOUR DAD WAS... IS...VERY PROUD OF YOU.
YEAH? HE TELL YOU THAT? BECAUSE THE MOST HE EVER TALKED TO ME WAS YESTERDAY BEFORE HE WENT BACK TO THE "MOTHER SHIP."
HE DIDN'T "TELL" ME ANYTHING. HE PROGRAMMED ME.
WHAT DOES THAT MEAN EXACTLY?
YOUR DAD CAN'T TAKE CREDIT FOR THE CUBE TECHNOLOGY, BUT HE CAN FOR THE APPLICATION OF IT. HE OBVIOUSLY THOUGHT YOU'D NEED A CALM VOICE OF REASON AND A SOURCE OF WISDOM AND TRUSTWORTHY KNOWLEDGE, SO HE CREATED ME TO PROVIDE THAT FOR YOU.
SO WHEN I'M TALKING TO YOU, I'M TALKING TO MY DAD?
BUT FILTERED THROUGH THE LENS OF YOUR PERSONALITY. MY APPEARANCE AND ORATORY STYLE ARE WHAT YOU IMAGINE THEY SHOULD BE.
MY DAD COULDN'T TALK TO ME...SO HE CREATED YOU TO DO IT FOR HIM. GREAT.
BREAKFAST.
I GOTTA CALL APRIL.

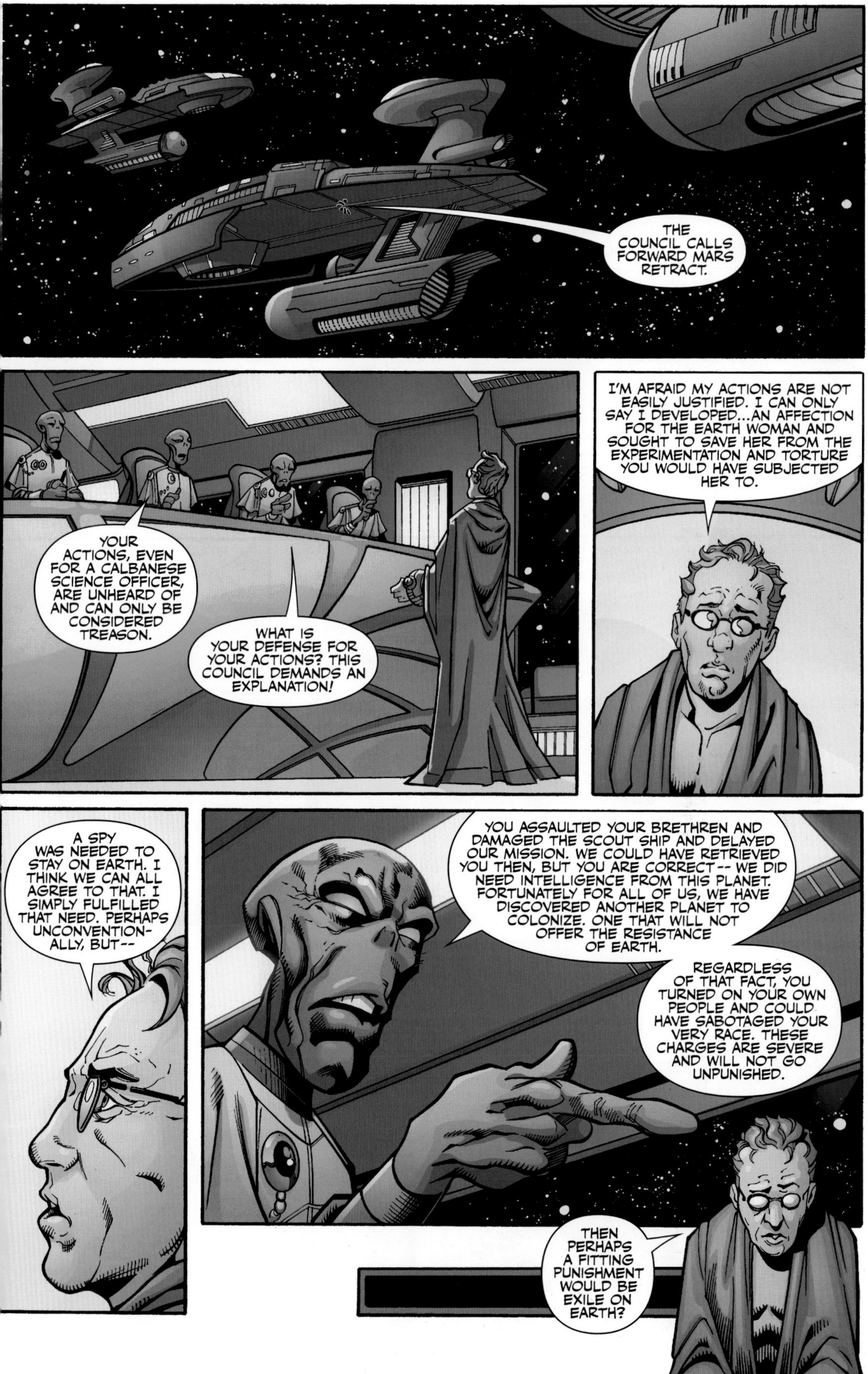
THE COUNCIL CALLS FORWARD MARS RETRACT.
YOUR ACTIONS, EVEN FOR A CALBANESE SCIENCE OFFICER, ARE UNHEARD OF AND CAN ONLY BE CONSIDERED TREASON.
WHAT IS YOUR DEFENSE FOR YOUR ACTIONS? THIS COUNCIL DEMANDS AN EXPLANATION!
I'M AFRAID MY ACTIONS ARE NOT EASILY JUSTIFIED. I CAN ONLY SAY I DEVELOPED...AN AFFECTION FOR THE EARTH WOMAN AND SOUGHT TO SAVE HER FROM THE EXPERIMENTATION AND TORTURE YOU WOULD HAVE SUBJECTED HER TO.
A SPY WAS NEEDED TO STAY ON EARTH. I THINK WE CAN ALL AGREE TO THAT. I SIMPLY FULFILLED THAT NEED. PERHAPS UNCONVENTION-ALLY, BUT--
YOU ASSAULTED YOUR BRETHREN AND DAMAGED THE SCOUT SHIP AND DELAYED OUR MISSION. WE COULD HAVE RETRIEVED YOU THEN, BUT YOU ARE CORRECT -- WE DID NEED INTELLIGENCE FROM THIS PLANET. FORTUNATELY FOR ALL OF US, WE HAVE DISCOVERED ANOTHER PLANET TO COLONIZE. ONE THAT WILL NOT OFFER THE RESISTANCE OF EARTH.
REGARDLESS OF THAT FACT, YOU TURNED ON YOUR OWN PEOPLE AND COULD HAVE SABOTAGED YOUR VERY RACE. THESE CHARGES ARE SEVERE AND WILL NOT GO UNPUNISHED.
THEN PERHAPS A FITTING PUNISHMENT WOULD BE EXILE ON EARTH?

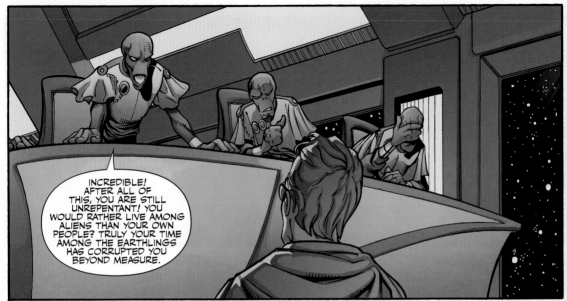

INCREDIBLE! AFTER ALL OF THIS, YOU ARE STILL UNREPENTANT! YOU WOULD RATHER LIVE AMONG ALIENS THAN YOUR OWN PEOPLE? TRULY YOUR TIME AMONG THE EARTHLINGS HAS CORRUPTED YOU BEYOND MEASURE.

MARS RETRACT, YOU WILL BE RECONSTRUCTED TO YOUR NATURAL FORM AND HELD IN CUSTODY UNTIL THE COUNCIL CAN DETERMINE A SUITABLE SENTENCE FOR YOUR ACTIONS. YOU WILL ACCOMPANY US TO OUR NEW WORLD AND YOU WILL PAY FOR YOUR TREASON.

WE EXPECT YOUR FULL COOPERATION DURING YOUR DEBRIEFING CONCERNING YOUR STAY ON THIS PLANET. WHAT INFORMATION YOU GATHERED DURING YOUR TIME HERE MAY STILL PROVE BENEFICIAL TO US.

BUT KNOW THIS, FORMER SCIENCE OFFICER RETRACT—FAIL TO FULLY COOPERATE WITH US, AND YOUR SENTENCE WILL MOST CERTAINLY RESULT IN YOUR SLOW AND AGONIZING...

...DEATH.

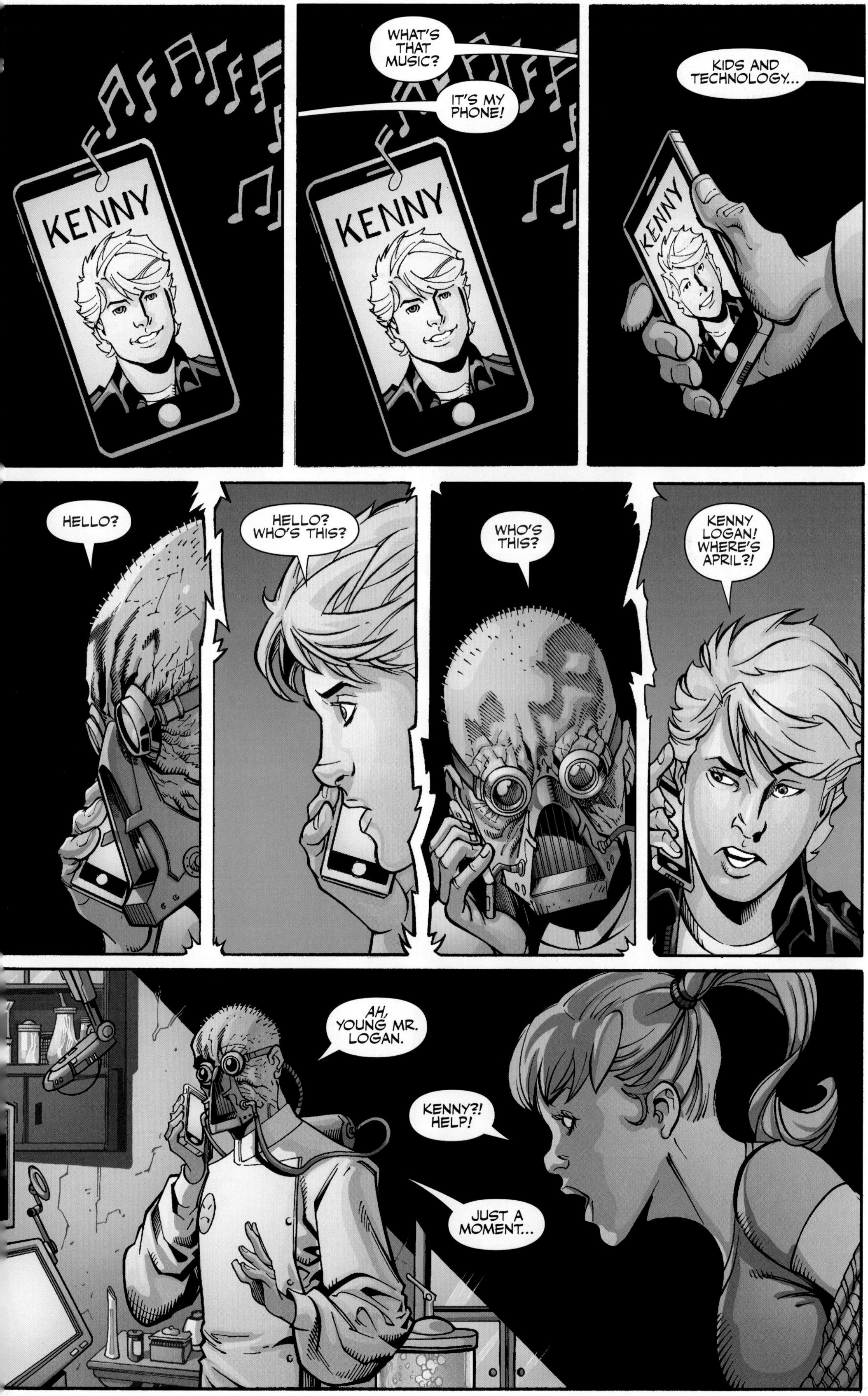
KENNY
WHAT'S THAT MUSIC?
IT'S MY PHONE!
KENNY
KIDS AND TECHNOLOGY...
KENNY
HELLO?
HELLO? WHO'S THIS?
WHO'S THIS?
KENNY LOGAN! WHERE'S APRIL?!
AH, YOUNG MR. LOGAN.
KENNY?! HELP!
JUST A MOMENT...

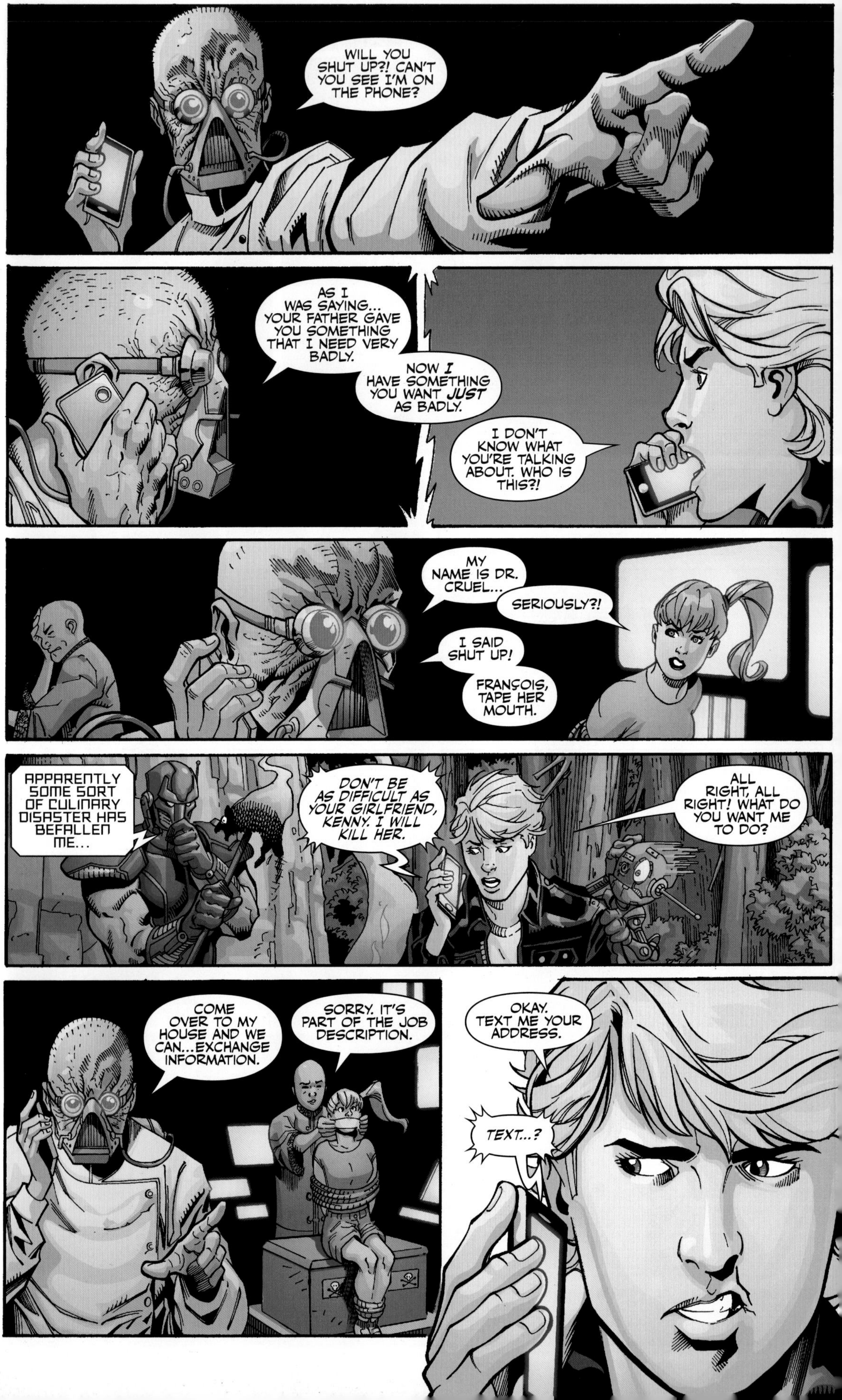
WILL YOU SHUT UP?! CAN'T YOU SEE I'M ON THE PHONE?
AS I WAS SAYING... YOUR FATHER GAVE YOU SOMETHING THAT I NEED VERY BADLY.
NOW *I* HAVE SOMETHING YOU WANT *JUST* AS BADLY.
I DON'T KNOW WHAT YOU'RE TALKING ABOUT. WHO IS THIS?!
MY NAME IS DR. CRUEL...
SERIOUSLY?!
I SAID SHUT UP!
FRANÇOIS, TAPE HER MOUTH.
APPARENTLY SOME SORT OF CULINARY DISASTER HAS BEFALLEN ME...
DON'T BE AS DIFFICULT AS YOUR GIRLFRIEND, KENNY. I WILL KILL HER.
ALL RIGHT, ALL RIGHT! WHAT DO YOU WANT ME TO DO?
COME OVER TO MY HOUSE AND WE CAN...EXCHANGE INFORMATION.
SORRY. IT'S PART OF THE JOB DESCRIPTION.
OKAY. TEXT ME YOUR ADDRESS.
TEXT...?

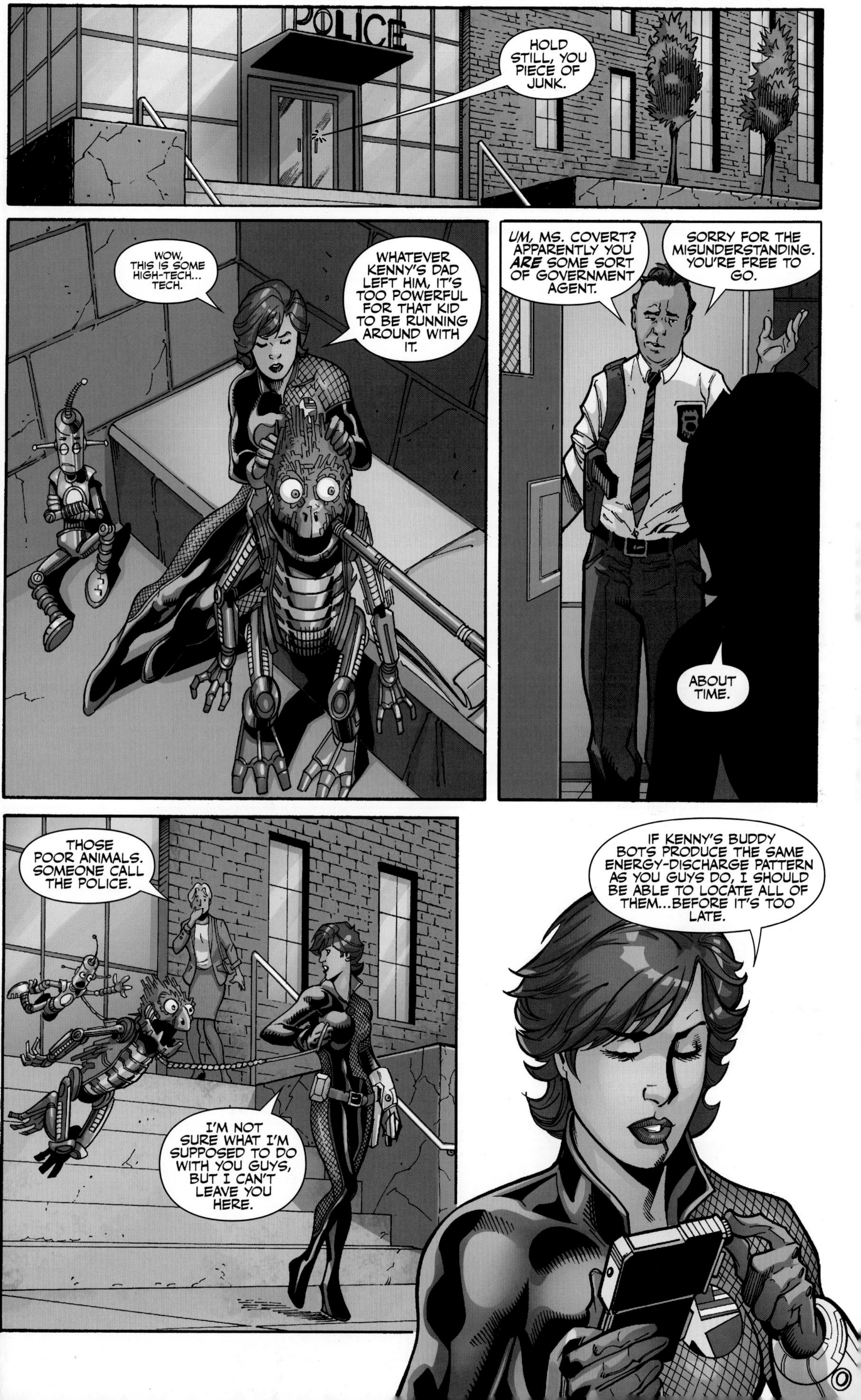

HOLD STILL, YOU PIECE OF JUNK.
WOW, THIS IS SOME HIGH-TECH... TECH.
WHATEVER KENNY'S DAD LEFT HIM, IT'S TOO POWERFUL FOR THAT KID TO BE RUNNING AROUND WITH IT.
UM, MS. COVERT? APPARENTLY YOU ARE SOME SORT OF GOVERNMENT AGENT.
SORRY FOR THE MISUNDERSTANDING. YOU'RE FREE TO GO.
ABOUT TIME.
THOSE POOR ANIMALS. SOMEONE CALL THE POLICE.
I'M NOT SURE WHAT I'M SUPPOSED TO DO WITH YOU GUYS, BUT I CAN'T LEAVE YOU HERE.
IF KENNY'S BUDDY BOTS PRODUCE THE SAME ENERGY-DISCHARGE PATTERN AS YOU GUYS DO, I SHOULD BE ABLE TO LOCATE ALL OF THEM...BEFORE IT'S TOO LATE.

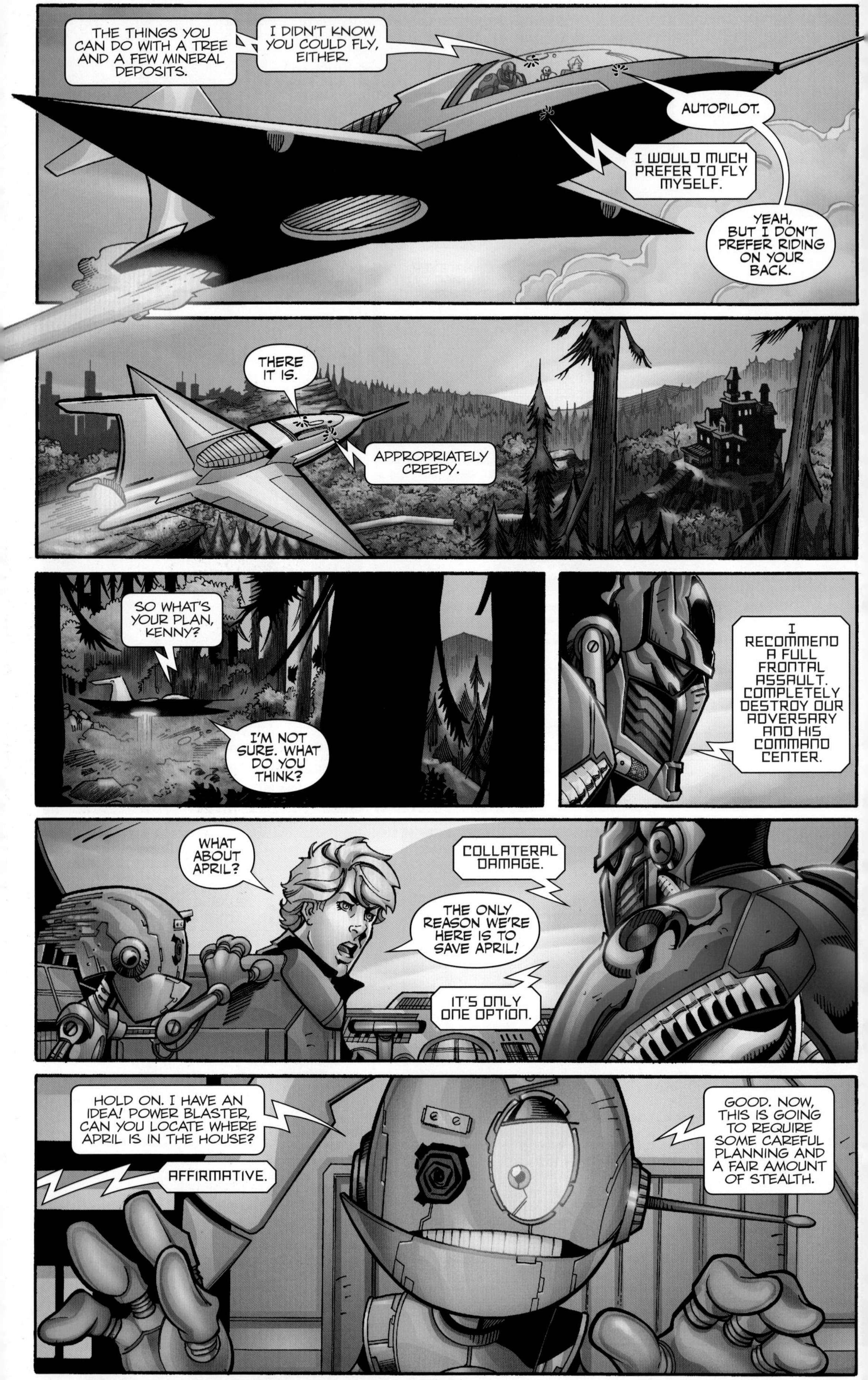

THE THINGS YOU CAN DO WITH A TREE AND A FEW MINERAL DEPOSITS.
I DIDN'T KNOW YOU COULD FLY, EITHER.
AUTOPILOT.
I WOULD MUCH PREFER TO FLY MYSELF.
YEAH, BUT I DON'T PREFER RIDING ON YOUR BACK.
THERE IT IS.
APPROPRIATELY CREEPY.
SO WHAT'S YOUR PLAN, KENNY?
I'M NOT SURE. WHAT DO YOU THINK?
I RECOMMEND A FULL FRONTAL ASSAULT. COMPLETELY DESTROY OUR ADVERSARY AND HIS COMMAND CENTER.
WHAT ABOUT APRIL?
COLLATERAL DAMAGE.
THE ONLY REASON WE'RE HERE IS TO SAVE APRIL!
IT'S ONLY ONE OPTION.
HOLD ON. I HAVE AN IDEA! POWER BLASTER, CAN YOU LOCATE WHERE APRIL IS IN THE HOUSE?
AFFIRMATIVE.
GOOD. NOW, THIS IS GOING TO REQUIRE SOME CAREFUL PLANNING AND A FAIR AMOUNT OF STEALTH.

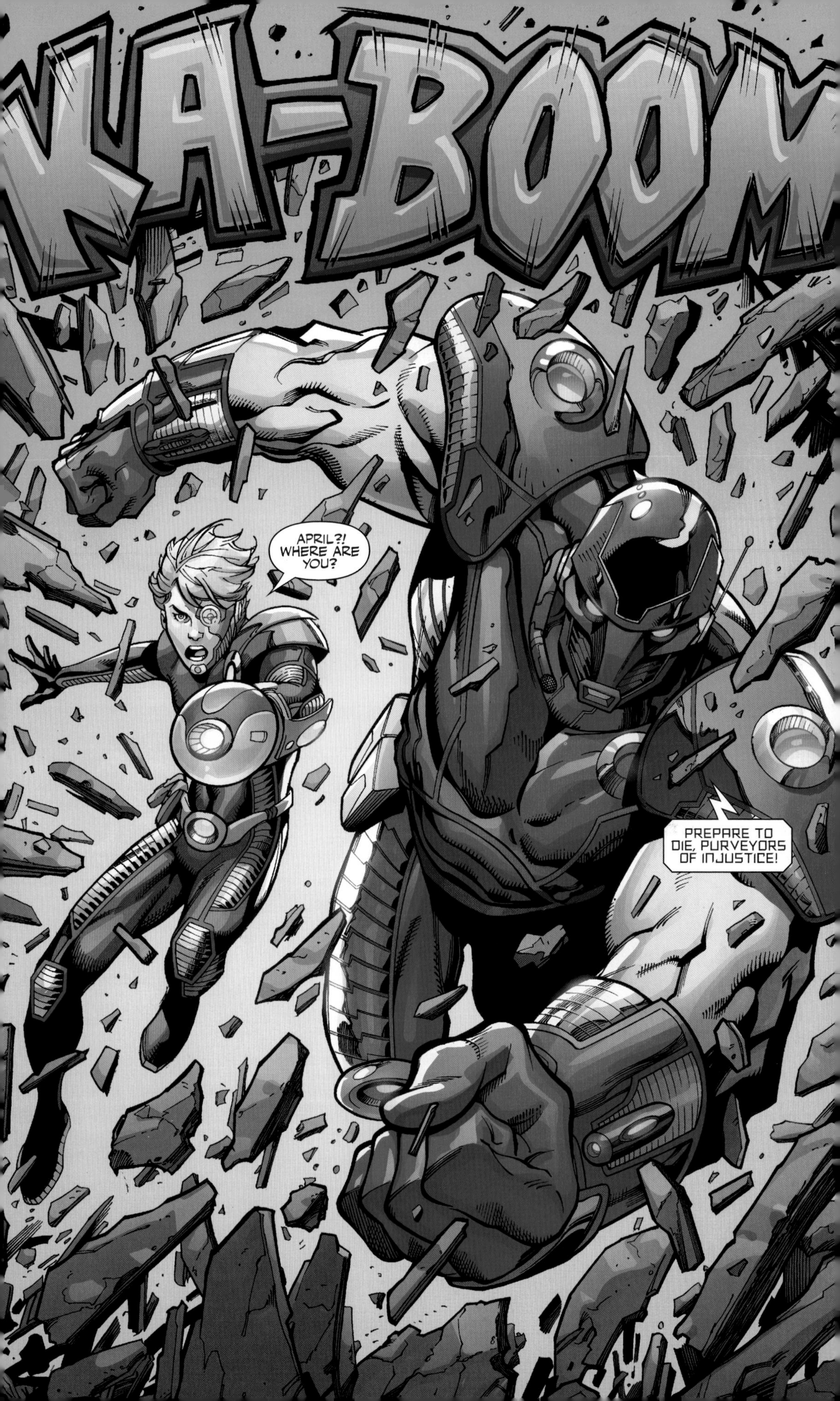
KA-BOOM
APRIL?! WHERE ARE YOU?
PREPARE TO DIE, PURVEYORS OF INJUSTICE!

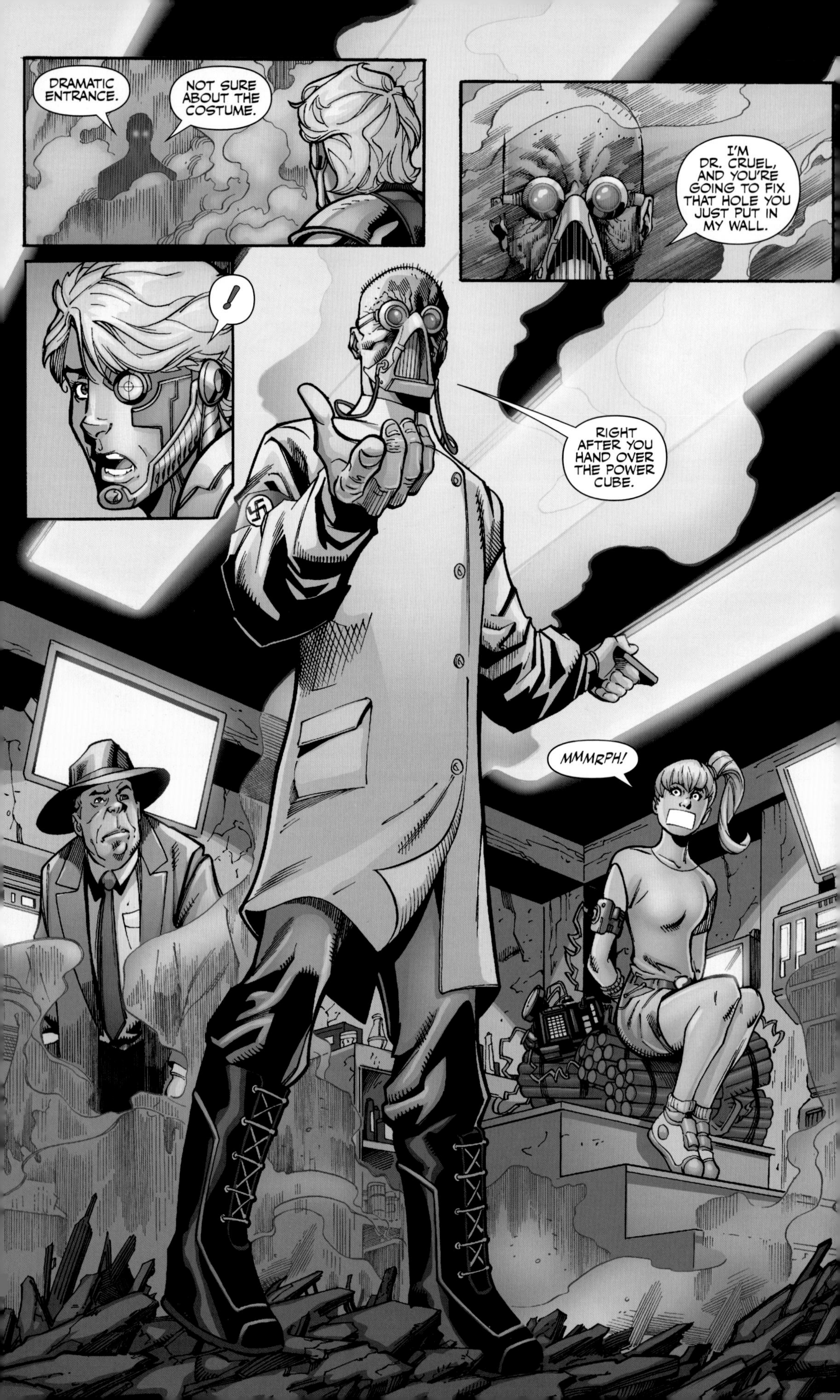

DRAMATIC ENTRANCE.
NOT SURE ABOUT THE COSTUME.
I'M DR. CRUEL, AND YOU'RE GOING TO FIX THAT HOLE YOU JUST PUT IN MY WALL.
!
RIGHT AFTER YOU HAND OVER THE POWER CUBE.
MMMRPH!

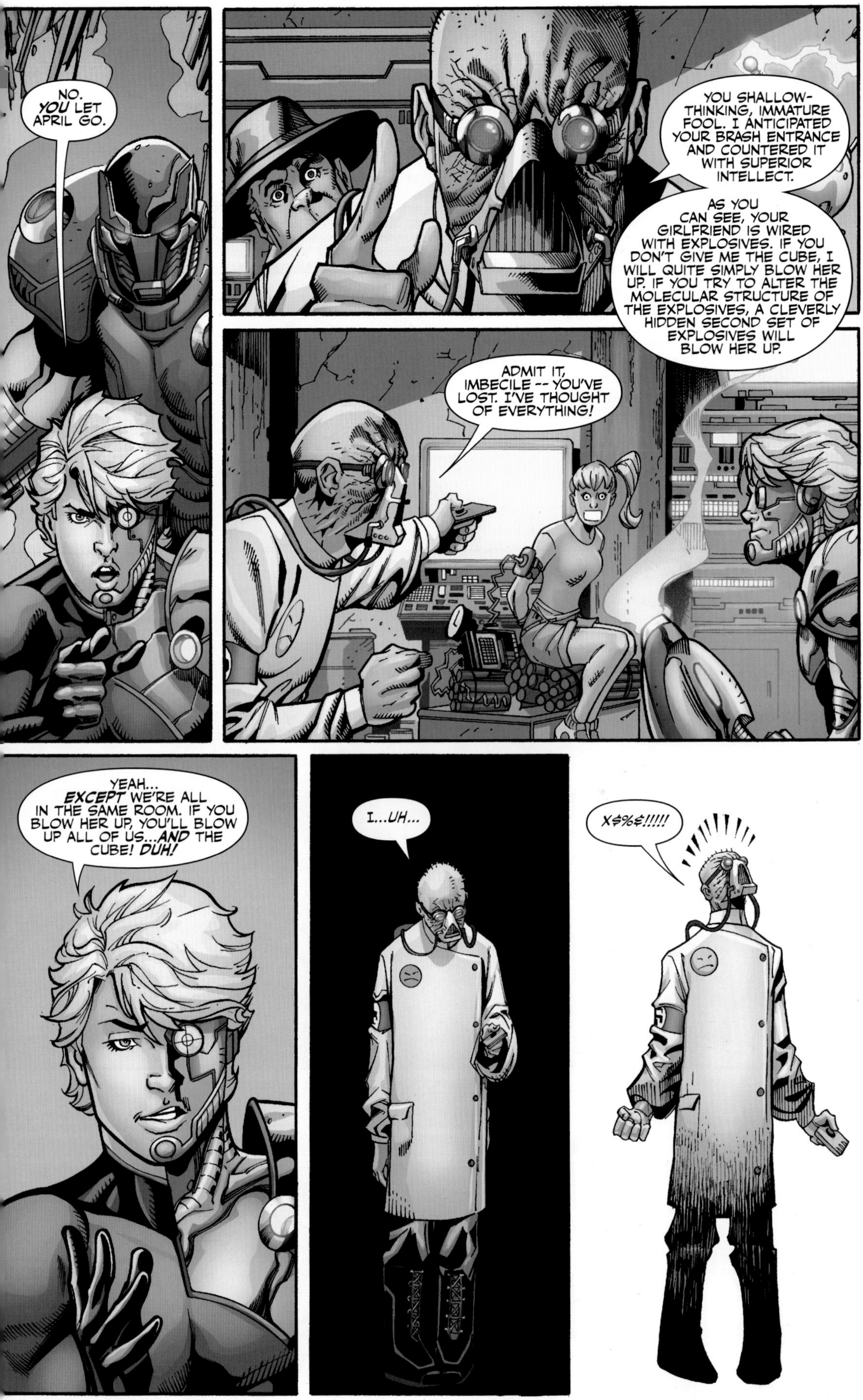

NO. *YOU* LET APRIL GO.
YOU SHALLOW-THINKING, IMMATURE FOOL. I ANTICIPATED YOUR BRASH ENTRANCE AND COUNTERED IT WITH SUPERIOR INTELLECT.
AS YOU CAN SEE, YOUR GIRLFRIEND IS WIRED WITH EXPLOSIVES. IF YOU DON'T GIVE ME THE CUBE, I WILL QUITE SIMPLY BLOW HER UP. IF YOU TRY TO ALTER THE MOLECULAR STRUCTURE OF THE EXPLOSIVES, A CLEVERLY HIDDEN SECOND SET OF EXPLOSIVES WILL BLOW HER UP.
ADMIT IT, IMBECILE -- YOU'VE LOST. I'VE THOUGHT OF EVERYTHING!
YEAH... *EXCEPT* WE'RE ALL IN THE SAME ROOM. IF YOU BLOW HER UP, YOU'LL BLOW UP ALL OF US... *AND* THE CUBE! *DUH!*
I... *UH*...
X$%¢!!!!!

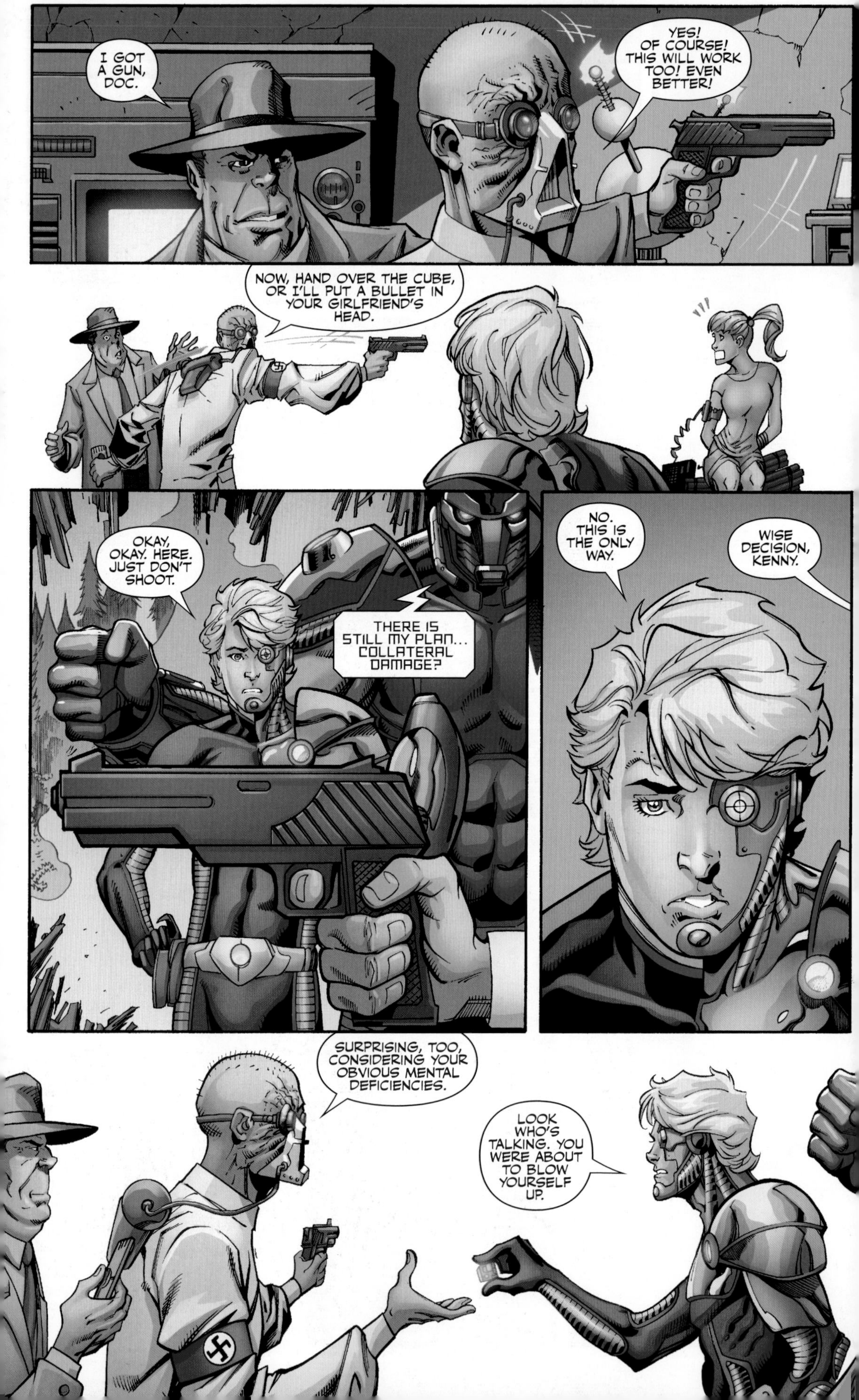
I GOT A GUN, DOC.
YES! OF COURSE! THIS WILL WORK TOO! EVEN BETTER!
NOW, HAND OVER THE CUBE, OR I'LL PUT A BULLET IN YOUR GIRLFRIEND'S HEAD.
OKAY, OKAY. HERE. JUST DON'T SHOOT.
THERE IS STILL MY PLAN... COLLATERAL DAMAGE?
NO. THIS IS THE ONLY WAY.
WISE DECISION, KENNY.
SURPRISING, TOO, CONSIDERING YOUR OBVIOUS MENTAL DEFICIENCIES.
LOOK WHO'S TALKING. YOU WERE ABOUT TO BLOW YOURSELF UP.

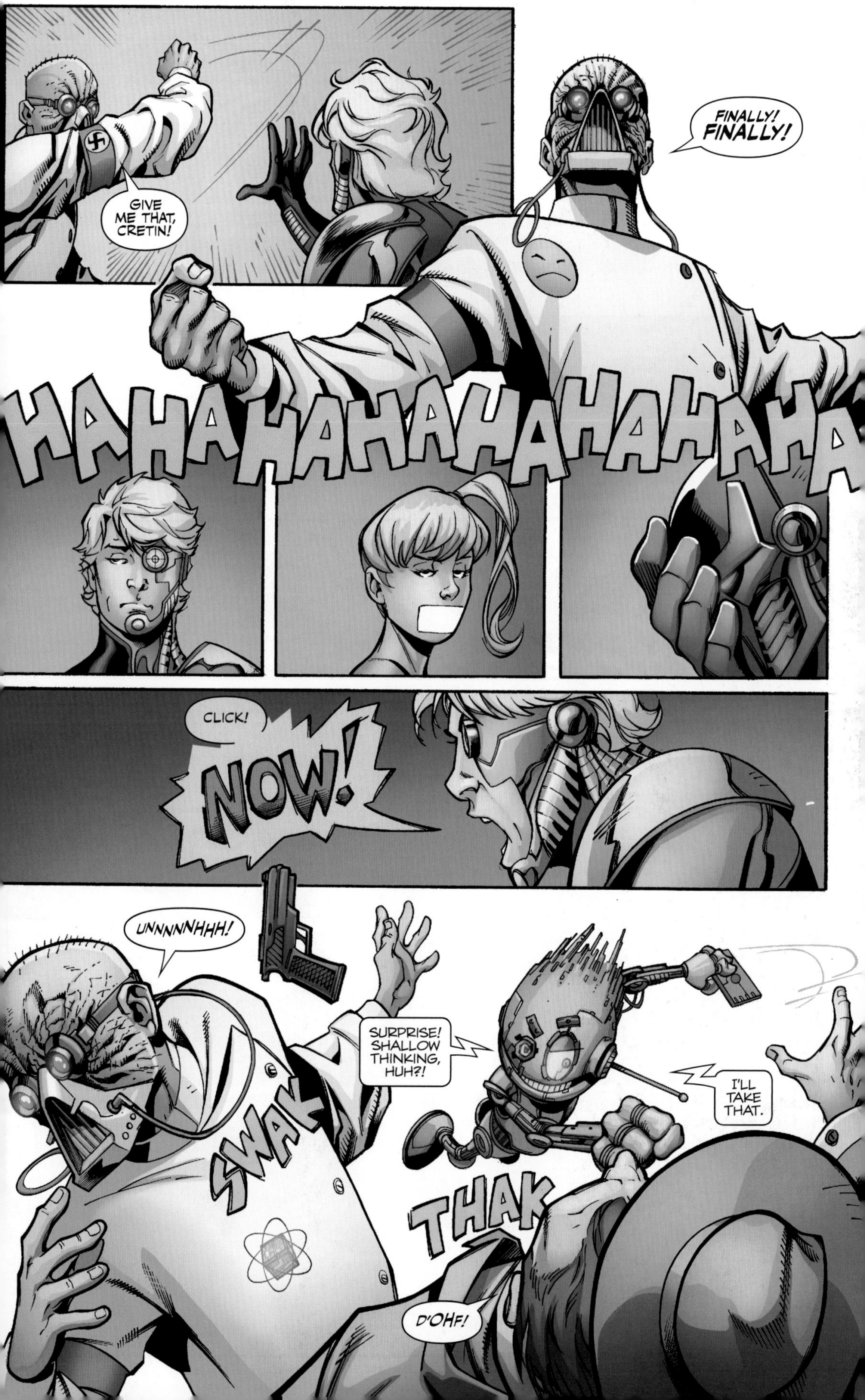
GIVE ME THAT, CRETIN!
FINALLY! FINALLY!
HAHAHAHAHAHAHAHAHAHAHAHA
CLICK!
NOW!
UNNNNNHHH!
SURPRISE! SHALLOW THINKING, HUH?!
SWAK
I'LL TAKE THAT.
THAK
D'OHF!

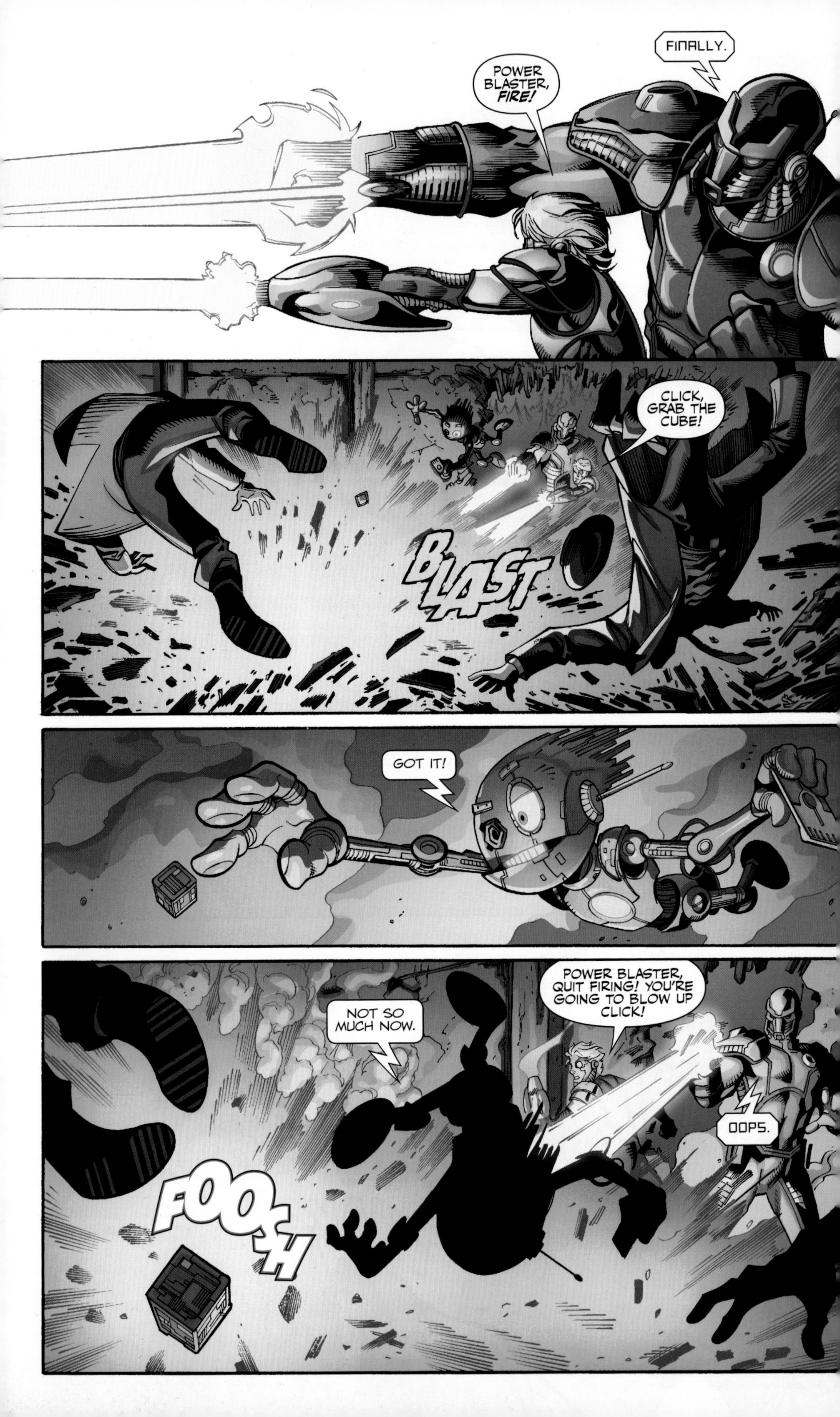
POWER BLASTER, FIRE!
FINALLY.
CLICK, GRAB THE CUBE!
BLAST
GOT IT!
NOT SO MUCH NOW.
POWER BLASTER, QUIT FIRING! YOU'RE GOING TO BLOW UP CLICK!
OOPS.
FOOSH

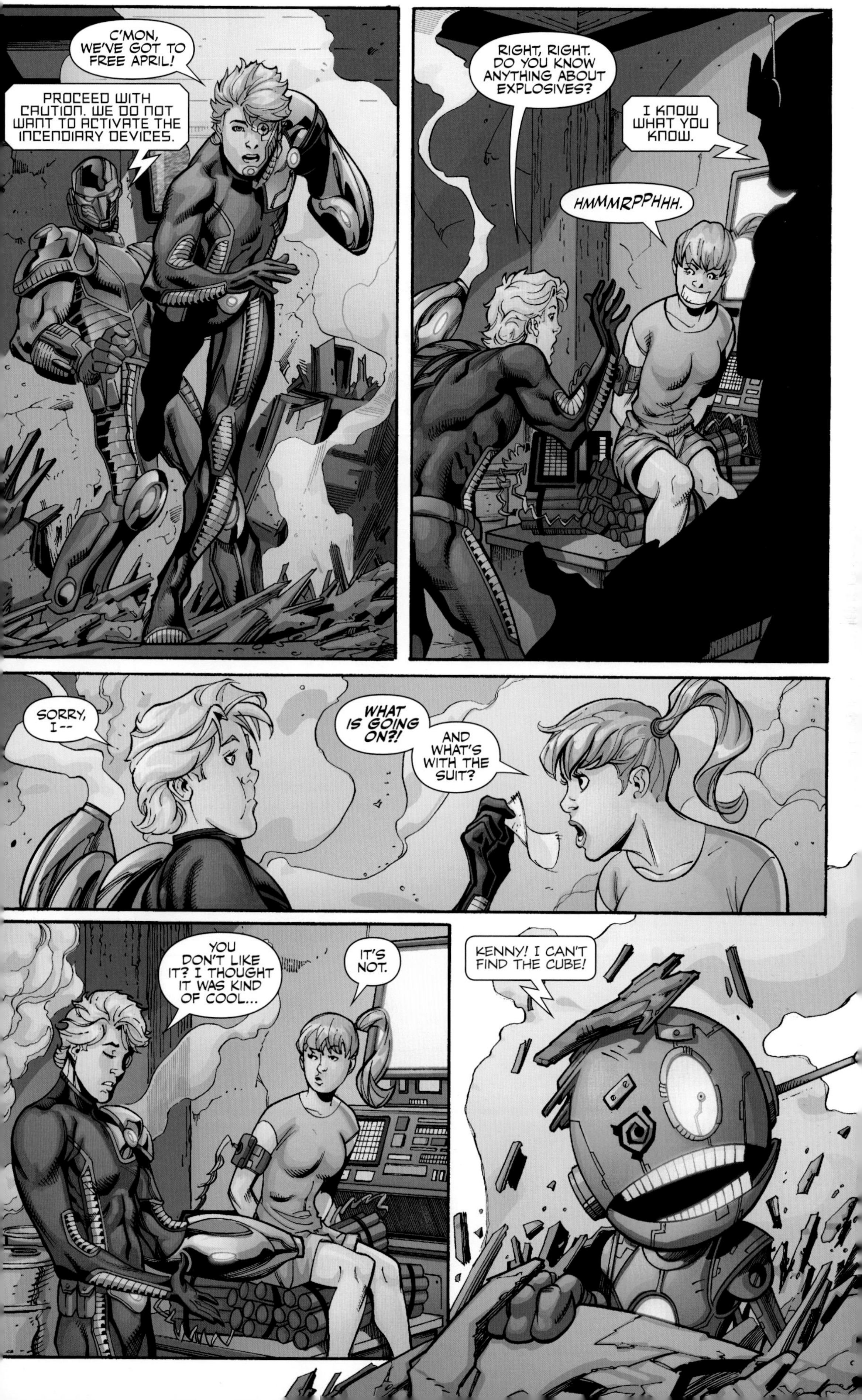

C'MON, WE'VE GOT TO FREE APRIL!
PROCEED WITH CAUTION. WE DO NOT WANT TO ACTIVATE THE INCENDIARY DEVICES.
RIGHT, RIGHT. DO YOU KNOW ANYTHING ABOUT EXPLOSIVES?
I KNOW WHAT YOU KNOW.
HMMMRPPHHH.
SORRY, I--
WHAT IS GOING ON?!
AND WHAT'S WITH THE SUIT?
YOU DON'T LIKE IT? I THOUGHT IT WAS KIND OF COOL...
IT'S NOT.
KENNY! I CAN'T FIND THE CUBE!

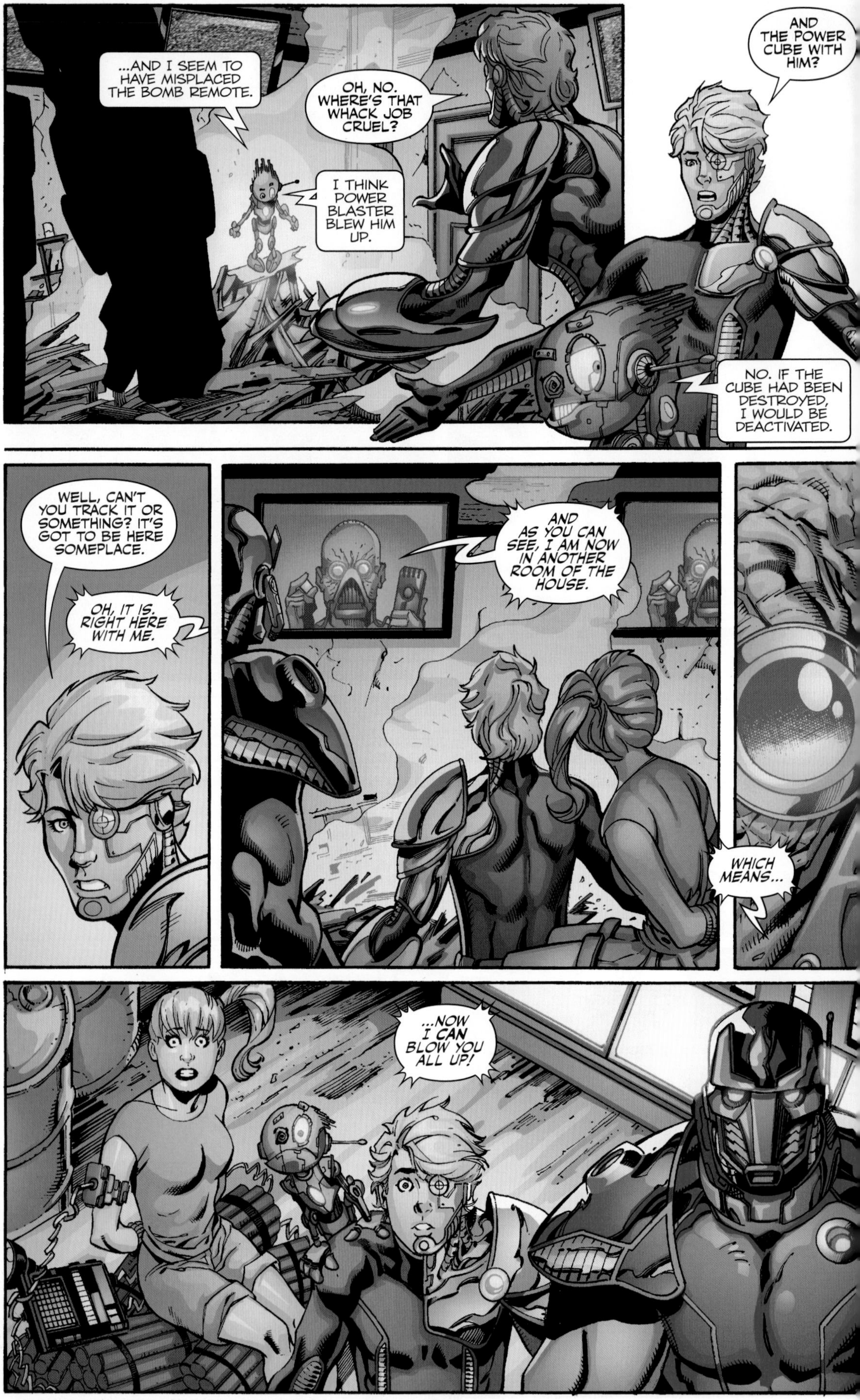
...AND I SEEM TO HAVE MISPLACED THE BOMB REMOTE.
OH, NO. WHERE'S THAT WHACK JOB CRUEL?
I THINK POWER BLASTER BLEW HIM UP.
AND THE POWER CUBE WITH HIM?
NO. IF THE CUBE HAD BEEN DESTROYED, I WOULD BE DEACTIVATED.
WELL, CAN'T YOU TRACK IT OR SOMETHING? IT'S GOT TO BE HERE SOMEPLACE.
OH, IT IS. RIGHT HERE WITH ME.
AND AS YOU CAN SEE, I AM NOW IN ANOTHER ROOM OF THE HOUSE.
WHICH MEANS...
...NOW I CAN BLOW YOU ALL UP!

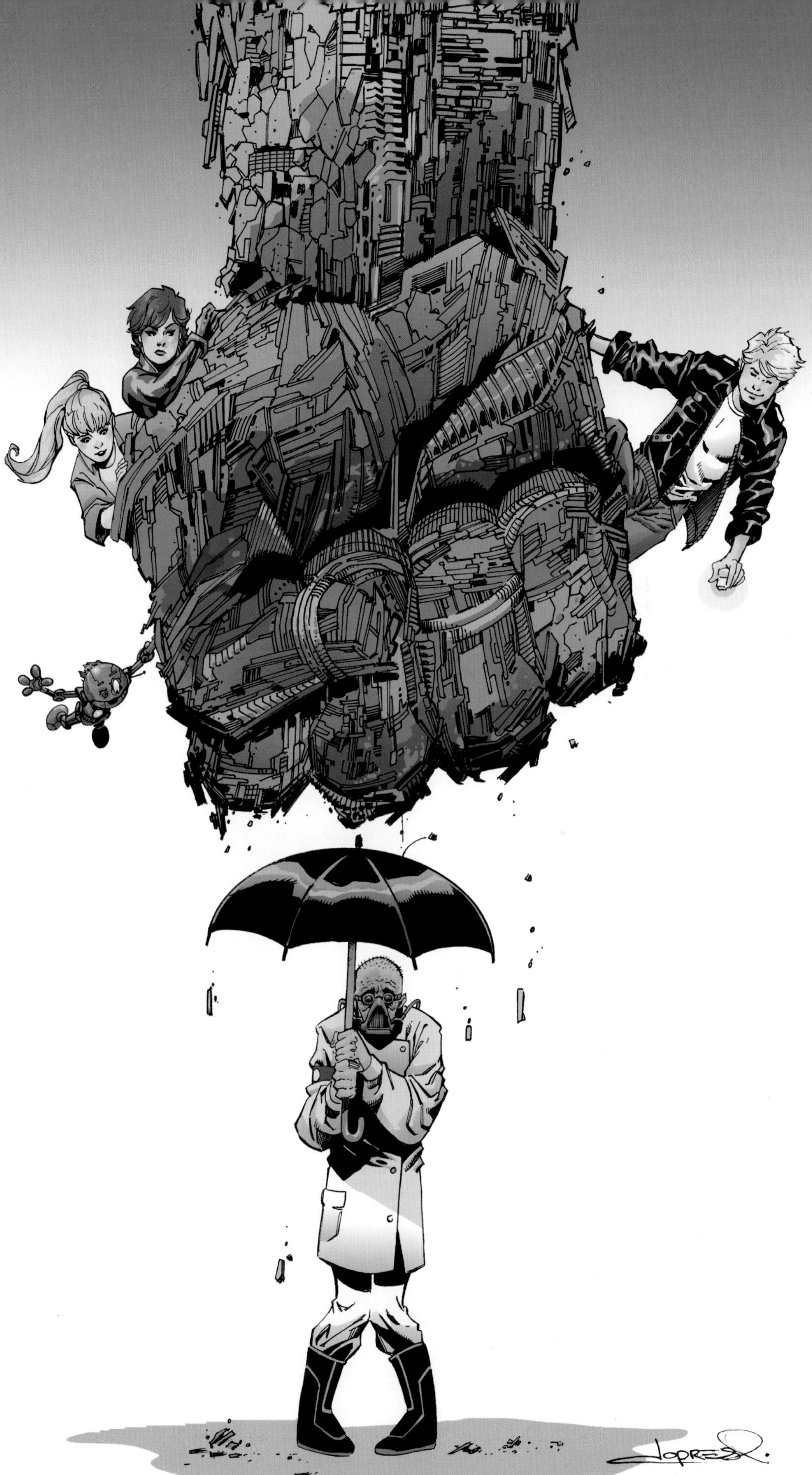

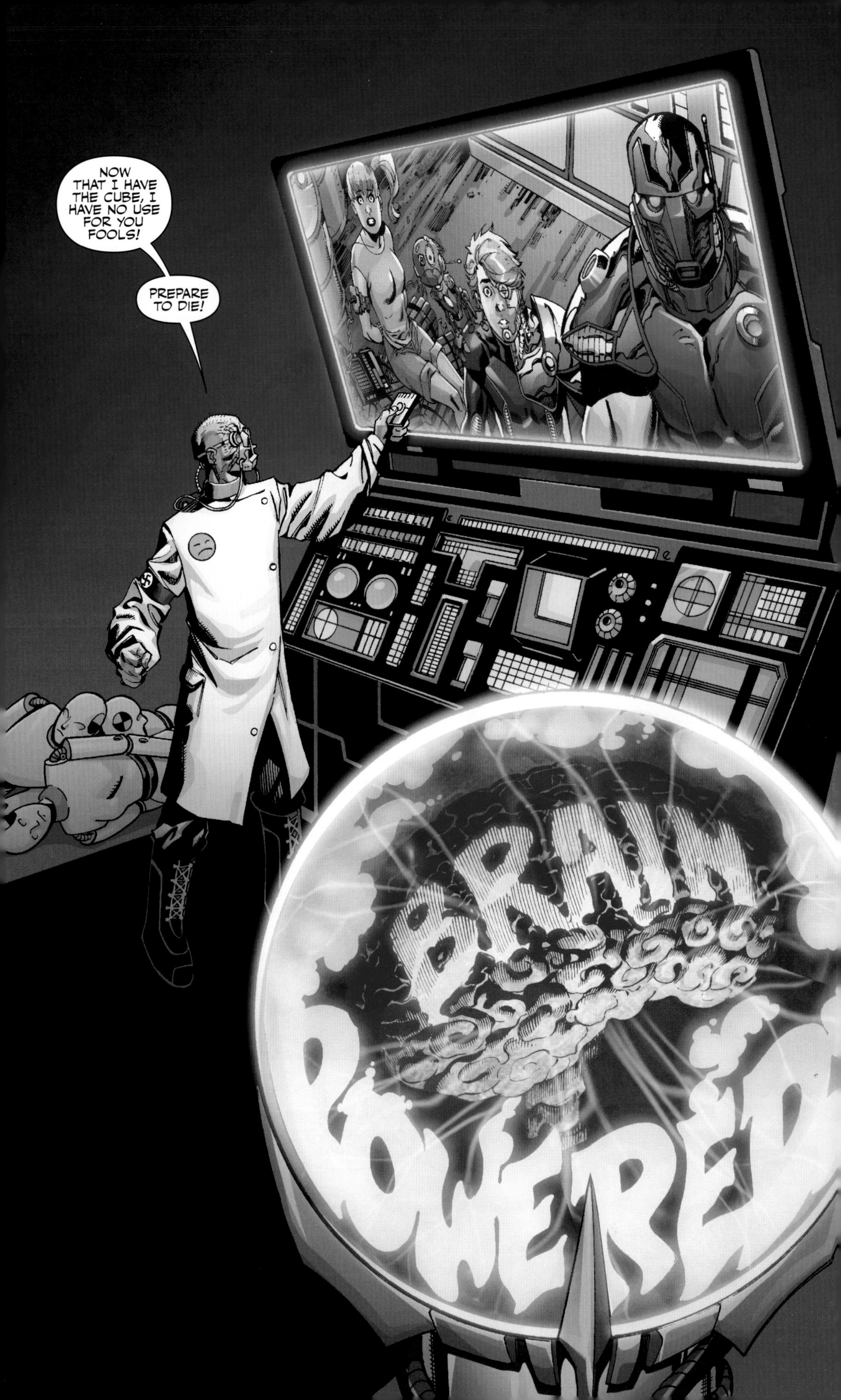
NOW THAT I HAVE THE CUBE, I HAVE NO USE FOR YOU FOOLS!
PREPARE TO DIE!
POWERED

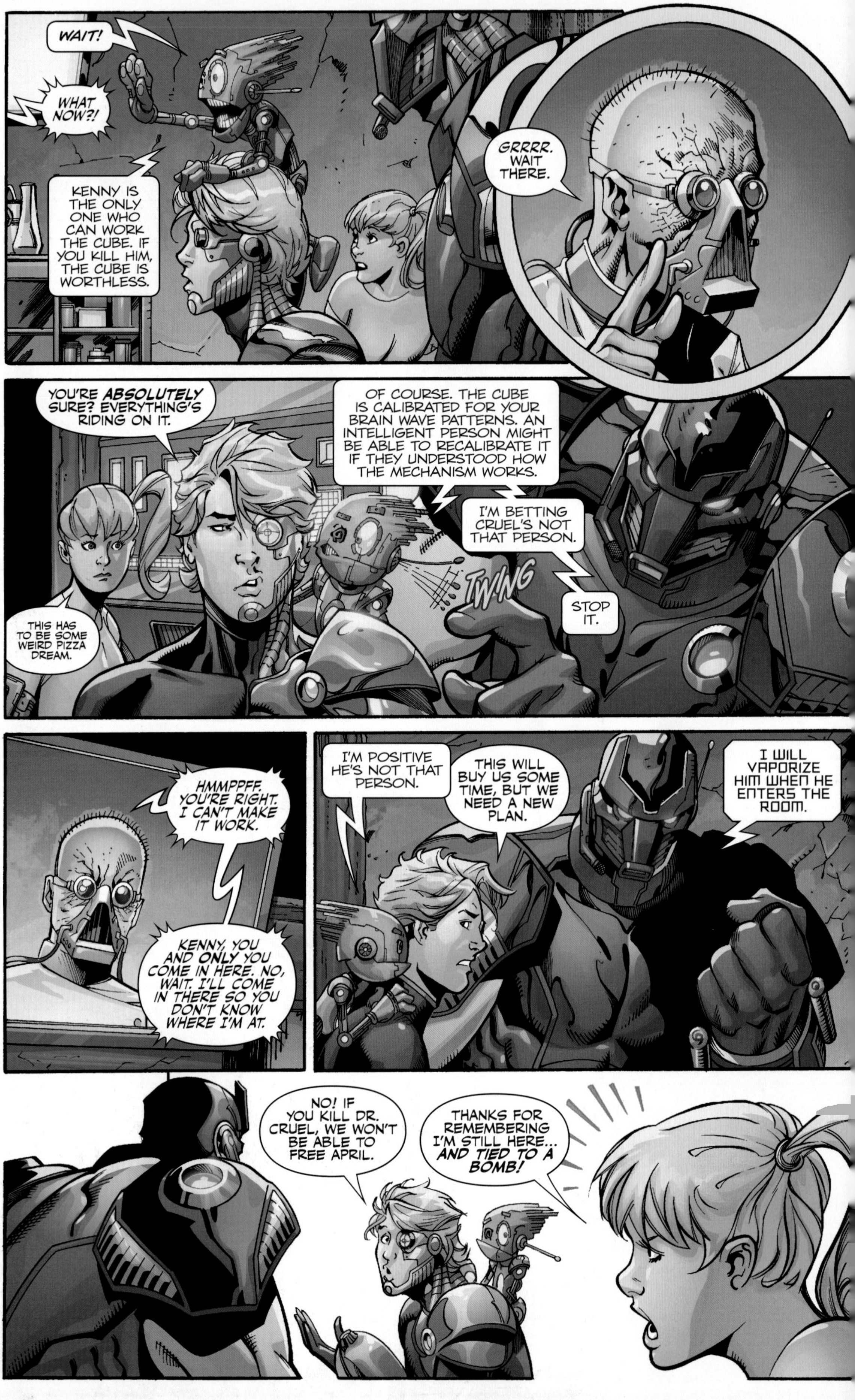

WAIT!
WHAT NOW?!
KENNY IS THE ONLY ONE WHO CAN WORK THE CUBE. IF YOU KILL HIM, THE CUBE IS WORTHLESS.
GRRRR. WAIT THERE.
YOU'RE ABSOLUTELY SURE? EVERYTHING'S RIDING ON IT.
OF COURSE. THE CUBE IS CALIBRATED FOR YOUR BRAIN WAVE PATTERNS. AN INTELLIGENT PERSON MIGHT BE ABLE TO RECALIBRATE IT IF THEY UNDERSTOOD HOW THE MECHANISM WORKS.
I'M BETTING CRUEL'S NOT THAT PERSON.
TWING
STOP IT.
THIS HAS TO BE SOME WEIRD PIZZA DREAM.
HMMPPFF. YOU'RE RIGHT. I CAN'T MAKE IT WORK.
KENNY, YOU AND ONLY YOU COME IN HERE. NO, WAIT. I'LL COME IN THERE SO YOU DON'T KNOW WHERE I'M AT.
I'M POSITIVE HE'S NOT THAT PERSON.
THIS WILL BUY US SOME TIME, BUT WE NEED A NEW PLAN.
I WILL VAPORIZE HIM WHEN HE ENTERS THE ROOM.
NO! IF YOU KILL DR. CRUEL, WE WON'T BE ABLE TO FREE APRIL.
THANKS FOR REMEMBERING I'M STILL HERE... AND TIED TO A BOMB!

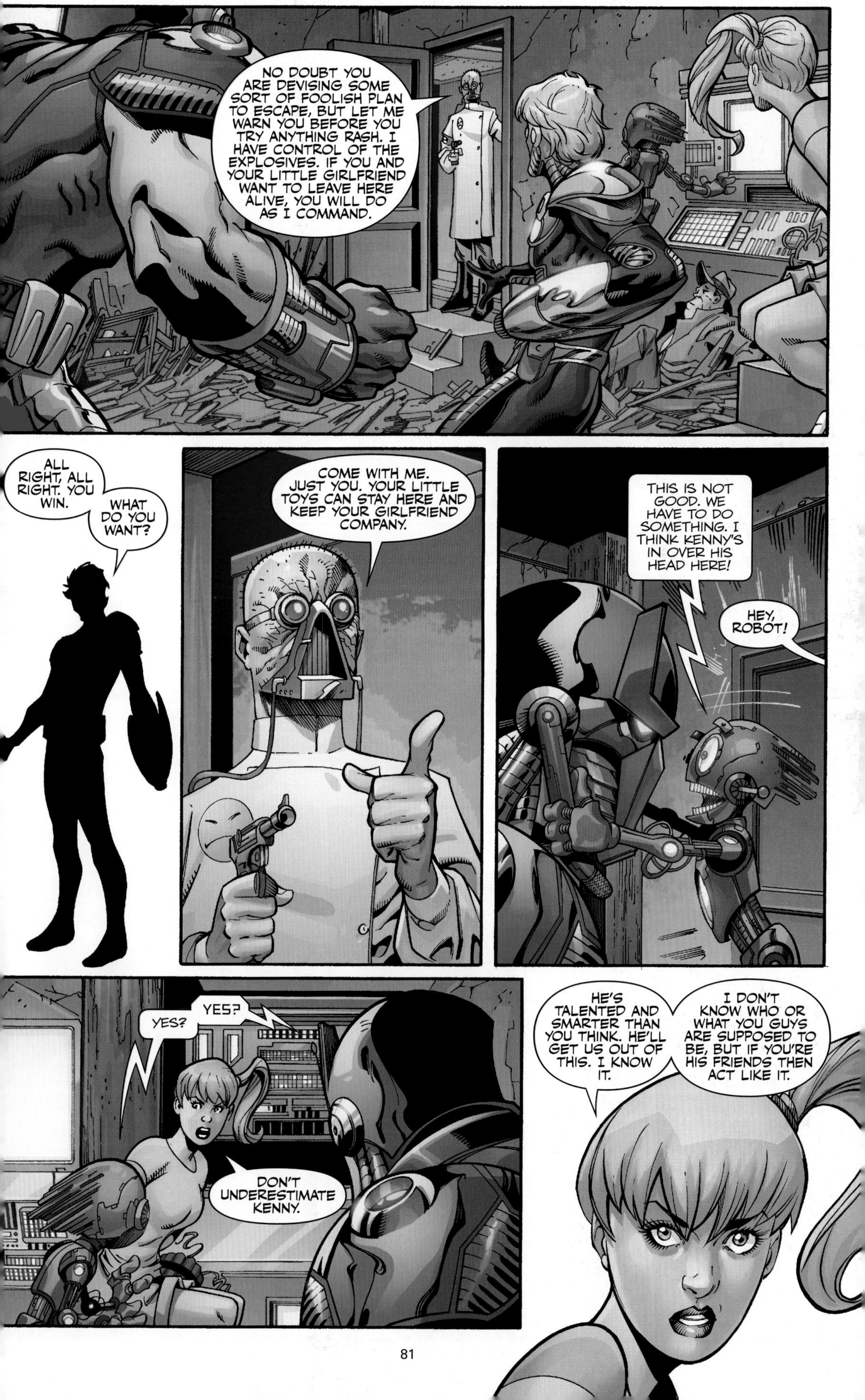
NO DOUBT YOU ARE DEVISING SOME SORT OF FOOLISH PLAN TO ESCAPE, BUT LET ME WARN YOU BEFORE YOU TRY ANYTHING RASH. I HAVE CONTROL OF THE EXPLOSIVES. IF YOU AND YOUR LITTLE GIRLFRIEND WANT TO LEAVE HERE ALIVE, YOU WILL DO AS I COMMAND.
ALL RIGHT, ALL RIGHT. YOU WIN.
WHAT DO YOU WANT?
COME WITH ME. JUST YOU. YOUR LITTLE TOYS CAN STAY HERE AND KEEP YOUR GIRLFRIEND COMPANY.
THIS IS NOT GOOD. WE HAVE TO DO SOMETHING. I THINK KENNY'S IN OVER HIS HEAD HERE!
HEY, ROBOT!
YES?
YES?
DON'T UNDERESTIMATE KENNY.
HE'S TALENTED AND SMARTER THAN YOU THINK. HE'LL GET US OUT OF THIS. I KNOW IT.
I DON'T KNOW WHO OR WHAT YOU GUYS ARE SUPPOSED TO BE, BUT IF YOU'RE HIS FRIENDS THEN ACT LIKE IT.

NOW CREATE A BODY FOR MY BRAIN, FOOL!

WHAT?

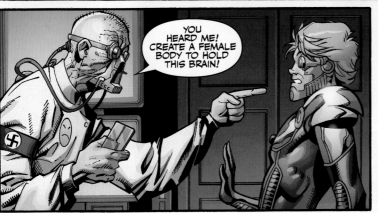

YOU HEARD ME! CREATE A FEMALE BODY TO HOLD THIS BRAIN!

ENOUGH WITH THE INSANITY! SERIOUSLY, I CAN'T TAKE IT!

I'M DONE UNTIL I KNOW WHAT'S GOING ON AROUND HERE! I DON'T CARE IF YOU KILL ME TWICE! I WANT TO KNOW WHO YOU ARE, AND WHAT'S THE DEAL WITH THAT BRAIN?!

DON'T YOU SASS ME! ALL I HAVE TO DO IS PUSH THIS BUTTON...

ALL RIGHT, FINE! I'LL TELL YOU MY DARK PLAN OF GENIUS.

TO BE HONEST, I'VE BEEN DESPERATE TO TELL THE STORY. IT'S REALLY A VILLAIN'S PRIVILEGE TO TELL HIS PLANS TO THE HERO. ALTHOUGH CASTING YOU IN THE ROLE OF THE HERO IS A RIDICULOUS STRETCH.

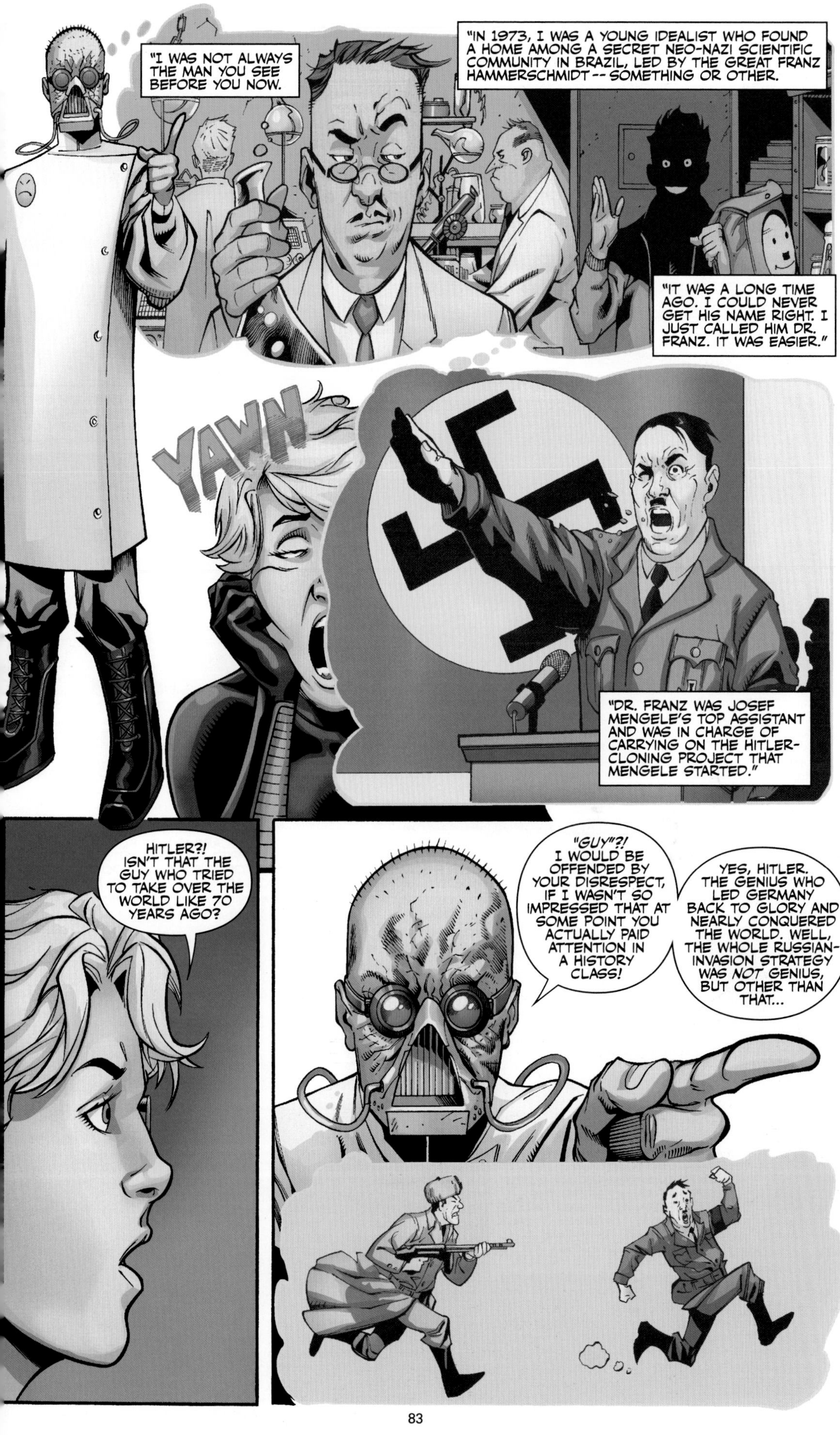
"I WAS NOT ALWAYS THE MAN YOU SEE BEFORE YOU NOW.
"IN 1973, I WAS A YOUNG IDEALIST WHO FOUND A HOME AMONG A SECRET NEO-NAZI SCIENTIFIC COMMUNITY IN BRAZIL, LED BY THE GREAT FRANZ HAMMERSCHMIDT -- SOMETHING OR OTHER.
"IT WAS A LONG TIME AGO. I COULD NEVER GET HIS NAME RIGHT. I JUST CALLED HIM DR. FRANZ. IT WAS EASIER."
YAWN
"DR. FRANZ WAS JOSEF MENGELE'S TOP ASSISTANT AND WAS IN CHARGE OF CARRYING ON THE HITLER-CLONING PROJECT THAT MENGELE STARTED."
HITLER?! ISN'T THAT THE GUY WHO TRIED TO TAKE OVER THE WORLD LIKE 70 YEARS AGO?
"GUY"?! I WOULD BE OFFENDED BY YOUR DISRESPECT, IF I WASN'T SO IMPRESSED THAT AT SOME POINT YOU ACTUALLY PAID ATTENTION IN A HISTORY CLASS!
YES, HITLER. THE GENIUS WHO LED GERMANY BACK TO GLORY AND NEARLY CONQUERED THE WORLD. WELL, THE WHOLE RUSSIAN-INVASION STRATEGY WAS *NOT* GENIUS, BUT OTHER THAN THAT...

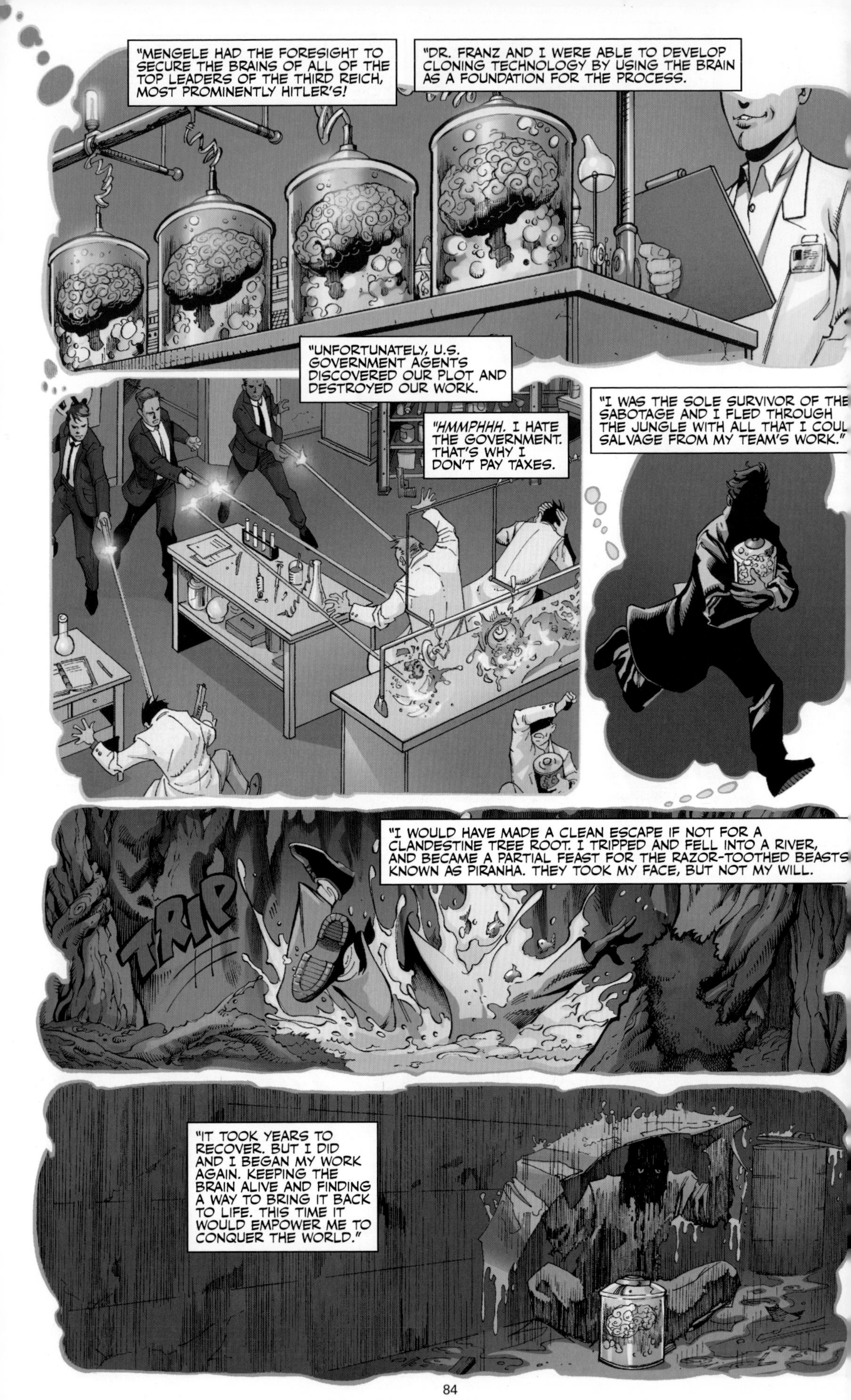
"MENGELE HAD THE FORESIGHT TO SECURE THE BRAINS OF ALL OF THE TOP LEADERS OF THE THIRD REICH, MOST PROMINENTLY HITLER'S!
"DR. FRANZ AND I WERE ABLE TO DEVELOP CLONING TECHNOLOGY BY USING THE BRAIN AS A FOUNDATION FOR THE PROCESS.
"UNFORTUNATELY, U.S. GOVERNMENT AGENTS DISCOVERED OUR PLOT AND DESTROYED OUR WORK.
HMMPHHH. I HATE THE GOVERNMENT. THAT'S WHY I DON'T PAY TAXES.
"I WAS THE SOLE SURVIVOR OF THE SABOTAGE AND I FLED THROUGH THE JUNGLE WITH ALL THAT I COUL SALVAGE FROM MY TEAM'S WORK."
"I WOULD HAVE MADE A CLEAN ESCAPE IF NOT FOR A CLANDESTINE TREE ROOT. I TRIPPED AND FELL INTO A RIVER, AND BECAME A PARTIAL FEAST FOR THE RAZOR-TOOTHED BEASTS KNOWN AS PIRANHA. THEY TOOK MY FACE, BUT NOT MY WILL.
TRIP
"IT TOOK YEARS TO RECOVER. BUT I DID AND I BEGAN MY WORK AGAIN. KEEPING THE BRAIN ALIVE AND FINDING A WAY TO BRING IT BACK TO LIFE. THIS TIME IT WOULD EMPOWER ME TO CONQUER THE WORLD."

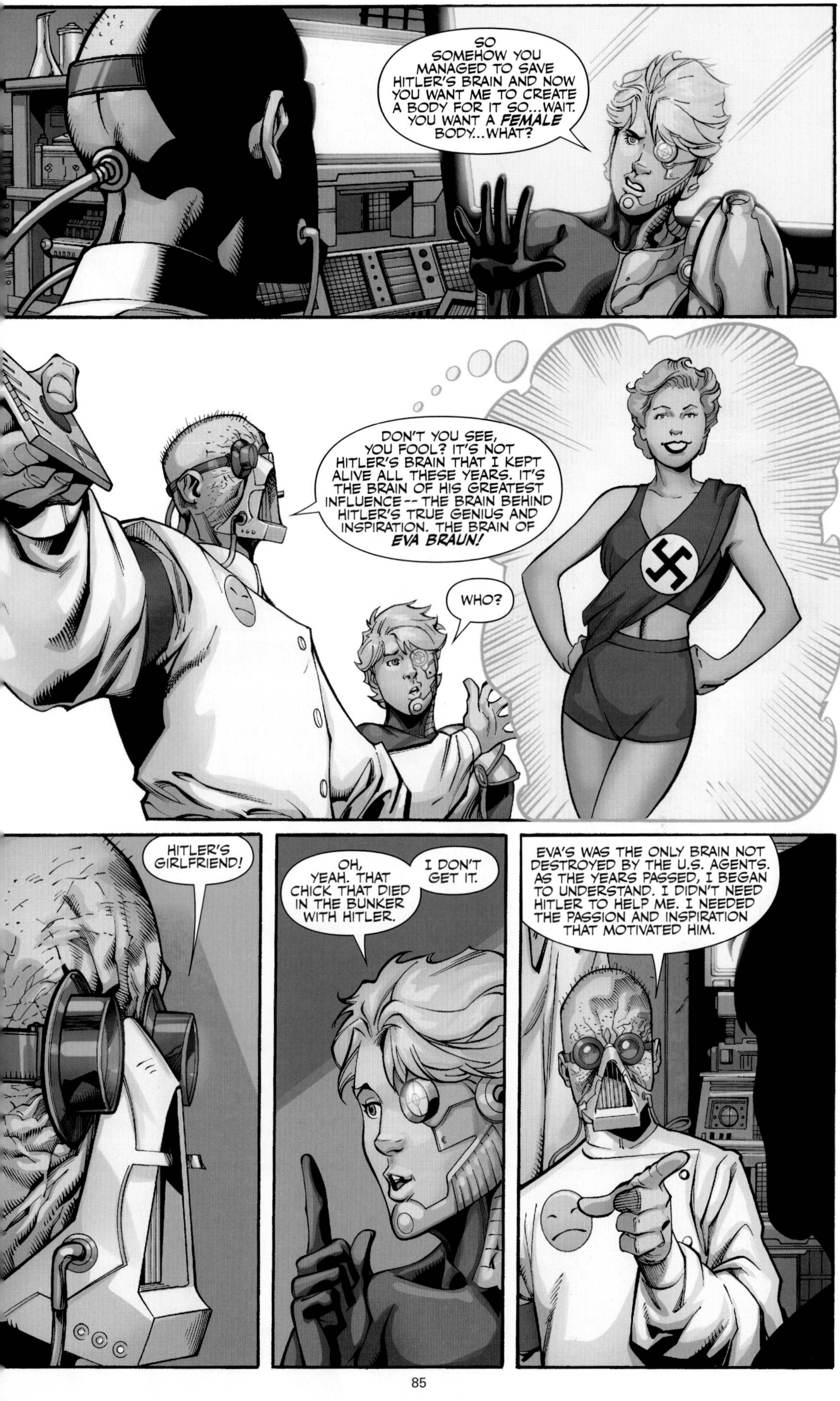
SO SOMEHOW YOU MANAGED TO SAVE HITLER'S BRAIN AND NOW YOU WANT ME TO CREATE A BODY FOR IT SO...WAIT. YOU WANT A *FEMALE* BODY...WHAT?
DON'T YOU SEE, YOU FOOL? IT'S NOT HITLER'S BRAIN THAT I KEPT ALIVE ALL THESE YEARS. IT'S THE BRAIN OF HIS GREATEST INFLUENCE-- THE BRAIN BEHIND HITLER'S TRUE GENIUS AND INSPIRATION. THE BRAIN OF ***EVA BRAUN!***
WHO?
HITLER'S GIRLFRIEND!
I DON'T GET IT.
OH, YEAH. THAT CHICK THAT DIED IN THE BUNKER WITH HITLER.
EVA'S WAS THE ONLY BRAIN NOT DESTROYED BY THE U.S. AGENTS. AS THE YEARS PASSED, I BEGAN TO UNDERSTAND. I DIDN'T NEED HITLER TO HELP ME. I NEEDED THE PASSION AND INSPIRATION THAT MOTIVATED HIM.

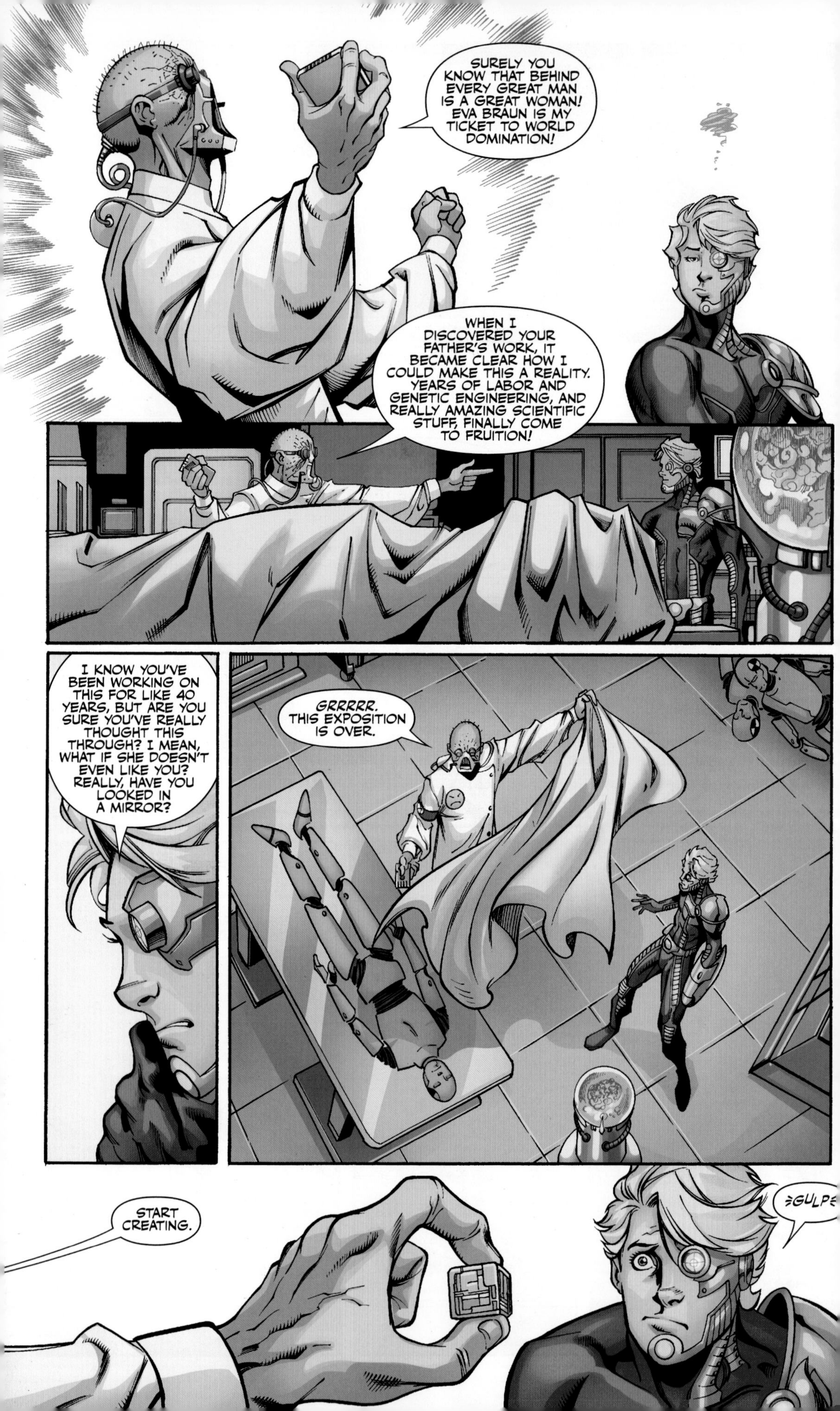
SURELY YOU KNOW THAT BEHIND EVERY GREAT MAN IS A GREAT WOMAN! EVA BRAUN IS MY TICKET TO WORLD DOMINATION!
WHEN I DISCOVERED YOUR FATHER'S WORK, IT BECAME CLEAR HOW I COULD MAKE THIS A REALITY. YEARS OF LABOR AND GENETIC ENGINEERING, AND REALLY AMAZING SCIENTIFIC STUFF, FINALLY COME TO FRUITION!
I KNOW YOU'VE BEEN WORKING ON THIS FOR LIKE 40 YEARS, BUT ARE YOU SURE YOU'VE REALLY THOUGHT THIS THROUGH? I MEAN, WHAT IF SHE DOESN'T EVEN LIKE YOU? REALLY, HAVE YOU LOOKED IN A MIRROR?
GRRRRR. THIS EXPOSITION IS OVER.
START CREATING.
GULP

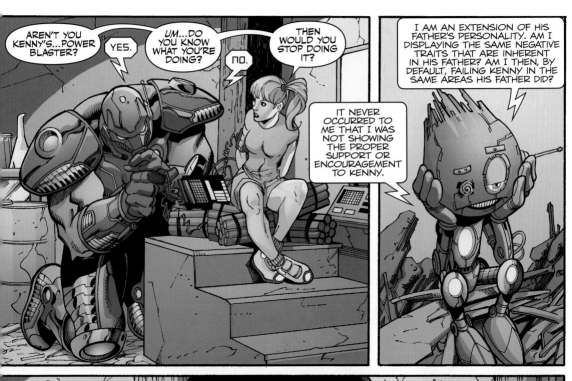

AREN'T YOU KENNY'S...POWER BLASTER?

YES.

UM...DO YOU KNOW WHAT YOU'RE DOING?

NO.

THEN WOULD YOU STOP DOING IT?

I AM AN EXTENSION OF HIS FATHER'S PERSONALITY. AM I DISPLAYING THE SAME NEGATIVE TRAITS THAT ARE INHERENT IN HIS FATHER? AM I THEN, BY DEFAULT, FAILING KENNY IN THE SAME AREAS HIS FATHER DID?

IT NEVER OCCURRED TO ME THAT I WAS NOT SHOWING THE PROPER SUPPORT OR ENCOURAGEMENT TO KENNY.

LOOK, I DIDN'T MEAN TO RUIN YOUR DAY. I WAS JUST TRYING TO POINT OUT THAT KENNY HAS A LOT OF GREAT QUALITIES AND IS STRONGER THAN YOU MIGHT THINK.

I REALLY THINK HIS DAD BELIEVED IN HIM. I JUST DON'T THINK HE KNEW HOW TO EXPRESS IT. YOU GUYS JUST HAVE TO LOOK BEYOND WHAT YOU THINK YOU KNOW...AND HAVE SOME FAITH.

SURPRISINGLY INSIGHTFUL FOR A TEENAGE GIRL.

...WHATEVER...

PERHAPS I CAN EXPAND BEYOND MY ORIGINAL PROGRAMMING AND EVOLVE. ACTUALLY LEARN AND GROW AND BECOME MORE THAN I WAS EVER CREATED TO BE! WHAT A FASCINATING POSSIBILITY!

KENNY, HURRY UP AND SAVE ME!

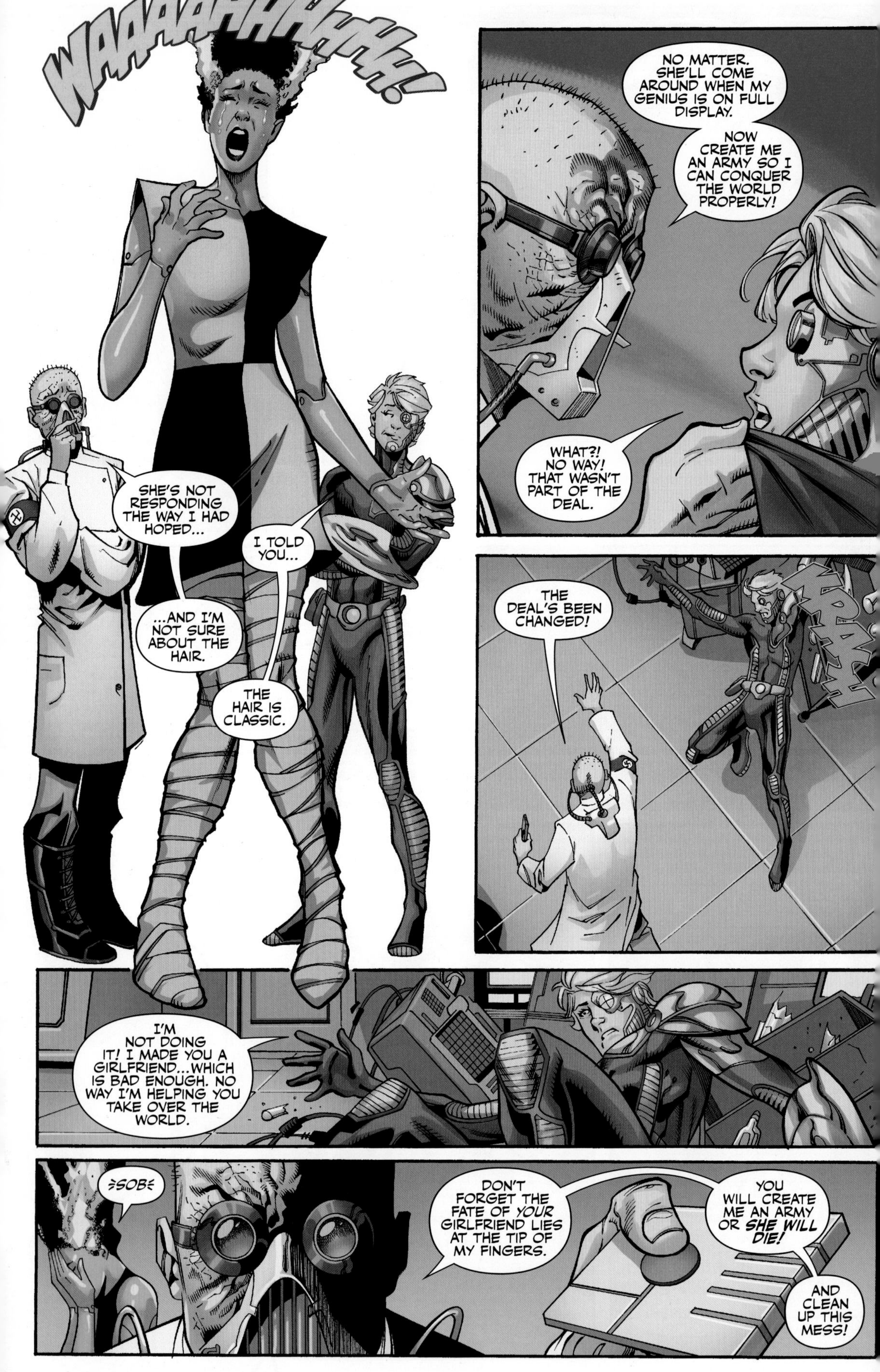
WAAAAHHHHHH!
SHE'S NOT RESPONDING THE WAY I HAD HOPED...
...AND I'M NOT SURE ABOUT THE HAIR.
I TOLD YOU...
THE HAIR IS CLASSIC.
NO MATTER. SHE'LL COME AROUND WHEN MY GENIUS IS ON FULL DISPLAY.
NOW CREATE ME AN ARMY SO I CAN CONQUER THE WORLD PROPERLY!
WHAT?! NO WAY! THAT WASN'T PART OF THE DEAL.
THE DEAL'S BEEN CHANGED!
I'M NOT DOING IT! I MADE YOU A GIRLFRIEND...WHICH IS BAD ENOUGH. NO WAY I'M HELPING YOU TAKE OVER THE WORLD.
SOB
DON'T FORGET THE FATE OF YOUR GIRLFRIEND LIES AT THE TIP OF MY FINGERS.
YOU WILL CREATE ME AN ARMY OR SHE WILL DIE!
AND CLEAN UP THIS MESS!

THAT ROBOT'S ION EXHAUST TRAIL IS GETTING STRONGER. I MUST BE GETTING CLOSE.

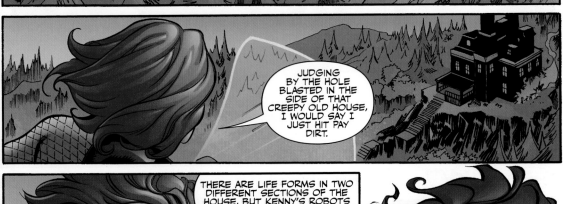

JUDGING BY THE HOLE BLASTED IN THE SIDE OF THAT CREEPY OLD HOUSE, I WOULD SAY I JUST HIT PAY DIRT.

THERE ARE LIFE FORMS IN TWO DIFFERENT SECTIONS OF THE HOUSE, BUT KENNY'S ROBOTS SEEM TO BE CONCENTRATED NEAR THE BLAST SITE. I'LL START THERE.

THE SCANNER IS PICKING UP VIDEO MONITORING EVERYWHERE. I'LL JUST DISRUPT THE ELECTRICAL FEED INTO THE HOUSE WITH MY OWN LITTLE ENERGY-DAMPENING FIELD. I LOVE GOVERNMENT TECH.

THIS TIME, THE ELEMENT OF SURPRISE IS MINE.

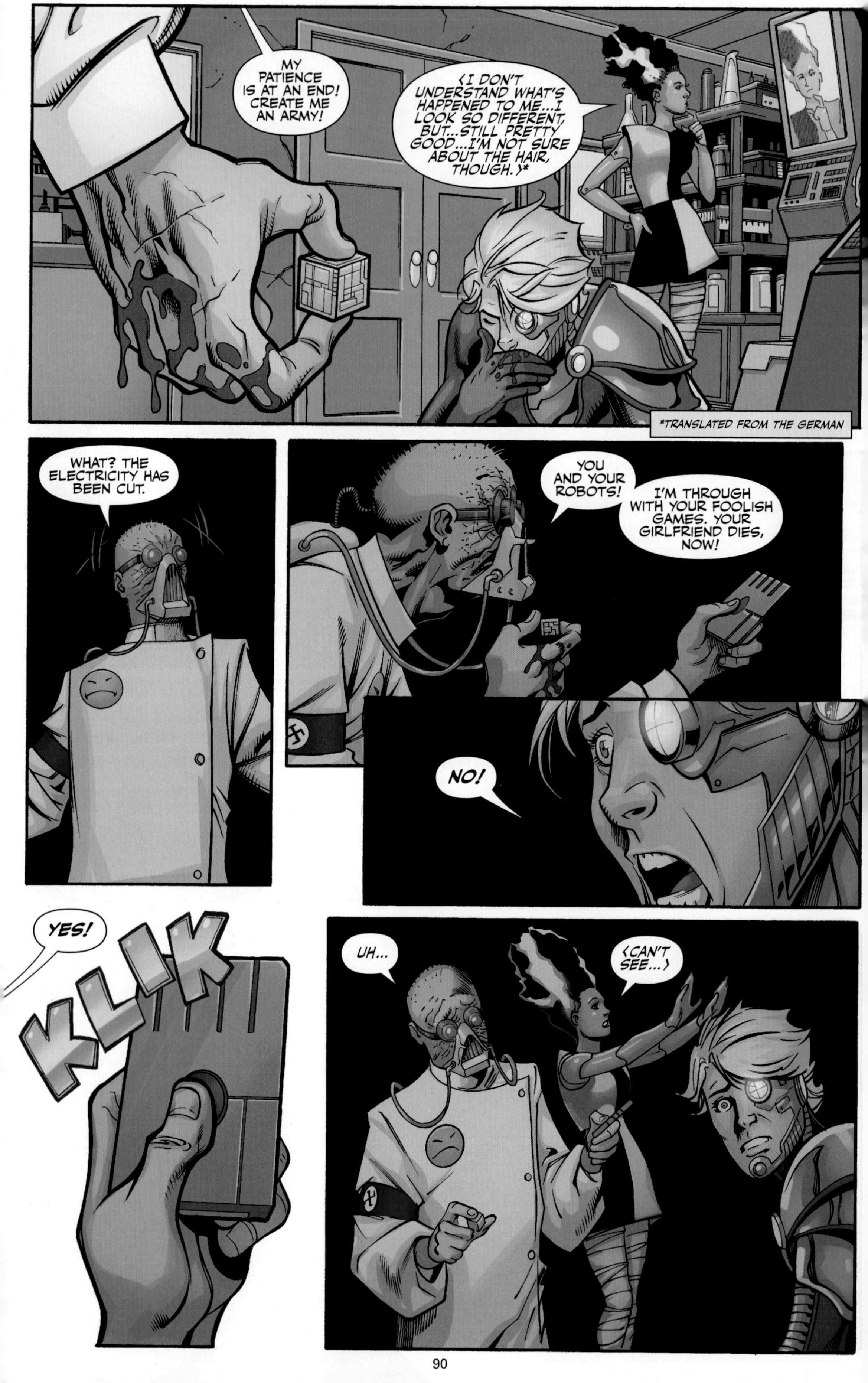
MY PATIENCE IS AT AN END! CREATE ME AN ARMY!
<I DON'T UNDERSTAND WHAT'S HAPPENED TO ME...I LOOK SO DIFFERENT, BUT...STILL PRETTY GOOD...I'M NOT SURE ABOUT THE HAIR, THOUGH.>*
*TRANSLATED FROM THE GERMAN
WHAT? THE ELECTRICITY HAS BEEN CUT.
YOU AND YOUR ROBOTS!
I'M THROUGH WITH YOUR FOOLISH GAMES. YOUR GIRLFRIEND DIES, NOW!
NO!
YES!
KLIK
UH...
<CAN'T SEE...>

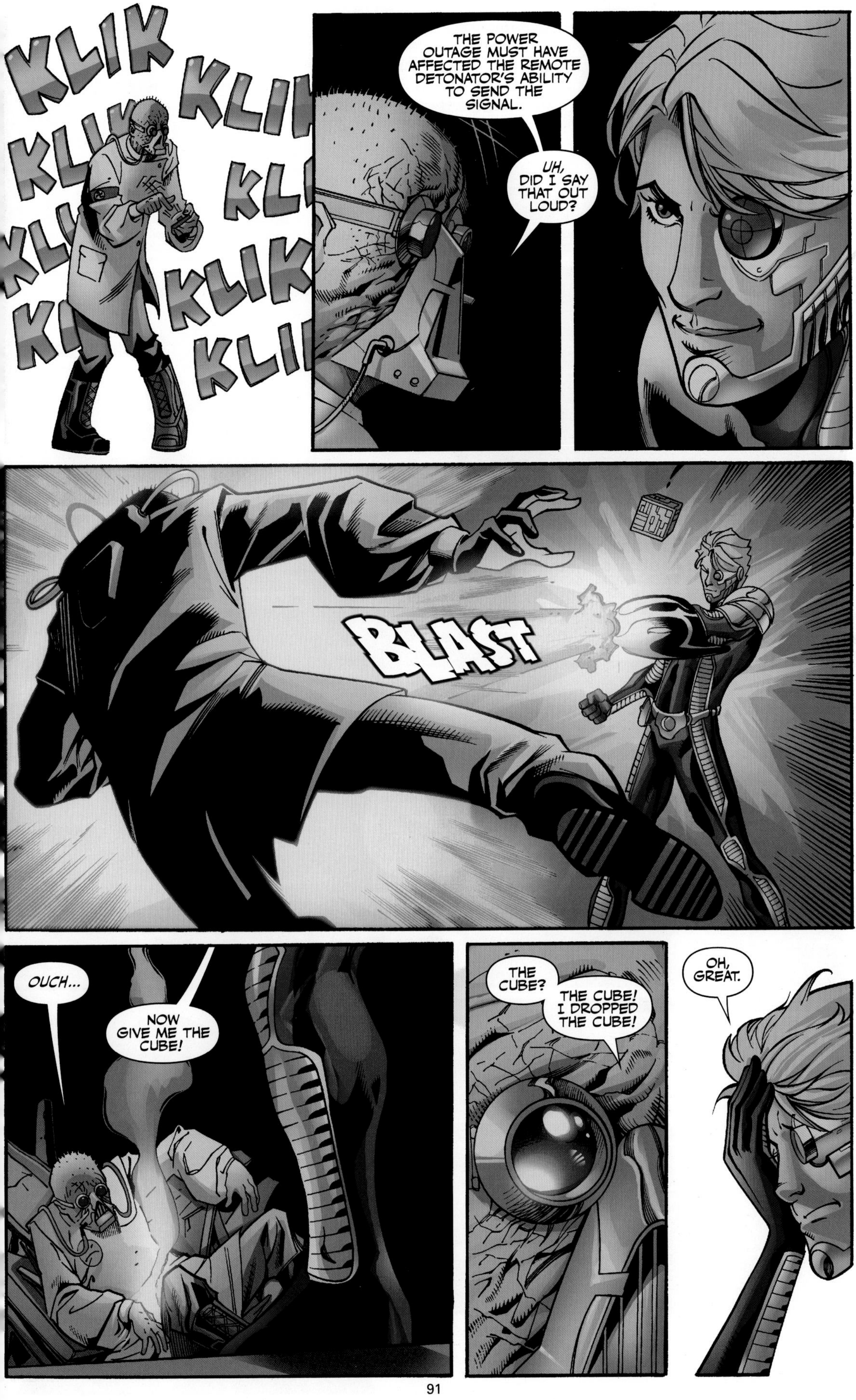
KLIK KLIK KLIK KLIK KLIK KLIK KLIK KLIK KLIK
THE POWER OUTAGE MUST HAVE AFFECTED THE REMOTE DETONATOR'S ABILITY TO SEND THE SIGNAL.
UH, DID I SAY THAT OUT LOUD?
BLAST
OUCH...
NOW GIVE ME THE CUBE!
THE CUBE?
THE CUBE! I DROPPED THE CUBE!
OH, GREAT.

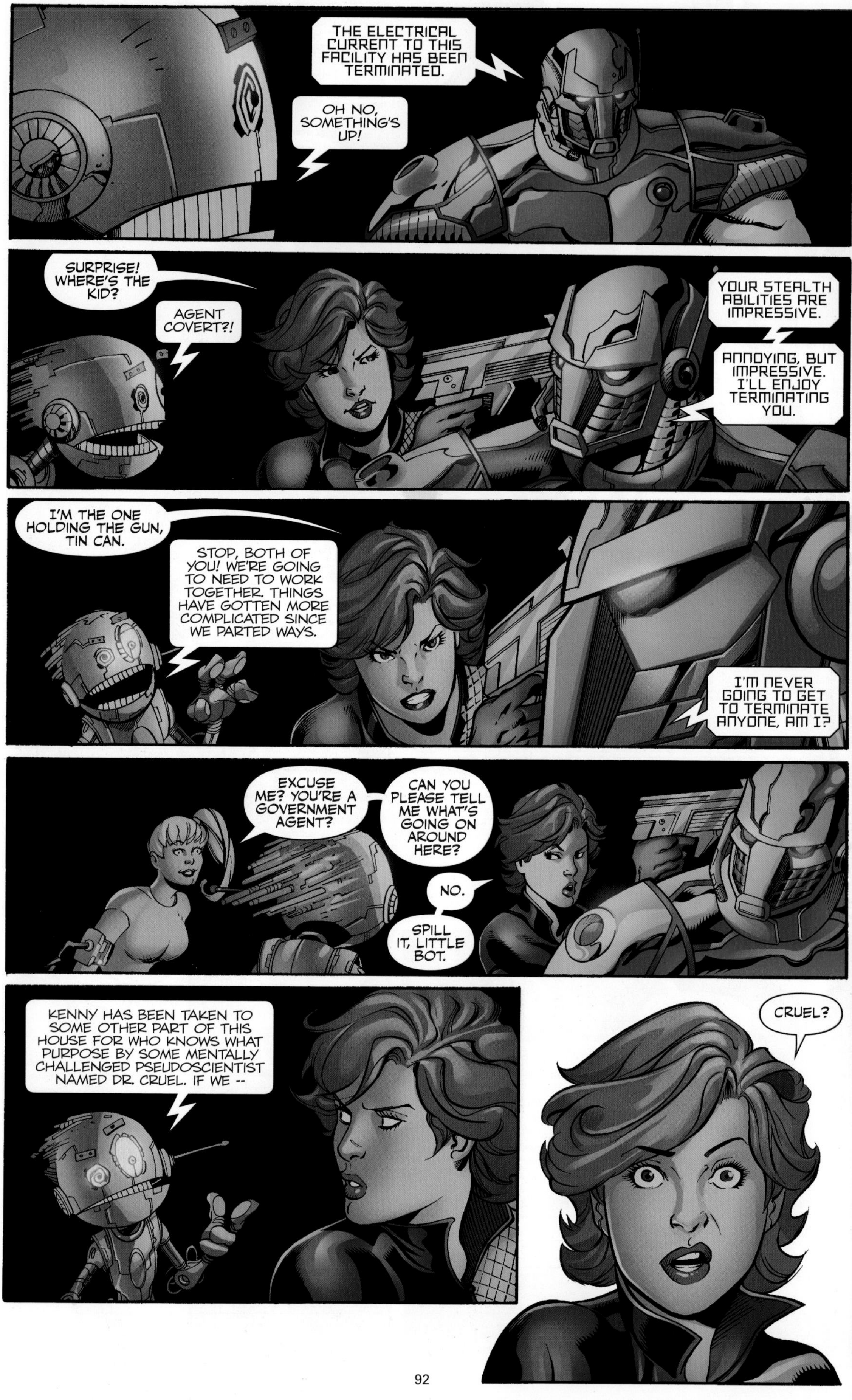

THE ELECTRICAL CURRENT TO THIS FACILITY HAS BEEN TERMINATED.
OH NO, SOMETHING'S UP!
SURPRISE! WHERE'S THE KID?
AGENT COVERT?!
YOUR STEALTH ABILITIES ARE IMPRESSIVE.
ANNOYING, BUT IMPRESSIVE. I'LL ENJOY TERMINATING YOU.
I'M THE ONE HOLDING THE GUN, TIN CAN.
STOP, BOTH OF YOU! WE'RE GOING TO NEED TO WORK TOGETHER. THINGS HAVE GOTTEN MORE COMPLICATED SINCE WE PARTED WAYS.
I'M NEVER GOING TO GET TO TERMINATE ANYONE, AM I?
EXCUSE ME? YOU'RE A GOVERNMENT AGENT?
CAN YOU PLEASE TELL ME WHAT'S GOING ON AROUND HERE?
NO.
SPILL IT, LITTLE BOT.
KENNY HAS BEEN TAKEN TO SOME OTHER PART OF THIS HOUSE FOR WHO KNOWS WHAT PURPOSE BY SOME MENTALLY CHALLENGED PSEUDOSCIENTIST NAMED DR. CRUEL. IF WE --
CRUEL?

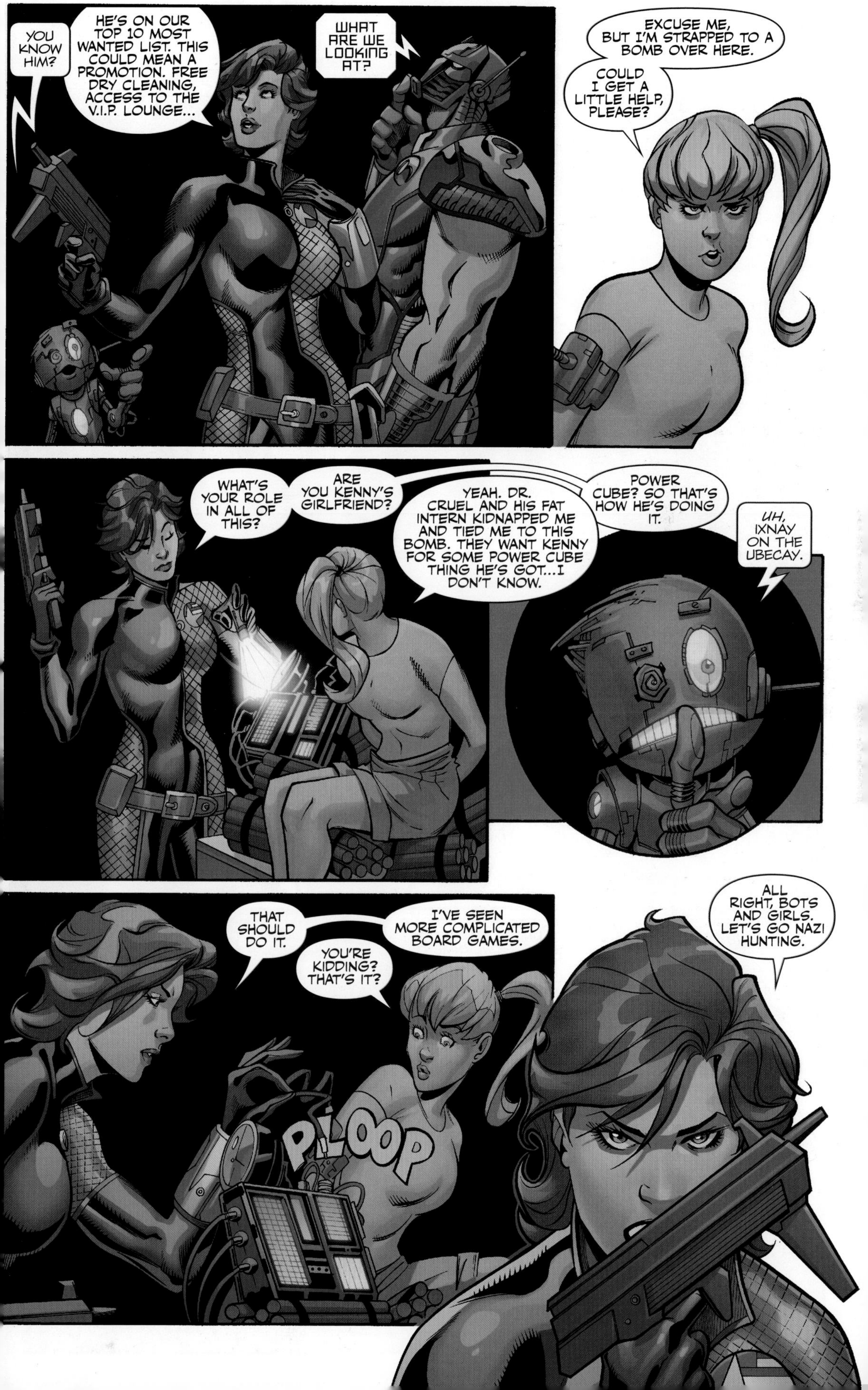

YOU KNOW HIM?
HE'S ON OUR TOP 10 MOST WANTED LIST. THIS COULD MEAN A PROMOTION. FREE DRY CLEANING, ACCESS TO THE V.I.P. LOUNGE...
WHAT ARE WE LOOKING AT?
EXCUSE ME, BUT I'M STRAPPED TO A BOMB OVER HERE.
COULD I GET A LITTLE HELP, PLEASE?
WHAT'S YOUR ROLE IN ALL OF THIS?
ARE YOU KENNY'S GIRLFRIEND?
YEAH. DR. CRUEL AND HIS FAT INTERN KIDNAPPED ME AND TIED ME TO THIS BOMB. THEY WANT KENNY FOR SOME POWER CUBE THING HE'S GOT...I DON'T KNOW.
POWER CUBE? SO THAT'S HOW HE'S DOING IT.
UH, IXNAY ON THE UBECAY.
THAT SHOULD DO IT.
I'VE SEEN MORE COMPLICATED BOARD GAMES.
YOU'RE KIDDING? THAT'S IT?
PLOOP
ALL RIGHT, BOTS AND GIRLS. LET'S GO NAZI HUNTING.

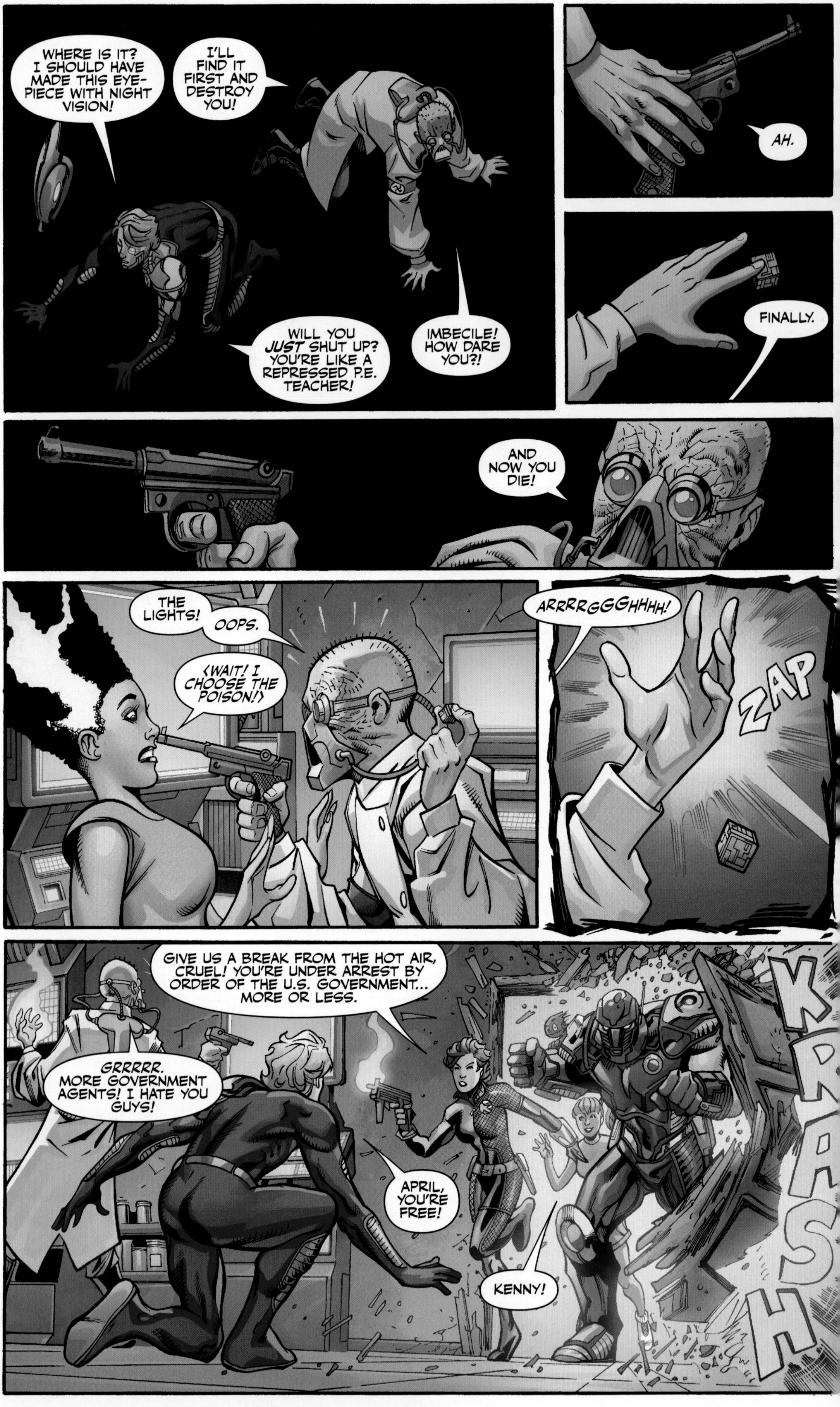

WHERE IS IT? I SHOULD HAVE MADE THIS EYE-PIECE WITH NIGHT VISION!
I'LL FIND IT FIRST AND DESTROY YOU!
WILL YOU JUST SHUT UP? YOU'RE LIKE A REPRESSED P.E. TEACHER!
IMBECILE! HOW DARE YOU?!
AH.
FINALLY.
AND NOW YOU DIE!
THE LIGHTS!
OOPS.
‹WAIT! I CHOOSE THE POISON!›
ARRRRGGGHHHH!
ZAP
GIVE US A BREAK FROM THE HOT AIR, CRUEL! YOU'RE UNDER ARREST BY ORDER OF THE U.S. GOVERNMENT... MORE OR LESS.
GRRRRR. MORE GOVERNMENT AGENTS! I HATE YOU GUYS!
APRIL, YOU'RE FREE!
KENNY!
KRASH

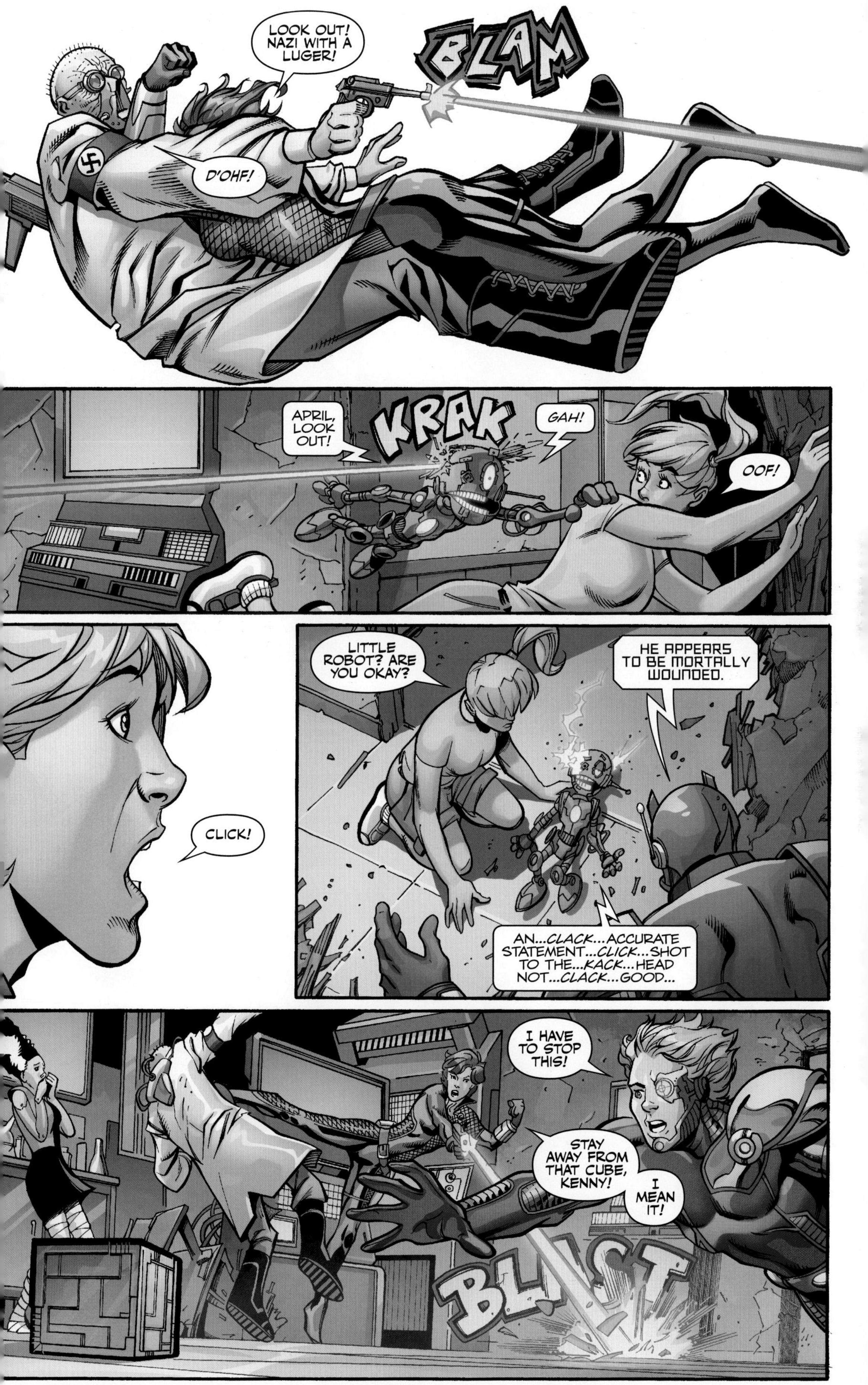
LOOK OUT! NAZI WITH A LUGER!
BLAM
D'OHF!
APRIL, LOOK OUT!
KRAK
GAH!
OOF!
CLICK!
LITTLE ROBOT? ARE YOU OKAY?
HE APPEARS TO BE MORTALLY WOUNDED.
AN...CLACK...ACCURATE STATEMENT...CLICK...SHOT TO THE...KACK...HEAD NOT...CLACK...GOOD...
I HAVE TO STOP THIS!
STAY AWAY FROM THAT CUBE, KENNY!
I MEAN IT!

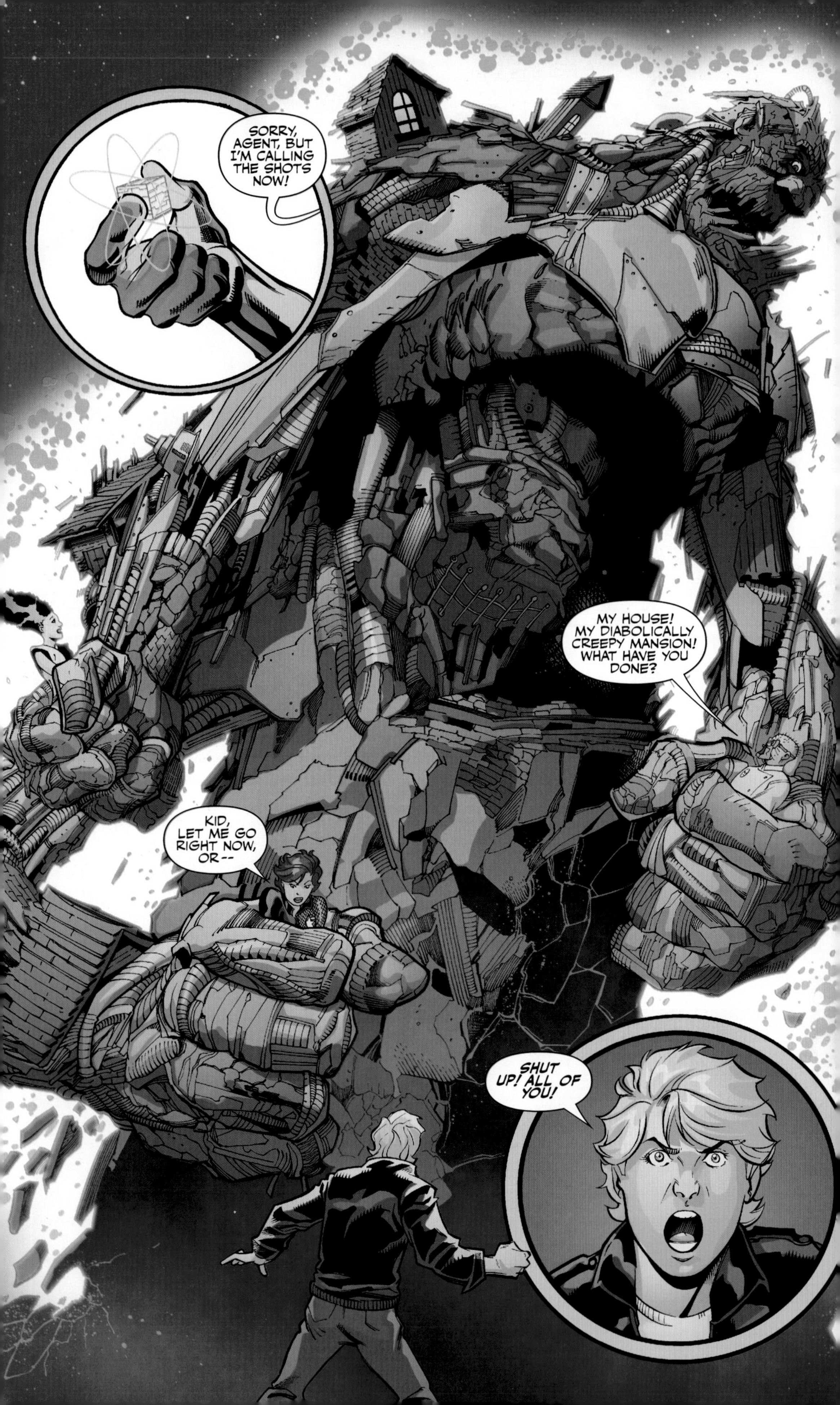
SORRY, AGENT, BUT I'M CALLING THE SHOTS NOW!
MY HOUSE! MY DIABOLICALLY CREEPY MANSION! WHAT HAVE YOU DONE?
KID, LET ME GO RIGHT NOW, OR--
SHUT UP! ALL OF YOU!

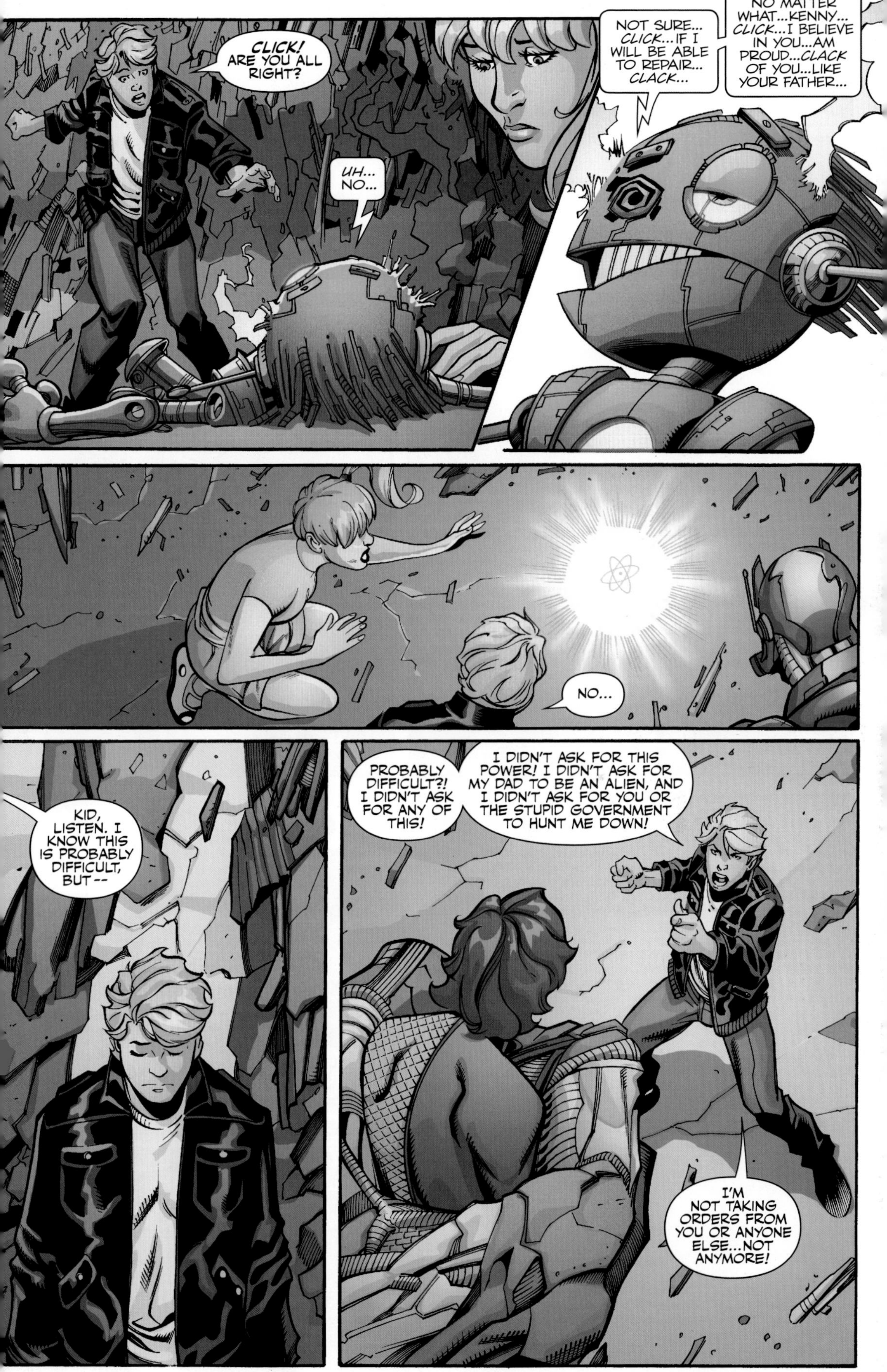
CLICK! ARE YOU ALL RIGHT?
UH... NO...
NOT SURE... CLICK...IF I WILL BE ABLE TO REPAIR... CLACK...
NO MATTER WHAT...KENNY... CLICK...I BELIEVE IN YOU...AM PROUD...CLACK OF YOU...LIKE YOUR FATHER...
NO...
KID, LISTEN. I KNOW THIS IS PROBABLY DIFFICULT, BUT--
PROBABLY DIFFICULT?! I DIDN'T ASK FOR ANY OF THIS!
I DIDN'T ASK FOR THIS POWER! I DIDN'T ASK FOR MY DAD TO BE AN ALIEN, AND I DIDN'T ASK FOR YOU OR THE STUPID GOVERNMENT TO HUNT ME DOWN!
I'M NOT TAKING ORDERS FROM YOU OR ANYONE ELSE...NOT ANYMORE!

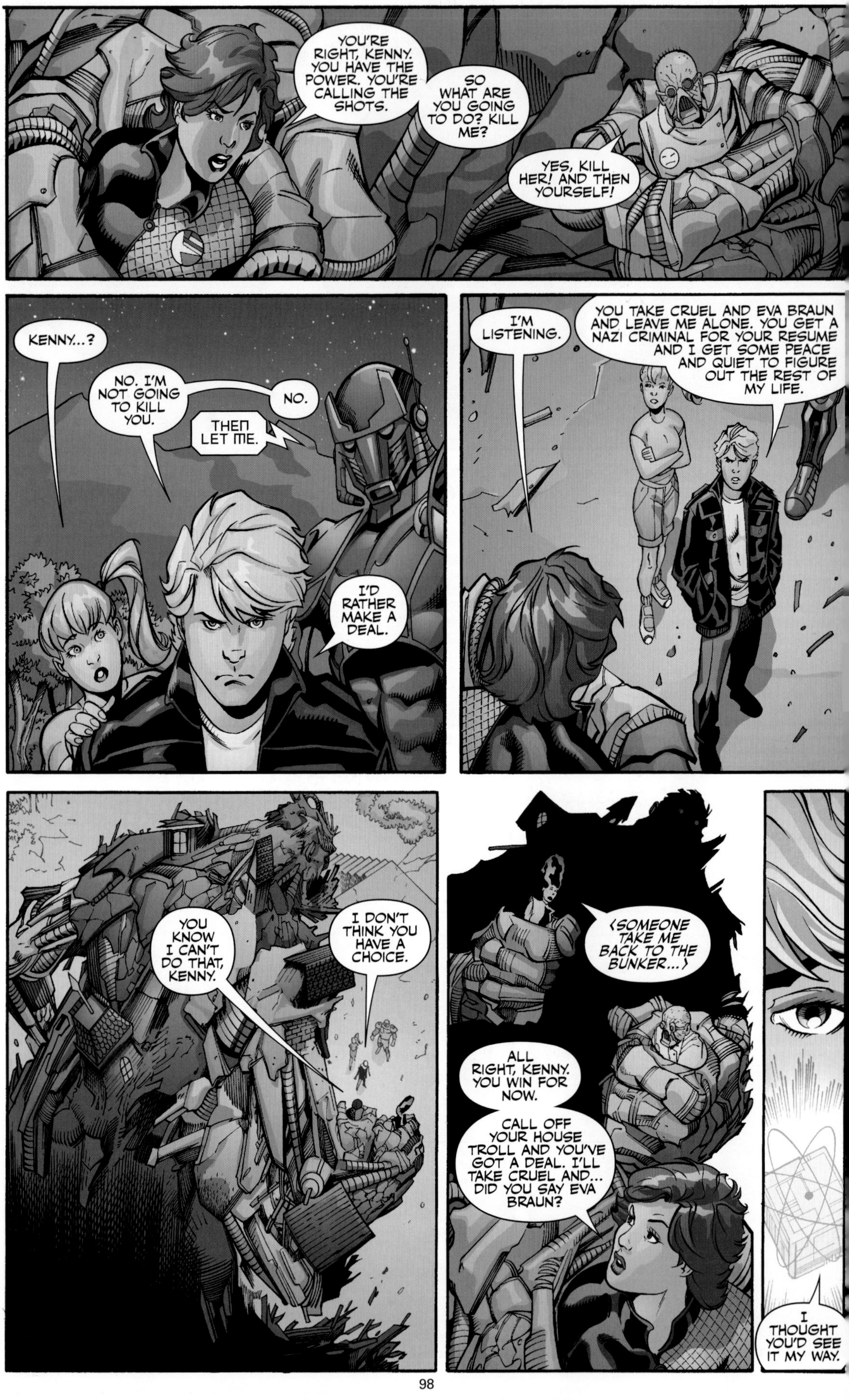
YOU'RE RIGHT, KENNY. YOU HAVE THE POWER. YOU'RE CALLING THE SHOTS.
SO WHAT ARE YOU GOING TO DO? KILL ME?
YES, KILL HER! AND THEN YOURSELF!
KENNY...?
NO. I'M NOT GOING TO KILL YOU.
NO.
THEN LET ME.
I'D RATHER MAKE A DEAL.
I'M LISTENING.
YOU TAKE CRUEL AND EVA BRAUN AND LEAVE ME ALONE. YOU GET A NAZI CRIMINAL FOR YOUR RESUME AND I GET SOME PEACE AND QUIET TO FIGURE OUT THE REST OF MY LIFE.
YOU KNOW I CAN'T DO THAT, KENNY.
I DON'T THINK YOU HAVE A CHOICE.
‹SOMEONE TAKE ME BACK TO THE BUNKER...›
ALL RIGHT, KENNY. YOU WIN FOR NOW.
CALL OFF YOUR HOUSE TROLL AND YOU'VE GOT A DEAL. I'LL TAKE CRUEL AND... DID YOU SAY EVA BRAUN?
I THOUGHT YOU'D SEE IT MY WAY.

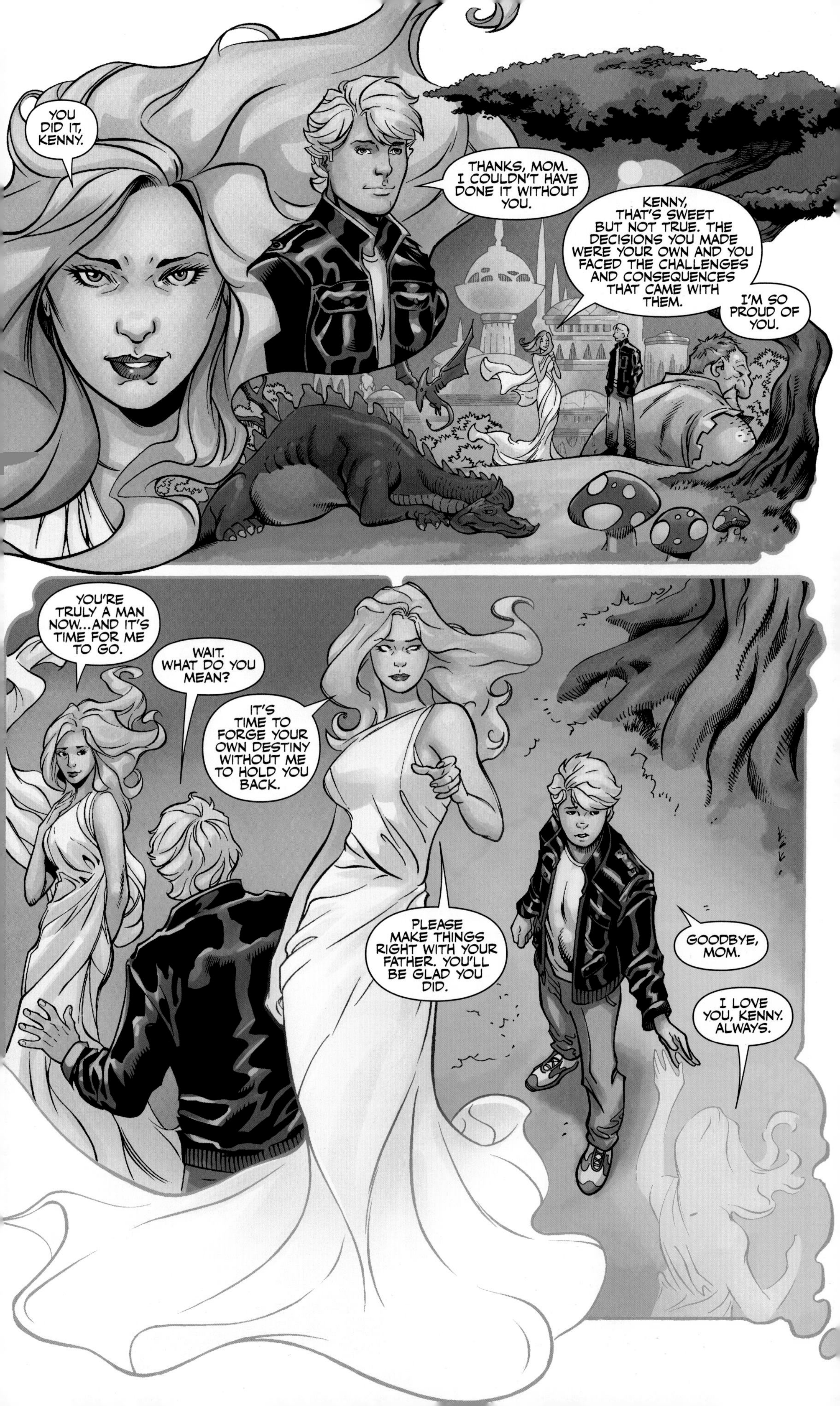
YOU DID IT, KENNY.
THANKS, MOM. I COULDN'T HAVE DONE IT WITHOUT YOU.
KENNY, THAT'S SWEET BUT NOT TRUE. THE DECISIONS YOU MADE WERE YOUR OWN AND YOU FACED THE CHALLENGES AND CONSEQUENCES THAT CAME WITH THEM.
I'M SO PROUD OF YOU.
YOU'RE TRULY A MAN NOW...AND IT'S TIME FOR ME TO GO.
WAIT. WHAT DO YOU MEAN?
IT'S TIME TO FORGE YOUR OWN DESTINY WITHOUT ME TO HOLD YOU BACK.
PLEASE MAKE THINGS RIGHT WITH YOUR FATHER. YOU'LL BE GLAD YOU DID.
GOODBYE, MOM.
I LOVE YOU, KENNY. ALWAYS.

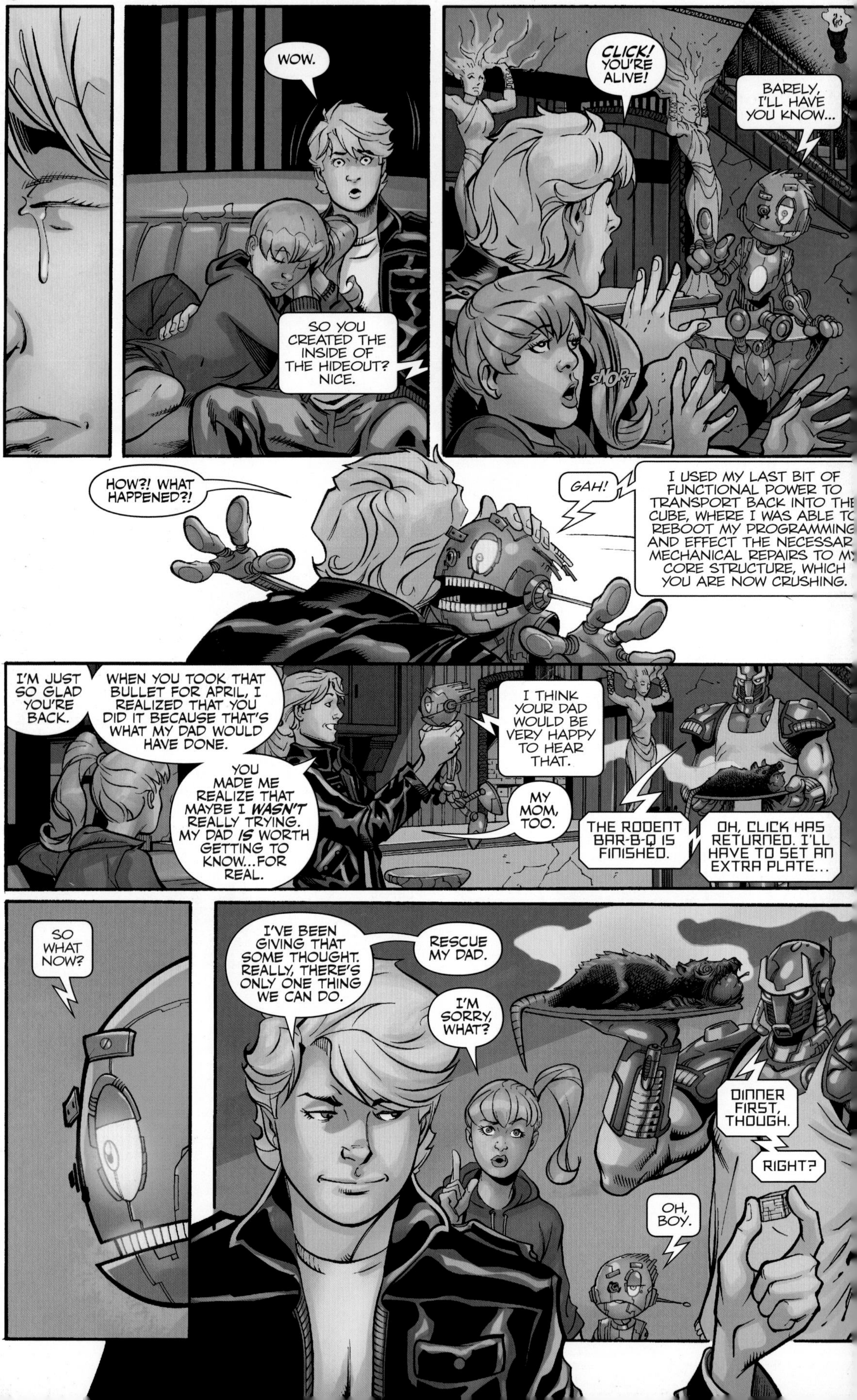

WOW.
SO YOU CREATED THE INSIDE OF THE HIDEOUT? NICE.
CLICK! YOU'RE ALIVE!
BARELY, I'LL HAVE YOU KNOW...
SNORT
HOW?! WHAT HAPPENED?!
GAH!
I USED MY LAST BIT OF FUNCTIONAL POWER TO TRANSPORT BACK INTO THE CUBE, WHERE I WAS ABLE TO REBOOT MY PROGRAMMING AND EFFECT THE NECESSARY MECHANICAL REPAIRS TO MY CORE STRUCTURE, WHICH YOU ARE NOW CRUSHING.
I'M JUST SO GLAD YOU'RE BACK.
WHEN YOU TOOK THAT BULLET FOR APRIL, I REALIZED THAT YOU DID IT BECAUSE THAT'S WHAT MY DAD WOULD HAVE DONE.
YOU MADE ME REALIZE THAT MAYBE I *WASN'T* REALLY TRYING. MY DAD *IS* WORTH GETTING TO KNOW...FOR REAL.
I THINK YOUR DAD WOULD BE VERY HAPPY TO HEAR THAT.
MY MOM, TOO.
THE RODENT BAR-B-Q IS FINISHED.
OH, CLICK HAS RETURNED. I'LL HAVE TO SET AN EXTRA PLATE...
SO WHAT NOW?
I'VE BEEN GIVING THAT SOME THOUGHT. REALLY, THERE'S ONLY ONE THING WE CAN DO.
RESCUE MY DAD.
I'M SORRY, WHAT?
DINNER FIRST, THOUGH.
RIGHT?
OH, BOY.

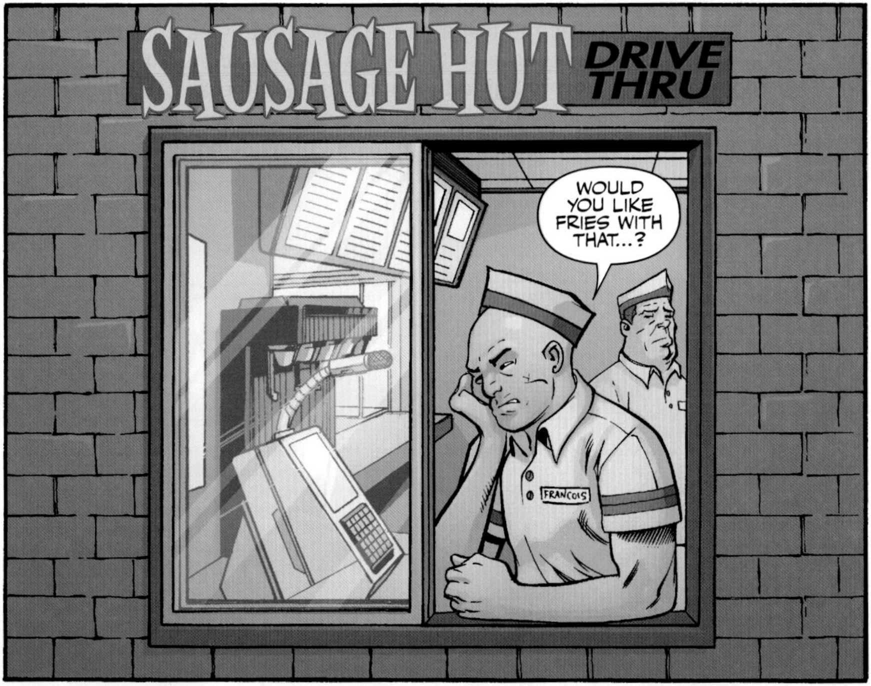
SAUSAGE HUT
DRIVE THRU
WOULD YOU LIKE FRIES WITH THAT...?
FRANCOIS

ology that allowed him to create anything he wanted. It was "high concept" and seemed emporary" and like something that might appeal to the modern comic audience more than aurs. Thus was born *Atomic Toybox*.

ished the first issue, and sales were reasonably good for a new book from a no-name r. Then I got orders on the second issue and realized that I was about to lose money, so I led it. For fifteen years readers came up to me at shows and conventions asking me if I was oing to finish *Atomic Toybox*. Imagine the guilt I felt leaving all of those readers hanging long! I always felt that the concept was a strong one and very marketable, so I kept it in ck of my mind until the opportunity arose to revisit it. When Mike Richardson approached out doing a creator-owned book for Dark Horse, I knew the time had arrived. So a couple rs later, here it is: renamed *Power Cubed* and finally complete. The guilt has lifted.

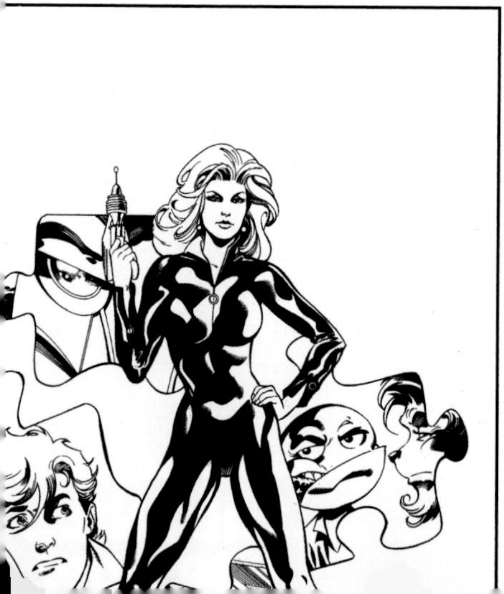

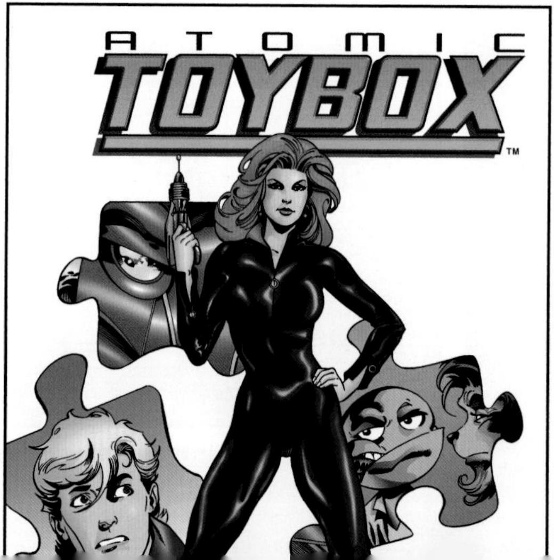
ATOMIC
TOYBOX
TM

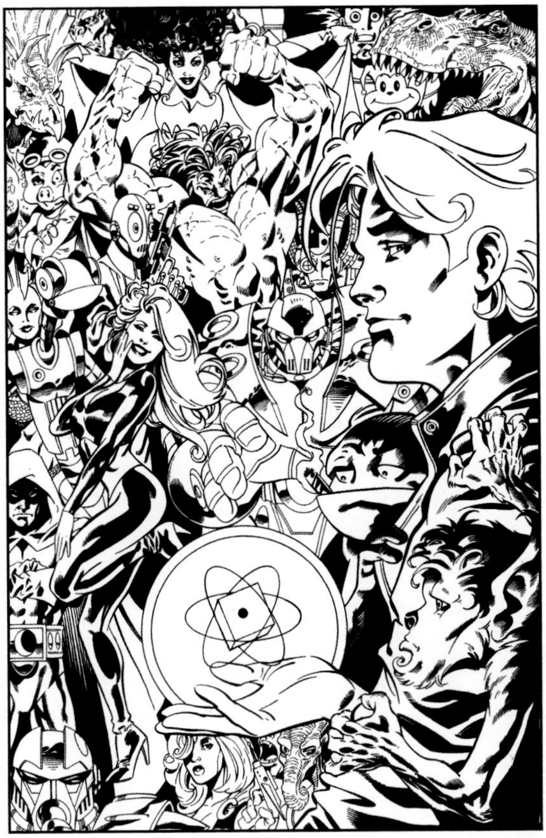

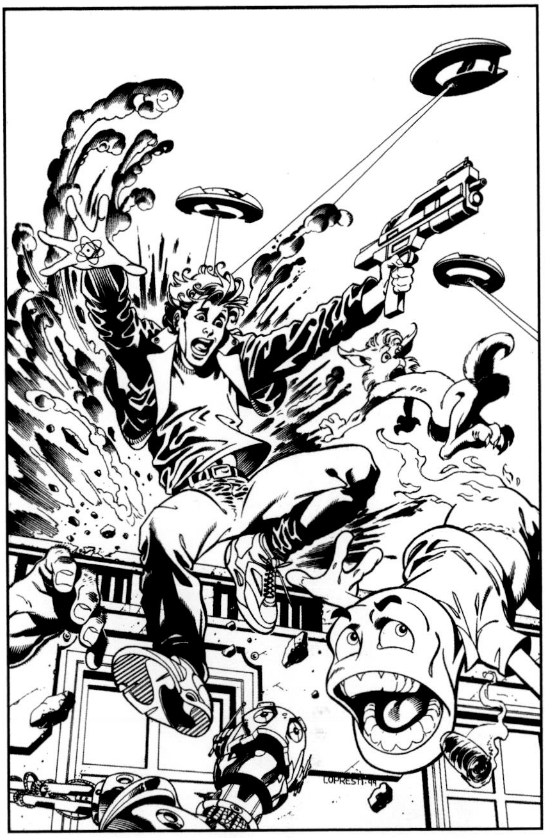

Left: The original but never used cover to issue #1 of *Atomic Toybox*. *Right:* A second version of the cover to *Atomic Toybox* #2. This was designed to be a wraparound cover with the back portion illustrated by Terry and Rachel Dodson.

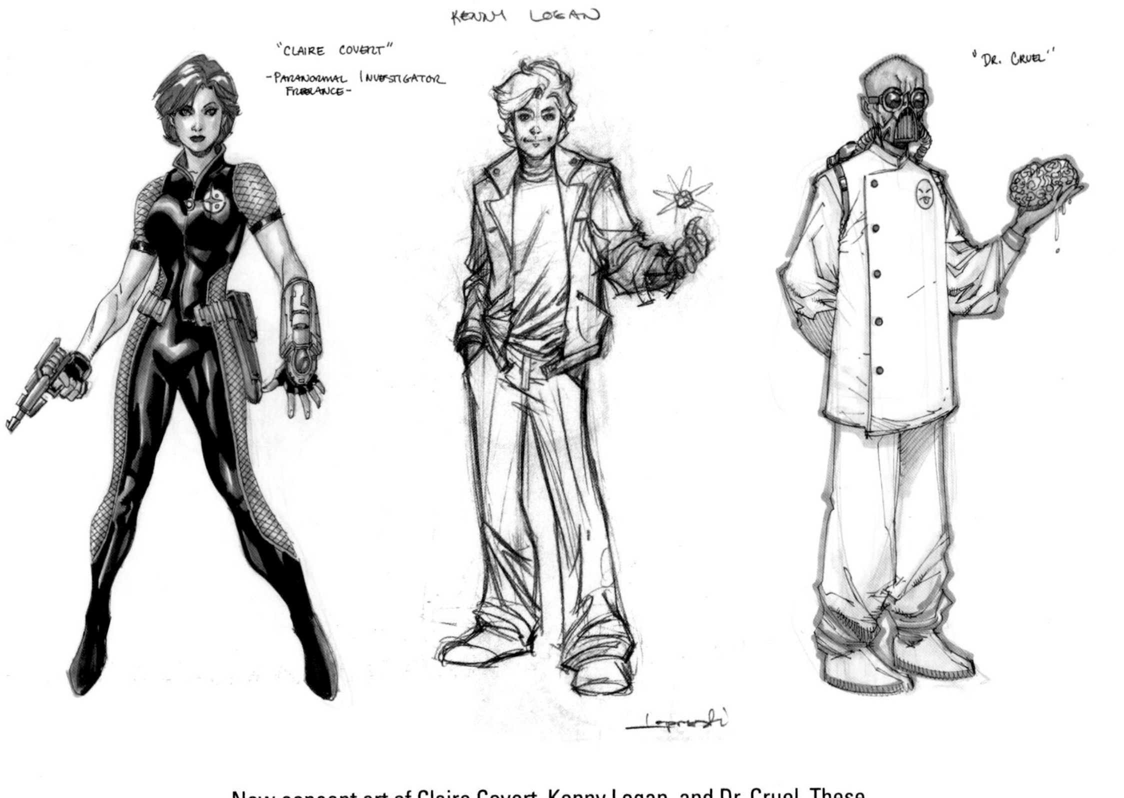
KENNY LOGAN
"CLAIRE COVERT"
-PARANORMAL INVESTIGATOR
FREELANCE-
"DR. CRUEL"

New concept art of Claire Covert, Kenny Logan, and Dr. Cruel. These were drawn post–*Atomic Toybox* but pre–*Power Cubed*.

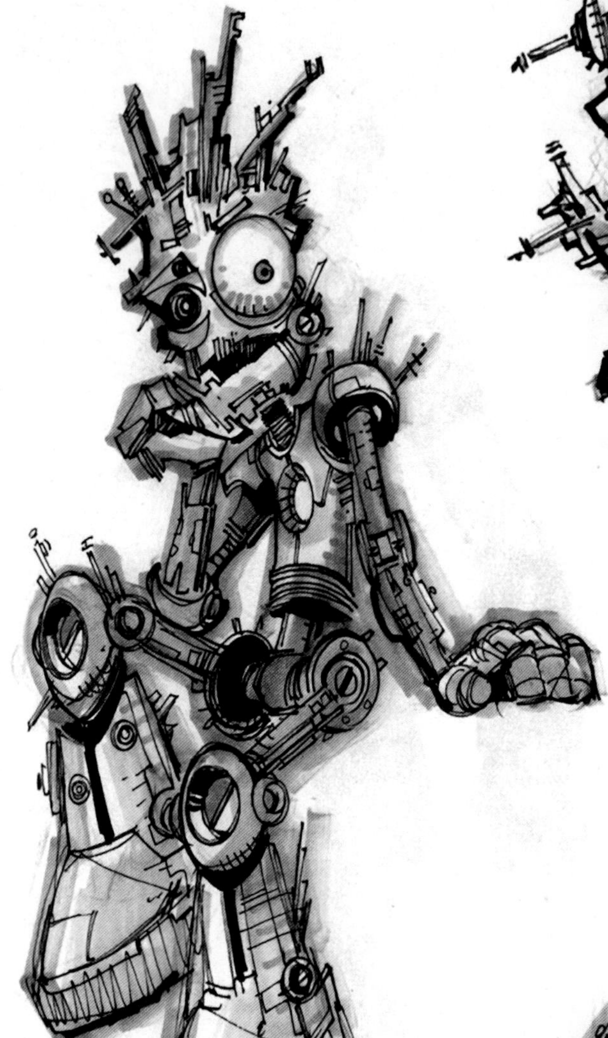

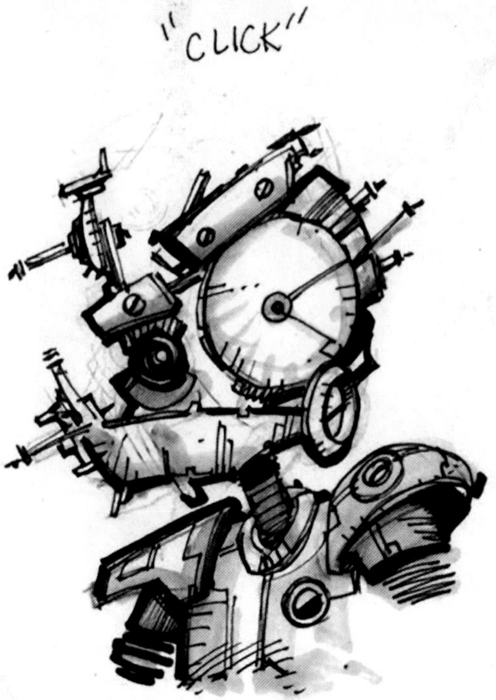
"CLICK"

My original concept drawings for Click, Kenny's sidekick.

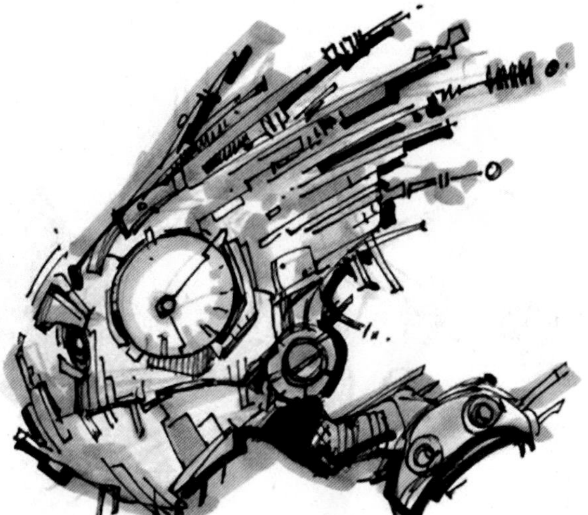